Landscapes of Fear

Landscapes of Fear

Yi-fu Tuan

Pantheon Books
New York

All rights reserved under International and Pan-American Copyright
Conventions. Published in the United States by Pantheon Books, a
division of Random House, Inc., New York, and simultaneously in
Canada by Random House of Canada Limited, Toronto.

Library of Congress Cataloging in Publication Data

Tuan, I-fu, 1930–
  Landscapes of fear.

  Includes index.
  1. Fear. 2. Landscape—Psychological aspects.
I. Title.
BF575.F2T8   152.4   79–1890
ISBN 0–394–42035–7

Design by Irva Mandelbaum

Grateful acknowledgment is made to the following for permission to
reprint previously published material:

Harper & Row Publishers, Inc., for two excerpts from *The Myth of the
Happy Child* by Carole Klein. Copyright © 1975 by Carole Klein.
Reprinted by permission of Harper & Row Publishers, Inc.

The University of Chicago Press for an excerpt from Thorkild Jacobsen, "The Cosmos as a State," in *The Intellectual Adventure of Ancient Man*. By permission of The University of Chicago Press. Copyright 1946 by University of Chicago.

Manufactured in the United States of America

First Edition

Contents

Acknowledgments

Writing a book on fear should not be a delightful experience. But it was, for various reasons, one of which is the sheer intellectual pleasure of exploring a large array of sources, ranging from exegeses on fairy tales to treatises on criminal law. To the authors of these specialized works I clearly owe a general debt, which I would like to acknowledge here. Another source of pleasure is the support of numerous friends, colleagues, and students. Among those who kindly supplied me with ideas and references are: Michael Albert, R. P. Beckinsale, Mark Bouman, R. W. Chambers, Stephen Daniels, Dennis Dingemans, Jack Flynn, Philip Gersmehl, Linda Graber, J. M. Houston, J. B. Jackson, James Hathaway, Jane Kelber, C. T. Kuan, Dana Noonan, P. W. Porter, Hugh Prince, R. H. Skaggs, Catherine Smiley, Nigel Thrift, Sze-Fu Tuan, and Ivor Winton.

Especially I wish to thank my editor, Tom Engelhardt. The faults of the book I naturally claim as my own, but insofar as it does have merits of clarity and coherence they reflect Tom's dedicated and imaginative editing.

Landscapes of Fear

1.

Introduction

Landscapes of fear? If we pause to reflect on what these are, surely swarms of images will come to mind: fear of the dark and of abandonment in childhood; anxiety in strange settings or on social occasions; dread of corpses and of the supernatural; fear of disease, war, and natural calamities; uneasiness at the sight of hospitals and prisons; fear of muggers in desolate streets and neighborhoods; anxiety at the prospect of the breakdown of world order.

Fears are felt by individuals and are in this sense subjective; some, however, have a clear source in a threatening environment, others do not. Certain kinds of fears haunt children, others emerge only with adolescence and maturity. Some fears burden "primitive" peoples who live in stressful environments, others appear in complex technological societies that have vast powers over nature.

In every study of the human individual and of human society, fear is a theme—either covert as in stories of courage and success, or explicit as in works on phobias and human conflict. Yet no one (so far as we know) has attempted to take "landscapes of fear" as a topic worthy of systematic exploration in its own right and for the light it may shed on questions of perennial interest: What is it to be human? What is it like to live in the world? We shall, in this book, attempt such an exploration, seeking in particular to trace links and resonances between various landscapes of fear.

Fear is not, of course, specific to human beings. All higher animals know it as an emotion that signals danger and is necessary to survival. We tend to suppress this fact from our consciousness, perhaps because we need to preserve "nature" as an area of innocence to which we can withdraw when discontented with people. For us, flowers and pebbles on the beach are images of serenity. Certain animals such as a cat nursing her kittens or a cow grazing in a field are pictures of mammary calm. Calm in the nonhuman world is, however, deceptive. An animal may feel safe at home, at the center of its territory; but, given the power of its distant sensors (smell, hearing, sight), it is aware of a much larger space which offers both temptations and threats. Few images of fear are as vivid as that of a rabbit that has just left its hole and confronts the open field: its ears shoot up and its body quivers in suspense. It is ready to run for its life at the breaking of a twig.

The intensity and frequency of fear differ greatly among species. Compared with the nervous rabbit, the lion surveying its domain of open savanna seems wholly unafraid. Preyed-upon animals have, of course, more reason to be nervously alert than animals that prey. Herbivores have many powerful enemies, from which they must escape if they are to survive. Evolution has provided herbivores with lateral eyes, which are an advantage because they give a nearly panoramic field of vision. The rabbit, defenseless and ever watchful, may actually have binocular overlap in the region behind the head as well as in that in front of it: "No one can sneak up on a rabbit."[1] Lions, like other beasts of prey, have frontal eyes. Their business is to hunt and kill; they have little cause to fear enemies coming up from behind. Vigilance must, however, be relaxed periodically in all animals. Who sleep well? "Those with a clear conscience," we would like to say, but the answer with far more general application is, "Those who can afford to be unafraid." Thus, predators such as cats sleep well, whereas species subject to heavy predation, such as rabbits, slumber poorly. Security of homeplace is also important. Bats in sheltered caves sleep more than sheep which doze in the open.[2]

Individuals within a species may well differ in feeling fear. Among humans—a highly polymorphous species—some people are naturally timid, whereas others are as naturally bold. We recognize temperamental variation in household pets, but are less sure how members within a wild species differ from each other, partly because observational data are lacking. Degree of polymorphism may serve, however, as a rough indicator. The bodies of individuals in some species (crows or seagulls, for example) are in fact very much alike, and it may be that the emotional responses of these animals show comparable uniformity.[3]

In estimating the kinds and range of fear known to an animal species, we need also to bear in mind that this emotion may change in the course of an animal's lifetime. Certain anxieties and alarms are learned. Although many birds instinctively recognize their enemies and shun them, young jackdaws have to be taught fear by their elders. Wolf whelps, in their vigorous but clumsy play, seem wholly unafraid, but as they grow into adolescence they must learn to be wary of the mature males of the species.[4] With human beings, there can be no doubt that different fears emerge or disappear at different stages in the life cycle. We tend to simplify our encounters with fear by suppressing unpleasant memories. An adult person, drifting through the routinized years of middle age, may barely recall the anxieties of youth, much less the night terrors of infanthood.

What is fear? It is a complex feeling of which two strains, alarm and anxiety, are clearly distinguishable. Alarm is triggered by an obtrusive event in the environment, and an animal's instinctive response is to combat it or run. Anxiety, on the other hand, is a diffuse sense of dread and presupposes an ability to anticipate. It commonly occurs when an animal is in a strange and disorienting milieu, separated from the supportive objects and figures of its home ground. Anxiety is a presentiment of danger when nothing in the immediate surroundings can be pinpointed as dangerous. The need for decisive action is checked by the lack of any specific, circumventable threat.

Alarm and anxiety are exhibited in all higher animals. Human beings have much in common with other primates both in the causes of these sensations and in their subsequent behavioral response. Where humans differ from other species, the reason lies in their greater emotional range and superior mind.

Emotional range is a gauge of the nervous system's complexity and hence, indirectly, of the mind. A jellyfish's repertoire of emotions is very limited compared with that of a complex animal like the rabbit, and the rabbit's range of feeling is narrow compared with that of a human being. An animal perhaps knows anger and sadness, but can it be wistful or melancholic? It shows alarm and signs of anxiety, but does it stand in dread of humiliation, of being shamed by its peers? A capacity for shame and guilt adds greatly to the scope of human fear. Can an animal living in its natural setting experience the macabre and the uncanny? Awareness of preternatural evil, unique to the human species, enables a person to see and live in phantasmagorial worlds of witches, ghosts, and monsters; these figures embody a weight of dread unknown to other animals. Fear of betrayal by a relative or friend is very different from fear of an enemy outside the familiar circle. Imagination adds immeasurably to the kinds and intensity of fear in the human world.

Our fertile minds are thus a mixed blessing. To apprehend is to risk apprehensiveness. If we did not know so much, we would have less to fear. Cardinal Newman, in the popular hymn "Lead, Kindly Light," asked not to see "the distant scene." "One step enough for me," he wrote. If we had less imagination, we would feel more secure. The Stoic philosopher Epictetus said to a fellow passenger, "You are afraid of this storm as if you were going to have to swallow the whole vast sea; but, my dear sir, it would take only a quart of water to drown you." Metaphysical terror, unique to human beings, cannot be assuaged anywhere in this world. Only God can provide relief. "Rock of Ages, cleft for me; let me hide myself in Thee." It is a desperate plea.[5]

Fear is in the mind but, except in pathological cases, has its origins in external circumstances that are truly threatening. "Landscape," as the term has been used since the seventeenth century, is a construct of the mind as well as a physical and measurable entity. "Landscapes of fear" refers both to psychological states and to tangible environments.

What are the landscapes of fear? They are the almost infinite manifestations of the forces for chaos, natural and human. Forces for chaos being omnipresent, human attempts to control them are also omnipresent. In a sense, every human construction—whether mental or material—is a component in a landscape of fear because it exists to contain chaos. Thus children's fairy tales as well as adults' legends, cosmological myths, and indeed philosophical systems are shelters built by the mind in which human beings can rest, at least temporarily, from the siege of inchoate experience and of doubt. Likewise, the material landscapes of houses, fields, and cities contain chaos. Every dwelling is a fortress built to defend its human occupants against the elements; it is a constant reminder of human vulnerability. Every cultivated field is wrested out of nature, which will encroach upon the field and destroy it but for ceaseless human effort. Generally speaking, every human-made boundary on the earth's surface—garden hedge, city wall, or radar "fence"—is an attempt to keep inimical forces at bay. Boundaries are everywhere because threats are ubiquitous: the neighbor's dog, children with muddy shoes, strangers, the insane, alien armies, disease, wolves, wind and rain.

Of course, a landscape of farmstead and cultivated fields does not directly evoke fear. On the contrary, it is a picture of peace. The farmstead is a haven, we say, but haven implies threat: one idea leads to the other. Consider now the hostile forces. Some of them, such as disease and drought, cannot be perceived directly with the naked eye. A landscape of disease is a landscape of disease's dire effects: deformed limbs, corpses, crowded hospitals and graveyards, and the gruesome attempts by authorities to combat an epidemic; these attempts, in the past, included armed *cordons sanitaires,* enforced incarceration of those suspected of being sick, and fires maintained in the streets day and night. Drought is the absence of rain, also not a visible phenomenon except indirectly in its devastations: shriveled crops, dead and dying animals, dead, emaciated, and panic-stricken people.

Other hostile forces, on the other hand, take clearly visible and tangible form: for example, the blizzard, the raging flood or fire, and the maddened human mob. To Europeans of an earlier age and to peoples of other traditions, mountains and sprawling forests were landscapes of fear. Unlike blizzards and floods, which might be conceived as pursuing their victims, mountains and forests injured only those who encroached upon their domain. Yet a mountain could also seem an active power; by its commanding and ominous presence it was able to induce dread in the people of subjacent valleys.

Many distinctive types of fearsome landscape exist. The differences between them, however, tend to blur in the experience of the individual victim because a dire threat in whatever form normally produces two powerful sensations. One is fear of the imminent collapse of his world and the approach of death—that final surrender of integrity to chaos. The other is a sense of personalized evil, the feeling that the hostile force, whatever its specific manifestation, possesses will. Before modern scientific ideas took hold, it seems that people nearly everywhere saw the forces of nature as animate beings, as deities and demons, good and evil spirits. Even today, when a snowstorm frustrates our long-laid plans we may find it difficult to regard the storm simply as a meteorologic event (with a probability of occurrence that statisticians can specify) and not also suspect it, however fleetingly, of perversity.

This deeply ingrained habit of anthropomorphizing nature follows from our prior and necessarily far deeper involvement with human beings. The first nurturing environment every human infant explores is its biological or adoptive mother. The first stable objects in the dawning consciousness of an infant are other people, and without objects a human sense of the world cannot emerge. Thus, from earliest experience we recognize our total dependence on other human beings for food and for a concept of reality. People are our greatest source of security, but also the most common cause of our fear. They can be indifferent to our needs, betray our trust, or actively seek to do us harm. They are ghosts, witches, murderers, burglars, muggers, strangers, and ill-wishers, who haunt our landscapes, transforming the countryside, the city streets, and the school-yard—themselves designed to nurture the human enterprise—into places of dread.

The nature of fear changes for a maturing child as it does for a society that in the course of time becomes more complex and sophisticated. Landscapes of fear are not permanent states of mind tied to invariant segments of tangible reality; no atemporal schema can neatly encompass them. We need to approach landscapes of fear, then, from the perspectives of both the individual and the group, and to place them—if only tentatively—in a historical frame.

In this book, we start with the child's world and explore how children shed their alarms and anxieties as they grow and gain confidence. Yet growth, by moving away from the known, creates risks; and the child, though acquiring power with greater knowledge, also becomes more aware of dangers, real and imagined. The child develops a sense of reality through intimate association with adults, particularly the mother. The mother is the familiar object and the nurturing base from which the child ventures forth to establish his or her own expanding world. But the mother or parental figure is not always dependable. She can turn wrathful and seem arbitrary in her moods and actions. In addition, adults often treat children as unformed human beings who must be controlled, as animals and untamed nature are controlled; and a common method used to discipline children is to teach them fear, including the fear of such vengeful figures as bogymen, witches, and ghosts.

Strength lies in numbers and in organization. By acting together, people are able to master the local environment and create a more or less stable world in which they feel at home. In the past and among tribal societies, this humanized world was perceived to be a small pocket of order and safety surrounded by a host of threats. The wall of a house or of a town provided both physical protection and magical defense against human enemies, demons, violent weather, and disease—forces that spelled chaos, dissolution, and death. No sharp lines were drawn between them: thus human enemies were demons; evil spirits assumed human shape and possessed human will; thunderclouds were armies of the dead or were caused by witches; and epidemics swept over cities as malevolent, death-dealing vapors and clouds.

As human power over nature is extended, fear of it declines. The built world of modern times effectively withstands the normal fluctuations of nature. An exceptional event, such as a flood, can still wreck a town, but the sensation of fear differs from that known in the past because natural forces tend no longer to be viewed as malicious—that is, possessed by the will to injure. Paradoxically, it is in the large city—the most visible symbol of human rationality and triumph over nature—that some of the old fears remain. The urban sprawl, for example, is seen as a jungle, a chaos of buildings, streets, and fast-moving vehicles that disorient and alarm newcomers. But the greatest single threat in the city is other people. Malevolence, no longer ascribed to nature, remains an attribute of human nature. Certain quarters are shunned because they are haunted by criminals and teen-age gangs. Mobs move and destroy with the impersonality of fire; they are "mindless," yet they consist of individuals with minds and wills—each with the mind and the will for chaos.

Although human beings create order and society by acting cooperatively, the mere fact of amassing in the same place sets off a situation that can result in violence. To rulers and governments people in swarms are potentially dangerous; like forces of nature they must be controlled. In the past, authorities attempted to subdue crowds by deliberately fostering an atmosphere of fear around the machinery of law and justice. They put up pillories and gallows at public places; they dramatized executions and established a highly visible landscape of punishment.

Focusing as we do on fear, we inevitably give the impression that human beings dwell on the earth precariously and are almost constantly afraid. This is surely a distortion. Drowsy habitude and the ordinariness of the daily round rather than fright and despair are the common human lot. Even when a society seems hedged in by superstitious fears, we cannot assume that the people, individually, live in dread most of the time. Superstitions are the rules by which a human group attempts to generate an illusion of predictability in an uncertain environment. Rules are effective in tempering anxiety; and the numerous rules themselves cease to be a conscious burden once they become habit. Even where the objective situation is truly horrible and threatening, people learn in time to adapt and ignore. Furthermore, there is a perverse streak in human nature that appreciates cruelty and grotesquerie if they pose no immediate danger to self. People flocked to public executions and ate picnic lunches under the shadow of the gibbet. Life from the four- teenth to the sixteenth century offered abundant spectacles of suffering and pain. Nevertheless, as if such dreadful sights were not enough, the French popular theater of the time was filled with tortures and executions that might last even longer on stage than they did in reality.[6]

It is a mistake to think that human beings always seek stability and order. Anyone who is open to experience must recognize that order is transient. Quite apart from the accidents of life and the impingement of external forces over which an individual has little control, life itself is growth and decay: it is change or it is not life at all. Because change occurs and is inevitable, we become anxious. Anxiety drives us to seek security, or, on the contrary, adventure—that is, we turn curious. The study of fear is therefore not limited to the study of withdrawal and retrench- ment; at least implicitly, it also seeks to understand growth, dar- ing, and adventure.

2.

Fear in the Growing Child

The child lives in a magical world of innocence and joy, a sheltered garden from which adults are expelled to their lasting sorrow. Vladimir Nabokov seems to believe in such a world. He confesses to an inordinate fondness for his earliest memories, but then argues that he has "reason to be grateful to them. They led the way to a veritable Eden of visual and tactile sensations."[1] No doubt there are fortunate people whose childhoods, like Nabokov's, are lived in bubbles of light and warmth. For the generality of humankind this is unlikely to be true. The pure happiness of the young is a creed of the Romantic era, and we who are its inheritors show a natural tendency to suppress the sorrow and recall the joy as we rummage through the storehouse of memory. Look casually at the baby in the crib, and "the sleep of innocence" comes to mind. Closer observation, however, reveals tiny movements of face and hands that suggest disturbed dreams. Night terrors afflict children one to two years old. The child wakes up from it trembling and drenched in sweat. What causes the terror? What has he or she seen?

Concern with childhood as a unique and uniquely important stage of human growth is a characteristic preoccupation of Western culture, with roots not much older than the seventeenth century. Far more common in the West and in other parts of the world as well has been the view that the child is a small and imperfect adult. For example, the initiation ceremony at puberty as practiced by many peoples expresses a belief in second birth: it marks the time when the youngster renounces his or her immature past and assumes the full dignity of a grown person. However fond parents are of their offspring, childhood is perceived as a rather awkward and fortunately transient state. Why focus on it? Given the fact that this attitude is common among peoples uninfluenced by Western values, it is not surprising that they have neglected to study the child. What we know of childish fears comes largely from the observation of children of European stock. Their fears, especially in the first year of life, may well be shared by the young of other cultural traditions. Whether this is the case will be considered briefly later.

Unlike many newborn primates the human infant cannot cling to the mother. The human mother has to maintain close contact with her child. But this biological incapacity to cling suggests that the human infant is adapted to tolerate brief periods of separation.[2] In the first few months of life he can be left alone for a while without showing signs of alarm or anxiety. If a person can ever be said to enjoy ignorant bliss and fearlessness, it is at the beginning of his or her life. Of course, unusual events can always induce fear. Like many other animals the human infant shows distress when confronted by sudden noise, loss of support, jerky movements, objects that rapidly expand or advance, and quick changes in luminescence. Generally, strangeness elicits alarm, but what constitutes "strangeness" alters as the child's world expands and he understands more of his environment. At first, specific events such as noise and sudden movements distress the child. Later, certain aspects in the visual setting cause unease. Still later, the child's fears no longer relate clearly to any objectively threatening part of the environment; they appear to be self-generated and presuppose a high order of imagination.

To be afraid of things in the environment the child must have a notion, however rudimentary, of objects that are permanent and exist independently of himself. The first enduring objects in the small child's unstable world are other human beings. Initially, the child does not distinguish between strange and familiar people: an infant two or three months old does not complain when he is moved from the mother's arm to that of a total stranger. Later, for a period lasting four to six weeks, the infant sobers at the sight of a strange face and stares at it uneasily. At about the eighth month (though it can be much earlier) the infant begins to show clear signs of consternation at the approach of an unknown person.[3] Fear increases noticeably with even a short distance from mother. On the mother's lap the infant is content, but he may display a wariness of the world when seated only four feet away from her. At the age when he begins to distrust strangers, he also begins to use his mother as a secure base from which to explore.[4]

An infant's world expands rapidly once he becomes mobile. He is exposed to exciting novelties many of which are potentially dangerous. Does any aspect of the topographic environment alert him to the possibility of harm? Experiments show that infants are able to recognize the "visual cliff." The older the infant, the more likely he is to refuse to cross a vertical gap covered with a glass plate even with the mother's encouragement. In one experiment nearly half of the infants aged between seven and eleven months are willing to crawl over to mother, but all those aged thirteen months and older refuse to cross the chasm. The younger infants trust their tactile senses: they pat and lick the glass plate and then, discarding the visual evidence, start to move over the edge of the cliff. The older infants, however, live in a more visual world and appear to be thinking, "If it looks dangerous, then it is, no matter what my hands tell me."[5]

Since time immemorial people have lived close to water. Young children might stumble into it and drown. Do they show a natural fear of water? They sometimes manifest fear when brought to the edge of the sea, especially when the waves are rolling in. With some this fear appears to be spontaneous and unlearned. Such distress, it is true, may be produced by the oncoming rush of waves and the crashing noise. Yet other children only two to three years old seem wholly without fear of the ocean and of going into the water. There is no consistent evidence that large bodies of water as such cause alarm.[6]

Many specific fears are, of course, learned and will differ from culture to culture. If we focus on natural disposition, what other general features in the natural environment are likely to trigger off a child's sense of danger? We can point confidently only to animals and darkness. Consider animals. During the first eighteen months of life few children are afraid of animals, but thereafter, fear of them becomes increasingly apparent until the age of five. What is it about an animal that precipitates alarm? The answer is not simple. Sudden movement is one cause; young children look at the frog with suspicion because it may jump unexpectedly.[7] Big furry animals, by virtue of their size and strange shape, elicit signs of distress. A small incident, such as tripping over a dog's leash, can change a child's attitude toward the canine species from wariness to acute fear. Children readily learn fear of animals through their ability to infer. They are taken to the zoo, where they appear to be enjoying themselves. They notice, however, that in the zoo animals are behind bars: the inference is that animals are dangerous. Why, then, are dogs in the neighborhood running free?

Fear of certain kinds of animals is hard to understand on rational grounds. A striking case is the widespread human aversion to the snake. Is this aversion innate or learned? Perhaps an answer might be found by studying our nearest relatives, the great apes. Tests at the London Zoo as early as 1835 revealed that a young chimpanzee became terrified when it caught a glimpse of a snake. In 1968 J. Van Lawick-Goodall observed that wild chimpanzees manifested fear both of a fast-moving snake and of a dying python.[8] Other ethologists have noted that in Old World monkeys and apes the tendency to be alarmed by reptiles is pronounced and, if learned, is long-lived in the absence of repeated experience. However, there are exceptions: a few chimpanzees brought up in captivity have been known not to show such fear. It may be, as Ramona and Desmond Morris say, that "the crude, generalized feeling of fear has to be awoken in the young ape in the first few months of life, if precise, specific fears are going to develop in the normal way."[9]

Children under two years old can look at snakes coolly even when these are slithering toward them across the floor. They become apprehensive as they grow older. Fear of snakes is strongly expressed at age four and increases to age six. Thereafter it shows a slight decline but remains strong throughout adulthood. In a television survey, 11,960 English children (ages four to fourteen) were asked to list the animals they disliked the most: snakes easily came first, followed by spiders, and then large, truly dangerous animals such as the lion and the tiger.[10] Whereas warm-blooded, furry beasts, however ferocious, are readily made admirable and appealing in legends and children's stories, reptiles and amphibians resist glamorization. People shun them less because they may be venomous than because they look repulsive and evil—not really like members of the animal kingdom. Prejudice against cold-blooded, hairless creatures that move on land is profound. Even Linnaeus wrote very unfavorably of what he called Amphibia, a term that included many more animals than are now so classified.

> These foul and loathsome animals are distinguished by a heart with a single ventricle and a single auricle, doubtful lungs and a double penis. Most Amphibia are abhorrent because of their cold body, pale colour, cartilaginous skeleton, filthy skin, fierce aspect, calculating eye, offensive smell, harsh voice, squalid hab-

itation, and terrible venom and so their Creator has not exerted His powers to make many of them.[11]

Fear of the dark is world-wide. It is not conspicuous during the first year of life, but even so, by the age of ten months, an infant is more likely to leave mother to enter and explore a brightly illuminated area than a dimly lit one. As the child grows, so does fear of the dark. Darkness creates a sense of isolation and of disorientation. In the absence of sharp visual details and with the ability to move curtailed, the mind is free to conjure up images, including those of burglars and monsters, upon the slenderest perceptual cues. When adults try to recall their earliest fears, they forget those of infancy but remember the dread of darkness.[12] Yet too often parents, assumedly with just such memories, have punished children by locking them in dark rooms, which are haunted places and signify total abandonment.

Fear of darkness may lie dormant and be wakened accidentally by events that are not particularly frightening in themselves. This suggests a predisposition toward fear of the dark. Consider the following story of how a child learned to be afraid:

> A relative was left in charge of a five-year-old child one evening while the parents were away. With the best intentions, this relative told the child a bed-time story about angels. Kind angels, she said, would stand at the foot of the bed during the night and watch over the child and protect him from harm. The child, who until this time had apparently had no instruction about angels, and who had no notion that danger might lurk in the bedroom, became much disturbed, and he protested against going to bed for several nights thereafter.[13]

In Western as well as in modern Oriental societies, a growing child enters school and encounters a new environment of noisy youngsters, strange adults, and confusing topography. The child is fearful of getting lost in the large school building and wary of rough playmates. He or she develops new social fears, which presuppose a self-consciousness that dawns at about the age of three. The new schoolboy or schoolgirl is leery of competitive games in which physical awkwardness is exposed to the ridicule of peers, and dreads tests that invite the scorn of teachers. A middle-class school-age child in an industrial society is under heavy pressure to win approval from the disparate constituencies of classmates, teachers, and parents.

Greta is only six years old and already she suffers from bad dreams that reflect a plaguing discomfort with the challenges of the first grade. "I wish," she says in tearful desperation, "I wish I knew . . . everything! If I knew everything, I could"—she takes a deep breath and comes up with an experience as bad as school —"I could sleep with the lights out."[14] Here is poignancy, the belief that if one had knowledge, physical darkness and school itself would hold no terror.

Alfred Kazin, recalling his childhood in Brownsville, wrote:

> When I passed the school, I went sick with all my old fear of it. With its standard New York public-school brown brick courtyard shut in on three sides of the square and the pretentious battlements overlooking that cockpit in which I can still smell the fiery sheen of the rubber ball, it looks like a factory over which has been imposed the façade of a castle. It gave me the shivers to stand up in that courtyard again; I felt as if I had been mustered back into the service of those Friday morning "tests" that were the terror of my childhood.[15]

Children show reluctance to play in certain areas; what they are really afraid of is not places as such, but people. Evil beings lurk almost everywhere. Children's view of human nature can be very Hobbesian. Ask a small American child why there are rules and laws, and he may well say, "So that people don't go around killing and robbing each other." The violence shown on television has undoubtedly increased the child's suspicion of the world, but even from his own experience the child knows that he can be humiliated or pummeled by the bigger kids on the block. A national survey of American children aged seven to eleven reveals that one-fourth of the sample of 2,258 youngsters are afraid to play outdoors and two-thirds of them fear someone will break into their homes and harm them. As for school, two-thirds of the children are anxious about tests and an equal number feel the shame of making mistakes. An unexpected result of the survey is that more than half of the children admit fear of classroom disorder: they object to the unruliness of their mates.[16] If school were authoritarian but orderly it might not be so frightening; a modern public school, however, can combine tyranny with the constant threat of chaos.

The world of small children is a fragile construct of fact and fantasy. Before they are seven or eight years old they often fail to distinguish between dreams (including daydreams) and external events. To the child, a nightmare can occur both in a person's head and out there in the room. An eight-year-old boy was able to explain how he saw the situation with the help of a sketch, which he voluntarily drew for the psychologist Jean Piaget. The boy said, "I dreamed that the devil wanted to boil me." In the sketch the boy shows himself in bed on the left; in the center is the devil and to his right is the boy again, standing in his nightshirt before the devil who is about to boil him. The fact that the boy is shown in his nightshirt suggests that the devil has pulled him out of bed. On being questioned the boy explained, "When I was in bed I was really there, and then when I was in my dream I was with the devil and I was really there as well."[17]

Because to children bad dreams are real events in the world, we must include them among their landscapes of fear. Nightmares are a common affliction. Their content changes with age, becoming more specific and differentiated as the child grows older. Children about two years old will describe what frightens them as menacing noises, animals, or machines. Biting animals and simple monsters predominate in the dreams of children aged two to five; when human figures appear they are not distinguished sexually. In still older children's dreams, monsters assume specific character.[18] Among the dreaded animals are crabs, spiders, and snakes. Horrible beings—more or less human—include ghosts, witches, vampires, werewolves, and deformed old men. It is clear that the dream images of older children are strongly affected by the folklore and beliefs of adults, who are known to evoke monsters deliberately for the purpose of gaining control over the children.

Childhood nightmares can show great variation in detail. Often what a child encounters in a bad dream reflects an experience earlier in the day or the day before. Certain themes, however, recur and may appear from time to time even in the dreams of adults. These include suffocation, being chased and devoured, wandering about lost in an empty room or in the woods, discovering a horrible thing behind the door, burglars and monsters outside the house threatening to enter, and abandonment.

Suffocation is a recurrent terror in childhood nightmares. A blanket may have been thrown inadvertently over an infant's face, or he may be so placed that his nose and mouth are buried in a soft pillow. Asphyxia suffered during infanthood can lead to an excessive fear of change in the environment in later life, and to claustrophobia in adulthood.[19] An older child, in a nightmare, may translate the feeling of suffocation into the terror of being buried alive. The sense of being rooted to a spot as danger approaches is fairly common in children's nightmares. Could it be caused by a memory of infant immobility and helplessness?

In the presence of parental figures, children are and feel secure. Alone, they feel vulnerable. The world seems a dangerous place, full of unaccountable noises and movements. Yet the shocks received in waking hours do not automatically produce nightmares in sleep. Bad dreams have complex sources. The physical threat usually needs to be complemented by one of a moral kind: the victim must feel that not only his body but his moral universe is in danger of collapse. A child, let us say, is chased by a bull across the field but comes to no harm. The experience in itself may cause a bad night's sleep, the effects of which will quickly pass. However, the nurse takes advantage of the incident to gain greater control over her charge. She warns, "If you are naughty, the bull will get you!" A simple physical fright is thus reinforced by moral disapprobation.[20] In the child's nightmare the threat of the bull is magnified because it addresses his sense of guilt as well as his body's vulnerability.

Parents and strange adults seem at times menacing to the child. On the other hand, the child himself can be an angry and devouring creature. As an infant he sucks milk ("life-blood") out of his mother and may bite the nipple in his passion. As a youngster two to five years old he entertains murderous impulses toward any one—including parents—who thwarts his pleasure and will. Such powerful and dangerous impulses are repressed. In dreams the child redirects his fury away from the figure on whom he depends toward his own self. Fury, whether perceived in another being or felt in himself, is personified as a monster, the shape of which probably depends on accidental daylight encounters of a disturbing sort. A common terror in the nightmares of young children is that of being eaten up or annihilated by such a monster.[21]

Children put away infantile fears as they mature, but gain new ones the subjugation of which calls for the power of imaginative play and of art. Death is a new fear. Children are more conscious of it than most adults realize. One way to cope with death is to act it out. Pretense can give children a sense of control, and with that assurance they may actually enjoy being frightened. Iona and Peter Opie report a game in which one child plays the corpse and lies on the ground under a pile of coats. The others walk around, pretending not to look at him, and shout, "Dead man, arise!" When least expected the child playing corpse jumps up and chases them.[22] There are, however, horrors too subtle to be acted out and for which the more adequate response is the spoken or written word. A ten-year-old girl, a nascent poet, describes her fear as

... like a cold night,
When the darkness begins to creep in
And the cup of hot cocoa in your hands is suddenly
Too cool to warm you . . .[23]

Children are not usually left alone to make sense of their experience. Since the eighteenth century, a resource available to Occidental children between the ages of five and ten has been the fairy tale. The fairy tale is the juvenile's myth, an articulated world that helps a youngster to understand his own life (awake and in dreams), his longings, fears, and need to grow. Consider such fears as betrayal, abandonment, disorientation, and the temptation of the unknown. A child is acquainted with evil. Life among peers is often rough. From playmates a child receives support and sympathy but also hard knocks and taunts. Mother is all-loving, but she can seem at times indifferent or turn suddenly into a towering figure of rage—a witch. In fairy tales the fact of human inconsistency, which feels like betrayal, is depicted but in a hidden manner acceptable to the young child: the two faces of the same individual become two persons—mother and stepmother (or witch), grandmother and wolf. "Once upon a time there was a dear little girl who was loved by every one who looked at her, but most of all by her grandmother, and there was nothing that she would not have given to the child." She gave the child a red cap, but also wanted (as wolf) to eat her up.[24]

The possibility of abandonment, a deep fear among children, occurs more often than adults care to admit, partly because they may have used it as an effective threat to control a recalcitrant youngster. Fairy tales recognize this threat and fear. Parents are depicted as having expelled their offspring under different kinds of duress. A man and his wife, in their greed for rampion in an enchantress's garden, promise her their first-born. When the enchantress comes to claim the child the parents make no strong protest. Hansel and Gretel are twice abandoned by their parents. In the tale "The Two Brothers," one brother accuses the young children of another of being in league with the devil. The father fears the devil, and painful as it is to him he nevertheless takes the twin boys deep into the forest, and with a sad heart leaves them there.

Children fear being lost. Even a seven-year-old may want to hold an adult's hand in strange surroundings, and feel resentful when it is withdrawn. The forest figures prominently in fairy tales. It is almost never a place for a stroll or games. It spells danger to the child, frightening by its strangeness—its polar contrast to the cozy world of the cottage. The forest also frightens by its vastness, its breadth and the size of its towering trees being beyond the scale of a child's experience. It is haunted by dangerous beasts. It is the place of abandonment—a dark, chaotic nonworld in which one feels utterly lost.

A healthy child is curious. He has the confidence to explore, yet curiosity is also prompted by anxiety. What is unknown is a potential threat. A child wants to know, for knowledge is power, but he also fears that what he discovers may overwhelm him. Parents encourage their young to explore, though within limits. Some of the limits are explained to the child and make sense to him; others are unexplained and seem to him arbitrary. In a dream the child approaches a closed door in dread. When he opens it, what will he see inside—treasure or monster? Such a forbidden door is a prominent theme in some fairy tales. In "Fitcher's Bird," for instance, a wizard abducts a child whom he treats well. One day he says, "I must journey forth, and leave you alone for a short time; here are the keys of the house; you may go everywhere and look at everything except into one room . . ." Of course, the child cannot resist the temptation. Curiosity lets her have no rest. She opens the door, and what does she see? "A great bloody basin stood in the middle of the room, and therein lay human beings, dead and hewn to pieces, and hard by was a block of wood, and a gleaming axe lay upon it."[25]

Terrible things do happen in fairy tales, but unlike those in ghost stories and folk legends, they thrill rather than terrify a healthy child five years of age or older. Why? One reason is the affectionate environment in which the stories are usually told. Another is the lack of detail in the descriptions: the horrors are notably clean and abstract, and where death occurs there is no hint of malodorous decay.[26] The wicked suffer cruel deaths under the most ingenious devices, but to the child the gruesome end of these powerful figures seems only a just revenge.

Scholars of the fairy tale believe that the genre helps children in two important ways.[27] It frankly describes the bad experiences that children know to be an intimate part of their lives but that adults seldom acknowledge. It shows the young that pain is necessary to growth, that one must pass through distressing thresholds to a higher state of being. To grow up, the child must leave the security of home and parents for the bewildering and frightening world beyond. Temptation to find one's way back home again must be resisted. In such stories as "Hansel and Gretel" and "The Little Earth-Cow," the children are able to return home by marking their paths in the forest with pebbles, but success of this kind is only temporary and cannot lead to lasting happiness. The castle or kingdom lies ahead, and even though the path to it may be through a dark forest, one is rarely without help; for in addition to wolves, giants, and witches, the forest harbors friendly animals, hunters, dwarfs, and fairies.

What are the fears of childhood in non-Western cultures? Do they differ significantly from those we have just noted? Confident answers will be given only when we know in detail the juvenile experiences of the non-Western world. We don't. Upbringing, of course, has a great impact on a child's perception. This is true within modern technological society as well as beyond it. Yet if we may still generalize and speak of the Western child (overlooking the cultural differences between social classes and nationalities), we may also be allowed to speak of *the* child on the ground that biology transcends culture in certain key phases of juvenile growth.

Infants universally encounter three kinds of stimuli that are potentially dangerous: strange persons, heights, and moving (or animate) objects.[28] Whether the infants are born and raised in Switzerland or in the Kalahari Desert, they become shy of strangers at about eight months old; at around thirteen months, they hesitate to cross the visual cliff, and are easily upset by sudden jerky movements such as those a potentially dangerous animal may make.

How these emotions are displayed no doubt differs from one type of upbringing to another, from habitat to habitat. Bushman infants show fear of people they don't know at about the same age as their Western peers, but the reaction is markedly more extreme: they scream, rush headlong to mother even when she is only a few feet away, and seek consolation in nursing. Again like Western infants, Bushman babies begin to explore their environment as soon as they are mobile, but by European standards they are more hesitant and more strongly attached to mother. These behavioral traits of small children in the Kalahari Desert suggest that they live in a more menacing world than do their Western counterparts.[29]

What other fears cut across cultures? We may safely assume that fear of disorientation—of getting lost—is universal. Above all, the small child needs to feel anchored in a center of nurture and of security. Beyond the home base is a threatening and confusing world: this may be forest, bush country, or desert. Transcending these geographical differences is night, which penetrates the center of home and makes even familiar objects seem strange. Fear of darkness is world-wide. Night is peopled with all kinds of malignant beings. Adults in many cultures are afraid to go out after dark; they transmit this fear to their children subconsciously, but also deliberately as a technique of discipline. European children dislike being sent to bed because they have to leave the well-lit playroom for the isolation and darkness of the nursery. Isolation is less of a problem for children of nonliterate societies, for they usually sleep in the same hut with adults. On the other hand, among the herders and farmers of East Africa, young children may be asked to retire early by themselves; when they show reluctance their parents may threaten them with such remarks as "I will throw you out to a hyena."[30]

Do children in non-Western societies fantasize or suffer from bad dreams and nightmares with a frequency comparable to that found among European children? Although factual data are lacking, we can provide tentative answers because it can be assumed that how adults feel about their offspring and behave toward them plays a key role in the way juvenile imagination develops. Consider the beliefs of poor, illiterate peasants from Kwantung province in China who have emigrated to Hong Kong. They hold that a pregnant woman is polluted. Pregnancy and childbirth are considered "poisonous" disorders similar in nature to cholera, dysentery, bubonic plague, and epilepsy. The victim of such disorders is *kwaai,* which means "queer" or "strange." A pregnant woman is strange for various reasons, among them being the possession of four eyes—two in the head and two in the stomach. In addition, the women think that if they behave badly toward someone, his soul will return in the body of their own child. Fetuses are viewed with ambivalence and even with hostility and alarm. The newborn remains an object of suspicion until it has proved its normality.[31] Under such circumstances a child is bound to doubt his welcome in the world, and it would be surprising if his fantasy life were not haunted by demons and monsters.

On the other hand, consider the sea-dwelling Manus of the Admiralty Islands, north of New Guinea, as Margaret Mead saw them. Their children were fed and provided with material support, but otherwise left much to themselves. The result was that the children romped in a safe, carefree environment *un*-imaginatively, without direction, like puppies. Their lives were neither darkened by demons nor illuminated by good spirits. Delight in listening to stories or telling them was absent. According to Mead, Manus children did not speculate about what was happening on the other side of the hill or what the fishes said. Their appetite for fantasy was uncultivated, though it did exist. For example, they pored eagerly over an old issue of Mead's *Natural History* magazine, which to them was full of wonders.[32]

Common sources of fear among children in large, complex societies are punishment by adults for failure at some task and humiliation by peers. In smaller societies such fears are often minimized or absent. However, we need to distinguish between people whose livelihood is based on animal husbandry (African cattle herders, for instance) and primitive foragers. Children in societies with large animals but no fences are asked to mind the herd. They have freedom in the performance of their task but also responsibility. A herd boy who lets his animals stray into a neighbor's garden is almost certain to be severely punished. By contrast, among hunters and gatherers young children have no economic function to perform. The boys hunt for their own pleasure and are not punished if they fail to obtain game.[33] Two other sources of strain are also absent. One is competition in team sports: a small band of foragers includes too few children for them to be organized into contending groups along age lines. The second is competition in learning: a boy need not measure himself against his peers, for he is taught individually by his father or uncle.[34] In large nonliterate societies, especially those imbued with a warrior ethos, boys do face severe competition in trials of manhood. Among many North American Indian tribes, a nonathletic or nonaggressive youth could escape the male role by becoming a berdache—assuming the dress and social role of a female.[35]

Many children fear school, a place of challenge where one's weaknesses are exposed to unsympathetic strangers. Fear of this kind was commonplace in the schools of early modern China. However, a striking change in educational attitude and atmosphere occurred under the rule of the People's Republic. Westerners who have visited China in recent years have repeatedly expressed surprise at the docility and friendliness of kindergarten and primary-school children. They look relaxed, appear to like their surroundings, and accept visiting foreigners with ease. How did such a transformation take place? An important step was the removal of the need to shine in the classroom at another's expense. Children gained confidence and poise when they no longer felt the lash of competition. Key words in the educational philosophy of recent years have been "cooperation" and "success": the two ideas are inseparable because success is the overcoming of difficulties with the support—moral, if not material—of one's peers; and the goal of success is never personal glory but the well-being of the people.[36] Moralistic stories repeatedly drive home this point. Compared with traditional Chinese folk tales, children's literature in the People's Republic tends to depict two-dimensional heroes and villains who lack the power, surely, to resolve whatever ambiguities of good and evil the children encounter in their personal lives.[37] Perhaps such shadows and doubts should simply be suppressed. Chinese children, after all, look healthy and bright. Still we wonder: What kinds of dreams and nightmares do they have? What is the quality of a fantasy life that has no touch of the supernatural?

Throughout the discussion of children's fears, we have avoided a detailed excursus into the role of culture. Thus far our focus has been on what fears children acquire and discard in the normal processes of maturation and of entry into adult society. We may now turn to the consideration of how much children's fears can be traced directly to adult behavior—to methods of upbringing and discipline sanctioned by custom.

3.

The Child as Unformed Nature

Children have reason to fear adults, even those closest to them. Throughout history and in widely different parts of the world, infants and young children have often been treated as of small account and with extraordinary cruelty. Killing the newborn child was an accepted practice in many societies. Until the fourth century A.D., neither law nor public opinion found infanticide wrong in Greece or Rome. Ancient writers could openly approve of the act. A man had the right to do what he wanted with his children. The Greek philosopher Aristippus (435–356 B.C.) asked, "Do we not cast away from us our spittle, lice, and such like, as things unprofitable, which nevertheless are engendered and bred out of our own selves?" The Roman philosopher Seneca (4 B.C.–A.D. 65) seemed to argue the reasonableness of infanticide with these words: "Mad dogs we knock on the head, the fierce and savage ox we slay; sickly sheep we put to the knife to keep them from infecting the flock; unnatural progeny we destroy; we drown even children who at birth are weakly or abnormal. Yet it is not anger, but reason, that separates the harmful from the sound."[1]

Why have people killed their own offspring? It seems to us a grotesque and unnatural act. But ideas on what constitutes a human personality change. Just as many people now question the full human status of the month-old fetus and argue that they should be allowed the choice to dispose of it, so many societies in the past denied human standing to the newborn child. Human dignity was granted only when the child reached a certain age. Perhaps the frequency of infant deaths in Europe until the late eighteenth century, as in the non-Western world even in our time, made it emotionally expedient for parents to withhold human status from an infant who might not survive. A widely shared feeling in the past was that one had several children in order to keep just one or two. Marcus Aurelius thought the wish "Let my dear children live" as unreasonable as the wish "Let all men praise whatever I may do."[2] Montaigne calmly observed, "I have lost two or three children in their infancy, not without regret, but without great sorrow." Many people probably felt, like Montaigne, that infants had "neither mental activities nor recognizable bodily shape."[3]

When there were too many children to be raised and not enough food and clothing to raise them with, some have had to be killed in order that others might live. Parents steeled themselves to loss; they grew callous. In the Orient, among the Chinese, the Japanese, and the Indians it was customary, as the Japanese peasants put it, to "thin the rows" of the population much as one thins the rows of growing vegetables. In Europe before the nineteenth century, infanticide was practiced on a substantial scale. One reason for its decline was the establishment of foundling hospitals, which allowed mothers to abandon rather than kill their unwanted offspring. Thomas Coram, an English sea captain, was so depressed by the daily sight of infant corpses thrown on the dustheaps of London that he worked for seventeen years to establish a hospital for foundlings. The hospital was chartered in 1739.[4] In 1756 it received the support of the English Parliament, which also recommended that asylums be opened in all the counties, ridings, and divisions of the kingdom. In France, Napoleon decreed in 1811 that there should be hospitals in every department. However, the demand for the service of such institutions far exceeded their resources.[5] By the 1830s, the situation in France had become desperate; in 1833 the number of babies left with the foundling hospitals reached the fantastic figure of 164,319.[6]

Killing and abandonment: parents have committed these two horrors against their children. Although statistical evidence is scanty, researchers have shown that both practices were far more common in Europe and in other parts of the world than we are willing to believe.[7] Extenuating circumstances explain much of the cruelty, of course, but were the circumstances always so extenuating? In Europe parents demonstrated remarkable readiness to part with their offspring when they were still at a young age. Poor folk might have had to farm out their young children to the care of strangers in order to find work, but the well-to-do and the rich did the same. During the Italian Renaissance, virtually every child born to a well-to-do city family was sent immediately upon baptism to a wet nurse in the country. There he or she stayed until age two, and sometimes much longer.[8]

From the medieval period to at least the seventeenth century, it was a common practice among all classes to apprentice their offspring at about the age of seven to other families. In the midst of strangers and in a strange setting the children worked as servants; they also learned manners, a trade, and (in aristocratic households) a little Latin.[9] Even in the middle of the twentieth century, upper-class English parents still send their young sons to boarding schools, where they perform menial tasks for senior pupils, pick up the habits of a gentleman, and acquire a formal education. The parents are following custom and probably mean well when they place their seven- and eight-year-olds in strange surroundings, but to the children—especially the more delicate and sensitive ones—this can feel like abandonment, which is a major cause of fear.

Why were children so often treated as beings of little account? One answer lies in the way adults in different cultures have viewed "human nature," "animal nature," and "the body." All human societies distinguish between "people" and "animals." Many groups limit the term "people" to their own members and suggest that other human beings are "raw," animal-like, not fully human. Being "human" is a matter of knowing how to behave properly, of making the right gestures and saying the right things. Now, by these criteria the young of every society are not fully human; they lack culture. Traditionally, adults have tended to see them more as bodies than as persons—bodies full of sudden and strong impulses, without the graces that only progressive training can bestow. Part of the ancient harshness toward children may be explained by adults' ambivalence toward the human body—their own and even more their children's. The body is in reality an ever-present division of wild nature; like other divisions, it is normally supportive, though also capable of turmoil and violent eruptions that destroy the peace and rationality of the mind. We begin to create a world by decorating the body: the earliest meaning of "cosmos" was "cosmetics"—that is, the art of arranging the hair.

The idea of the body as wild nature to be tamed may seem at first a little strange to us. This is because, under the influence of Romantic thought, we have come to feel that the "natural man" is to be admired and that culture distorts an ideal. However, even to Rousseau what commanded admiration was not a bawling baby or the naked human body. What was deserving of praise was a person with culture, but without the excesses of artifice that the civilization of Rousseau's time encouraged. It is worth noting that people who live close to nature do not necessarily agree with the French savant in his attitude toward the artificial. Consider a "primitive" tribe, the Mbaya Indians of Brazil: in them we find an extreme example of contempt for the natural. The Mbaya had a hierarchical society. Their nobles viewed human procreation with a feeling akin to disgust. Abortion and infanticide occurred so often as to seem almost normal; to ensure the continuation of their class the nobles resorted frequently to adoption. Faces were painted in elaborate arabesque designs that served as the equivalent of escutcheons; the designs deliberately cut across the contours of the face. Claude Lévi-Strauss observes that the Mbaya "by their art revealed a sovereign contempt for the clay of which we are made."[10]

In many cultures, children are regarded as unformed human beings whose behavior is erratic and animal-like. To the classical humanist, childhood is not so much the positive foundation of maturity as formlessness and chaos; and adulthood is the result of the imposition of an ideal form, by education, on the child's refractory matter. With the achievement of adulthood, childhood is decisively and happily forgotten.[11] This view is widely shared by other societies. The Balinese of Indonesia feel revulsion against any behavior that reminds them of the animal state. For this reason, Clifford Geertz observes, babies are not allowed to crawl, and at the main puberty rite the child's teeth are filed so that they do not look like animal fangs. To the fastidious Balinese, not only defecation but eating "is regarded as a disgusting, almost obscene activity, to be conducted hurriedly and privately, because of its association with animality. Even falling down or any form of clumsiness is considered to be bad for these reasons."[12]

To formlessness, clumsiness, and animality, dogmatists within the Christian church were able to add another defect in the child's nature: sinfulness and susceptibility to possession by the devil. Some church fathers claimed that if a baby merely cried it was committing a sin. A child who cried too much or was otherwise too demanding ran the risk of being considered a changeling. As late as 1676, Richard Allestree, the English divine and provost of Eton College, could describe the newborn infant as "full of the stains and pollution of sin, which it inherits from our first parents through our loins." The devil used to be exorcised as part of the baptismal rite, and long after the Reformation the child who bawled at his christening was said to be letting out the devil.[13]

Modern sentiment is horrified by such disparaging views of children, so much at odds with the belief that they come into the world trailing clouds of glory. Yet as a matter of simple observation, even the fondest parents must admit that young children are uncivilized and, in that sense, animal-like compared with adults, and that they have a great propensity for chaos. A baby lacks the skill to build but he has the ability to destroy. With a sweep of the arm he sends a tower of wooden blocks crashing to the floor. Creating chaos out of order is among the infant's earliest worldly achievements, to which he responds with proud, gleeful laughter. Older children can build things, but they retain a talent for making a mess wherever they play. In Europe, the capacity of children for chaos and violence is a historical fact. Schoolchildren have at times been armed. In seventeenth-century France, a five-year-old boy could already wear a sword, which was not simply for ornamentation or prestige. In England, school mutinies persisted until well into the nineteenth century, and some of these had to be quelled by troops with fixed bayonets.[14]

The birth of a child breaks up the orderly pattern of the parents' lives. Parents react by imposing discipline with varying degrees of harshness, depending on the current view of childhood's nature. In many societies, including those of Europe in an earlier age, the means used to control children verged on extreme cruelty. Swaddling is an example. Tying up the child in such restraining devices was popular in widely different parts of the world. Swaddling an infant might take as long as two hours. Its convenience to adults, however, was enormous; once infants were bundled up adults no longer had to pay much attention to them. Swaddled infants become passive; they cry less and sleep more. Historical sources dating back to the seventeenth and eighteenth centuries describe children in all kinds of humiliating positions. They were sometimes laid for hours behind a hot stove, hung on pegs on the wall, placed in tubs, and, in general, left like parcels in any convenient corner.

Bundling up infants tightly was encouraged by the old superstition that they could turn into malignant beings. Vestiges of this belief have lingered in the remoter parts of Eastern Europe to our day. The baby was thought to be animal-like and violent and to have a capacity for evil. It must be bound or it would tear off its own ears, scratch out its eyes, break its legs, or touch its genitals. One is reminded of Lewis Carroll's Alice, who learns that the "proper way of nursing" a baby is to "twist it up into a sort of knot, and then keep tight hold of its right ear and left foot, so as to prevent its undoing itself." (That baby soon after turns into a pig and runs off.)

Mechanical devices were used on older children. In the sixteenth century, youngsters one to three years old might be put in stool-like frames and made to stand in them for hours at a stretch. Adults believed that the stools helped the children learn to walk while preventing them from crawling like animals.[15] In the nineteenth century, highly esteemed and influential pedagogues such as Dr. Daniel Gottlieb Schreber created a whole armory of implements to discipline the growing child's body. The *Geradhalter* (straight-holder) was an iron crossbar designed to prevent the child from leaning forward while reading. The *Hopfhalter* (head-holder) was a device for preventing the child's head from falling forward or sideways: it consisted of a strap that tied the child's hair to his underwear in such a way that his hair was pulled if he did not hold his head straight. A "sleeping belt" strapped a child to his bed so that his body would remain supine and straight during sleep. There were numerous other implements, the most gruesome of which were designed to prevent masturbation. The human purpose behind all these instruments of torture was to discipline the body, and in the process to "uproot" and "exterminate" the weeds of the mind.[16]

The use of physical restraints against the young enjoyed a greater popularity in the machine-minded West than it did in other societies. Machines are not, however, really necessary. Adults can effectively train children by frightening them with words and dramatic gestures. Inflicting verbal threats and images of horror upon the child is sickeningly common throughout the world. Here are a few examples.

On the island of Bali, when a child learns to walk, his ventures away from home base are controlled by the mother mimicking terror. She calls him back with threats that are random in content: "tiger!" "policeman!" "snake!" "feces!" The result of such dramatic warnings is that the child learns to associate undefined space with lurking monsters.[17]

Joseph Lijembe lived his childhood among the herders and farmers of western Kenya. Looking back, he wrote:

> Yes, fear played a big part in the growing up of all of us from a very young age. Whenever my baby sister Alusa refused to suckle, I remember, my mother always forced her to do so by slapping her. If she continued to cry for a long time she would

be "thrown" out in the dark and my mother would invite *manani,* some wild beasts, to "come and eat her!" . . . As I grew older and had to sleep outside our home, I found it frightening to move about at night. I had to be given escort by either my mother or my father. I was afraid of the existence of night-runners, wild beasts, and even ghosts which my parents used to say haunted our home area.[18]

At Silwa, a Muslim village in Upper Egypt, adults are eager to make their children docile and filial. These are key values in education, and the method used to inculcate them is fear. Almost every young child knows the *silowa,* a monster that roams through the village at night on its way from the hills to the Nile to quench its thirst. The *silowa* eats children, as does the *ghool,* a huge hairy beast, which attacks them in the dark. Adults warn children against talking to or looking at their shadows, especially on moonlit nights, for this can make them insane. To ward off evil spirits, children are told to recite the Fatiha or any part of the Koran on passing near haunted sites. Sacred objects can bestow blessings, but they are also sources of danger. The child is warned against urinating near a saint's tomb or running about in the cemetery because such activities incur the saint's wrath.[19]

In the American Southwest, the Navaho child is sensitized at an early age to the ubiquitous menace in his world. As soon as he understands speech, he overhears adults whispering about witchcraft and discovers that the family suspects and fears certain fellow tribesmen. By age six the child is aware of the impotence of parents, grandparents, and other guardians, who must resort to prayers and songs to appease nature's spiritual beings. Fear and threats are used to control children. They are told that if they don't behave the big gray *yeibichai* will carry them off and eat them. Fear is driven home through dramatic devices. Masked figures come out and threaten the children at their initiation ceremony. Adults make "owls" of rushes and sticks and hang them at inconspicuous places around the hogan. In a dark night the child easily mistakes them for real beasts; he is warned that an owl may take him off. This threat is all the more sinister because owls are associated with ghosts and witches. In such a menacing milieu the child naturally comes to feel that the important thing in life is to be safe. And safety lies in circumspection—in behaving according to strict rules with respect to both supernatural and human agents.[20]

Occidental history contains many gruesome accounts of how adults have tried to subdue their young by means of fear. The ancient Greeks had their *lamia* and *striga* who, like their Hebrew prototype Lilith, ate children raw. According to the sainted Greek theologian Chrysostom (347–407?), monsters were "invented for the child's benefit to make it less rash and ungovernable."[21] By medieval times witches and devils took the front stage. After the Reformation, God himself was the major bogyman. Tracts written in baby language described the tortures God had in store for children in hell: "The little child is in this red-hot oven. Hear how it screams to come out."[22] Corpses dangling on the gibbet served to impress upon children the need to be moral and good. In the early years of the nineteenth century, school authorities might even dismiss a class so that their pupils could go and witness a public hanging. Parents themselves occasionally took advantage of a hanging to educate their youngsters, who were whipped when they returned home to make the lesson indelible.[23] In the eighteenth and nineteenth centuries, upper-class Europeans frequently left their young offspring in the care of nurses. Thus was created another route for instilling fear. Nurses who wanted to keep children in bed while they went off at night told their small charges fearsome ghost stories. To ensure obedience they might go the length of enacting them. In an eighteenth-century memoir, Susan Sibbald recalled how ghosts were a real part of her childhood.

> I remember perfectly when both the nursery maids at Fowey wished to leave the nursery one evening. . . . We were silenced by hearing the most dismal groanings and scratchings outside the partition next the stairs. The door was thrown open, and oh! horrors, there came in a figure, tall and dressed in white, with fire coming out of its eyes, nose and mouth it seemed. We were almost thrown into convulsions, and were not well for days, but dared not tell.[24]

In the more isolated parts of Europe, even into the 1960s, the parents themselves did not hesitate to threaten their offspring with a variety of ogres.

As the level of education rises, dependence on supernatural horrors in the enforcement of discipline declines. However, parents can and still do terrorize their children with the threat of abandonment. The threat to abandon a child, John Bowlby notes, can be expressed in a number of ways. One is that if a child is not good he will be sent to a reformatory, or be taken off by that secular ogre of the modern world, the policeman. A second way is that mother or father will go away and leave him. A third is that if a child misbehaves his parent will fall ill, or even die. A fourth is that the parent will commit suicide.[25] The proportion of parents who use such threats varies widely with their social status. One English study found that among the professional and managerial class 10 percent of the parents interviewed admitted to using threats of abandonment as a disciplinary technique. The proportion rose to 30 percent for parents of the lower-middle and working classes.[26] In reality, the frequency is probably higher, both parents and children being most reluctant to admit to these drastic breaches of human relationships.

Ghosts and ogres are specific terrors. Children are afraid to go out of their rooms for fear of what they might find there. The threat of abandonment, by contrast, induces a pervasive sense of anxiety. Yet the fear can also be intense and specific. Parents are known to dramatize their dire warnings. A miner's wife shame-facedly admitted to putting on a little drama for the benefit of their four-year-old son.

> I have said that if he makes me poorly when he's naughty I shall have to go away, and then he'll have no Mummy to look after him. . . . I know that's all wrong, but I do it. His Daddy'll say to him "Pack his bags—get that bag out, and get his toys, he's going!" And he has one time put some of his clothes and toys *in* the bag; and it made him nearly demented.[27]

Alfred Hitchcock often recalls a dramatic incident from his childhood. As punishment for a minor transgression committed when he was about five or six years old, his father sent him down to the police station with a note. The officer in charge read it and then locked him in a cell for five minutes, saying, "This is what we do to naughty boys."[28] Those five minutes must have seemed interminable. Here was total abandonment: to be delivered to an ogre—a policeman—and confined by him to a cell. Hitchcock retained a fear of the police into adult life. The anguish of arrest and confinement is a recurring theme in his films.

The drama of abandonment may also be put on to impress older children. A father took the step of drawing up a document which said that he and his wife irrevocably gave up all rights to their thirteen-year-old son, Eric, and that they wished him to be placed in one of the local authority's homes. "They then put Eric into the car and drove him to see the children's officer. It was lunch-time and his office was closed. The boy was thereupon taken backwards and forwards from office to car until he was in tears and almost hysterical." This incident—a punishment for the boy whom the father had accused of stealing—was deeply repressed in both the parents and the child. It was divulged by the child only when a psychiatrist put him under drugs.[29]

What are the reasons for the harsh and often cruel treatment of children? The reasons are no doubt complex. We may begin with the fact of parental hostility. In extreme cases, the hostility toward children appears to be a displacement of the parent's angry feelings toward his or her own parents. Thus cruelty is passed on from one generation to the next. More generally, young parents may see the newborn child as posing a threat to the tenuous security and peace of their own lives. The parents fear chaos, and the child seems to be a force for chaos. Related to this idea is the view that the child is like an animal, a bit of wild nature that needs to be tamed, using harsh means when required. The child, they feel, must learn obedience in order to become a respectable member of adult society. Finally, many adults themselves live in a world of fear. They half-believe in the monsters, witches, and ghosts they conjure up to frighten their children. They sense hostility in both the physical and the human environment and feel that an education in fear prepares the children to submit, adapt, and live.

4.

"Fearless" Societies

To survive, animals must be sensitive to danger signals; they must know fear. Human beings, individually and collectively, are no exception. In the heart of ancient Sparta was a temple dedicated to Fear. Other societies may not acknowledge the role of fear so explicitly, but nonetheless it is there in the midst of all human groups. Society as a whole dreads the capricious will of the gods, natural calamities, wars, and the collapse of social order; rulers fear dissension and rebellion; the ruled fear punishment and the arbitrary powers of authority. Although all societies know fear, its prevalence varies strikingly from one to another: some seem remarkably free of fear, others appear to live under its aegis.

Which societies are carefree and harmonious? Our answer to this question depends not only on the amount of ethnographic information available but also on how we choose to interpret it. Values and unacknowledged ideologies inescapably stand in the path of a wholly objective judgment. In the eighteenth century, for example, European savants reacted to the blight and tyranny of their own cultures by claiming to see Edenic and utopian societies on the islands of the South Pacific. In the nineteenth century, in reaction to the horrors of the industrial revolution, life in the traditional village and in the countryside was glamorized. In our time, scholars have shown a tendency to be critical not only of technological society but also of primitive hunters and gatherers, whose lives were thought to be strenuous and short. What captured the Western intellectual's affection was the Neolithic village, idealized as a place for communal living, and the Neolithic Age, idealized as a time of innovation during which techniques were created that enabled the people to transform their environment without destroying it.[1] In recent years still another trend is discernible: the tendency now is to denigrate village life for its superstition and envy, manifested in bitter factionalism and witch hunts, and to elevate the life of simple hunters and gatherers to a state approximating that of Eden. However, few people living in the manner of Paleolithic times remain on the scene for modern ethnographers to study. The recent literature is therefore focused on a few small and scattered groups, and it is not surprising that most of these are to be found in a nurturing tropical environment.

Of carefree and harmonious societies, perhaps the best documented is that of the Mbuti Pygmies in the northeastern corner of the Congo rain forest. Colin Turnbull has been the most diligent observer of this people, and the following account is based on his work.[2] An outstanding fact concerning the Mbuti Pygmies is that they have no concept of evil. Without such a concept there can still be alarm, but the special components of human fear—dread, suspicion, anxiety—are much diminished.

What is the rain forest like? Contrary to popular belief, which is distorted by images of the jungle, the undisturbed rain forest can be a very accommodating environment. The forest floor is uncluttered by undergrowth. Trees soar to a thick canopy, which filters out much of the intense sunlight so that the interior is well shaded without being gloomy, and is cool (less than 80° F.) even during the hottest part of the day. Flora and fauna provide the Pygmies with a year-round supply of food. The plant world offers an abundance of mushrooms, nuts, berries, roots, and fruits. Game is plentiful and accessible because it is not migratory except within small areas. Hunted animals include monkey, okapi, various kinds of antelope, forest pig, and elephant. In a normal hunt, enough game is obtained by the early afternoon to last a day or two. The long blocks of free time allow the Pygmies to repair their hunting nets, chat, play with the children, sing, and dance.

Society is egalitarian. Men and women help one another to raise the children, build their simple cone-shaped huts over the haphazardly cleared ground, and hunt. Net hunting is indeed a communal activity: men and youths join their nets to form one half of a ring, women and girls the other half; they converge, trapping the animal in between.

The routine of daily life shows little change through the year, which is unmarked by seasons. Even for the good-natured Pygmies, living close with the same people and doing much the same things month after month create a mounting sense of strain. Disputes arise even over trivia, but their virulence is defused at an early stage through the mediation of the clown— an indispensable member of every hunting band. The clown lampoons one or both parties in dispute. He takes upon himself the anger of the quarreling parties and laughs it off in song and dance. The clown can afford, as it were, to be the scapegoat, because he is an unmarried man and also a great hunter entitled to respect. For the band as a whole, communal strain is relieved by the honey season, which lasts two months and is a time of abundance when Pygmy families break off from the band. By living temporarily apart, they release the built-up tensions. When the time comes for families and friends to rejoin, they do so in a spirit of anticipation and of good will. The Mbuti consider honey a great delicacy. In the honey season the forest camps are filled with singing and dancing day and night.

To the Mbuti the rain forest is protector and life-giver. They call it sometimes "father," sometimes "mother." They have no need for sacred places because their sylvan world in its entirety is sacred. They live in the midst of an all-nurturing power, to which they become emotionally attached through symbolic rites such as bathing infants in water mixed with the juice of the forest vine. An idyllic moment in their lives (and seen by them as such) is when they make love in the forest under moonlight, or simply dance alone with gestures that suggest the dancer is courting the forest. The circumambient character of the Pygmies' world is emphasized by the importance they place on beautiful sounds, those of supernatural birds as well as those of their own making, rather than on visions that are tied to specific localities. Unlike most other peoples the Pygmies of the Congo forest live not so much in sacred space, a bounded area or volume, as in an all-encompassing medium. Therein lies a major source of their sense of security and freedom from fear.

How the Mbuti respond to death and the other inevitable crises of life provides eloquent testimony to their confidence in their world. When misfortune strikes, the Mbuti do not attribute it to malevolence, but rather to a lack of normal benevolence. The death of someone may cause intense personal grief but there is no formal mourning, no feeling of injury or suspicion of witchcraft. In case of sickness, death, or failure in hunting, the Pygmies will organize a festival, the purpose of which is to awaken the spirit of the forest, to draw its attention to the plight of the people. During the festival the Pygmies do not make specific requests; rather, the adult men gather at night and sing songs of praise: "The forest is kind, the forest is good." And on occasions of death: "Darkness is all around us . . . but if Darkness *is* (if the forest allows it), then Darkness is good."[3]

Acute awareness of time is a cause of tension and distress in contemporary Western society. Our dreams are more often haunted by time than by space: people dream of missing the boat or the train, and wake up in fright. Westerners are raised with the burden and challenge of a personal goal, which rests on the idea of time as an arrow pointing toward the successive deadlines of the future. In contrast, the Mbuti have a very weakly developed sense of time. They live in the present. Each day takes care of itself. The past and the future pale into insignificance when compared with the reality of the existential moment. The Pygmies' memories of their ancestors are short; their legends reveal a singular lack of interest in origins. Anticipation is a source of anxiety. The Pygmies do not make long-range plans. Although they have a detailed knowledge of useful plants and animals, there is a curious lacuna in their understanding of life, namely, its temporal dimension—the inevitable processes of growth, change, decay, and death.

Does any other primitive people compare with the Mbuti in their lack of strife and fear? The Tasaday of the Mindanao rain forest in the Philippines would seem to provide another illustration. They escaped the ubiquitous eye of the modern world for a long time because of their inaccessible location and the small size of their group—only twenty-six members at the time of discovery. We know as yet very little about them. Their existence was announced to the outside world in 1971. Since then, the media have catapulted this shy people into the limelight. Despite this, published scientific literature on the Tasaday remains limited and tentative in its findings.

Modern humans retain an old myth that speaks of a people, endearingly simple in their way of life, who can be found in a remote part of the earth. The Tasaday appear to fulfill certain specifications of that myth. Here are a few key facts.[4] Their material culture is among the simplest known to ethnography. The Tasaday are gatherers rather than hunters. Before discovery they did not know how to use the trap and the largest animal they killed was the frog. Their food consists mostly of plants such as the various roots, fruits, bamboo shoots, and palm pith. Protein is provided by a few small animals that can be "picked up"—tadpoles, frogs, fish, crabs, and palm grubs. On the average, an adult Tasaday spends only three hours a day foraging for food around the caves in which they live. Food therefore does not pose a problem, and much leisure time remains after the needs of the body are taken care of. On the other hand, there are periods when the two staples—a wild yam and the Caryota palm—become scarce, and the Tasaday have to abandon home base for long-range forays.[5] The forest is by no means a cornucopia to the Tasaday. Their daily intake of food amounts to less than 1,500 calories. They are underweight. Their health, however, is good: they appear not to suffer from malaria and tuberculosis even though malaria is endemic to the area and tuberculosis afflicts as many as 90 percent of the people in neighboring tribes.

The natural environment of the Tasaday is not quite so congenial as that of the Mbuti. The topography of interior Mindanao is more rugged. Elevation ranges from 3,500 to 4,500 feet, which means that at night and on certain days after heavy rain the air can feel unpleasantly chilly. The Tasaday do have taboos; they are not, for instance, to tamper with the trees and plants around their cave shelters. Violation can bring down punishment in the form of a torrential downpour and galelike winds.[6] The existence of ideas like taboo and punishment suggests that the Tasaday are less completely carefree in their rain forest than are the Mbuti in theirs. Yet the Tasaday are strongly attached to their small home territory and show no desire to explore beyond what is intimately known to them. Their incuriosity is such that they have no words for "sea" or "lake" although both features are less than forty miles away. Their sense of time is similarly curtailed. Important events of five or six years ago, such as the giving and taking of a bride, appear to be forgotten.

The Tasaday love peace. They have no weapons and appear to have no word in their language for "enemy" or "fighting." To them, all people in the forest are friendly, and the only unfriendly animal is the snake, which they try to avoid rather than kill. The Tasaday dislike "sharp looks" and loud noises. They are very affectionate. Infanticide seems unknown; indeed, they often express the wish for more children. Young children are constantly carried, nuzzled, and caressed. Much fondling takes place between adults. They speak to each other warmly, touch each other gently, and seem always ready to share what they have. Competitiveness is conspicuously absent among adults, although it can be discerned among young children. The Tasaday's favorite word is *mafeon,* which means "good and beautiful." When a couple decide to wed, the people gather around them and say "good, good, beautiful, beautiful," and that is all. The couple stay together until "their hair turns white."[7]

Western reporters have sometimes characterized the Tasaday as "flooded in happiness." Impromptu singing, day and night, promotes that impression. Yet the Tasaday are afraid of both snakes and thunderstorms. On days when the staple foods run short in the local area and the Tasaday have to search elsewhere, they undertake that step with reluctance. Their tie to the home area is so strong that it hints at an underlying anxiety. Finally, the Tasaday do not know how to cope with sickness and death. They lack medicines and medical charms; they have neither physical nor ceremonial means to alleviate their sense of helplessness and dread. The sick are left to die alone, and the fact of death itself is repressed.

Somewhat farther from Eden than the Mbuti and the Tasaday but nonetheless within its ambience are the Semang, a people of short stature living in the rain forest of interior Malaya. From the field observations of Paul Schebesta, who first visited the forest dwellers in 1924, we gain the impression of a shy but happy people ensconced in the bosom of nature.[8] The Semang material culture is very simple, comparable to that of the Mbuti but more elaborate than that of the Tasaday. The Semang construct lean-to shelters in their forest camps. Their most sophisticated artifact is the bamboo blowpipe, which they use to hunt small animals. They make no use of stone, and the few metal knives they have are obtained from their Malay neighbors.

The Semang depend primarily on plant foods which the women gather, supplemented by game and fish which the men provide. They move about frequently in their forest territory in small family groups. Social relationships are characteristically harmonious. Marriage is based on equal rights between man and woman, and genuine affection binds the married couple. The Semang are deeply fond of their children, who are not beaten even when, to a Western disciplinarian, they seem to deserve it. Old people enjoy respect and are never contradicted. War, murder, suicide, adultery, and theft—common ills of humanity—appear to lie outside the experience of these forest dwellers. Their idea of proper behavior extends to the animals. It is a great offense, punishable with a serious illness, to mistreat captured animals, or even to laugh at them. Game that has been brought down with a blowpipe must be killed quickly and without pain.[9] A sense of personal worth among the Semang is indicated by their attention to bodily cleanliness and by the enthusiasm with which both men and women use scented grass and flowers to decorate themselves.

Like the Mbuti the Semang are strongly bound to their sylvan environment. Its darkness gives them confidence, whereas the treeless plain makes them uneasy. "We must have trees round us, then all is well," a Semang explained to Schebesta, slapping a tree trunk. On the other hand, the Malayan interior is in some ways less hospitable to human dwellers than is the northeastern corner of the Congo basin. The Malayan forest is more of a jungle, difficult to penetrate, and full of blood-sucking leeches. Worse, it contains dangerous animals—in particular the tiger, the elephant, and black wasps—which the Semang greatly fear. In the Congo basin a thunderstorm can bring a dead tree crashing to the ground, and the Mbuti take it as a sign that the spirit of the forest is angry, but they are not much perturbed. A thunderstorm causes much greater distress among the Semang, who feel that they have offended the powerful thunder god. A blood sacrifice is necessary to propitiate him. As the storm rages, a Semang rushes out, stabs his or her calf with a bamboo splinter so that blood flows, collects the blood in a cup, and throws the mingled contents of blood and water into the air. The Semang suffer more often than the Mbuti from food shortages and endemic diseases; many are afflicted with a disfiguring and debilitating skin disorder. Perhaps because their earthly home is recognizably imperfect, the Semang, unlike the Mbuti, make room in their world-view for paradise, which is a place to the west where the sun never sets, where tigers, elephants, and diseases are unknown, and where people live forever.[10]

The tropical rain forest is a rich and nurturing milieu for hunters and gatherers. In general, food is not only plentiful but constantly available. We may think that the contentment, the social harmony, and the seeming lack of anxiety among these forest dwellers owe much to this dependability of food supply. But this idea is too simplistic. Consider the Bushmen who live on the edge of the Kalahari Desert. The biotic resources there are meager, and in contrast to the climatic constancy of the rain forest, the climate of the desert and veld is highly variable. October and November are months of intense heat and drought. The hard-baked plains sizzle under the sun, and the Bushmen are hard pressed to find any shade. Heroic means are necessary to conserve body moisture and to obtain water from pockets of wet sand. In July, the temperature plummets at night: water in the water holes may freeze, and cold winds from the Antarctic chill the naked Bushmen to the bone.

Emphasizing the hostility of the environment and the necessity for almost constant struggle to survive, early writings on the Bushmen tended to describe them as existing in a permanent state of semistarvation. Recent works paint a far more favorable picture; indeed, one prominent anthropologist characterized the !Kung Bushmen as the "original affluent society."[11] While "affluent" is an exaggerated epithet to apply to this desert people, there is no doubt that their environment is far more supportive than outsiders had previously realized. The materials the !Kung need to make a living lie in abundance around them and are free for anyone to take. Such materials include wood, reeds, bones for weapons and implements, fibers for cordage, and grass for shelters. The !Kung also have hides enough for garments and bags. They "can always use more ostrich eggshells for beads to wear or trade, but enough are found, at least, for every woman to have eight to ten shells for water-containers—all she can carry—and a goodly number of bead ornaments."[12]

Food is not plentiful, but the veld does offer a wide variety of edible plants. Some 85 species are available to the Bushmen of the Dobe area. As for animals, 54 species are classified as edible, although of these only 17 are regularly hunted. This broad range of foods allows the Bushmen to shift their subsistence strategies as environmental conditions alter. In fact, when persistent drought prevails, the hunters and gatherers are likely to suffer less than pastoral peoples and farmers who live on richer lands. However, does the search for food require ceaseless effort? Apparently not. Richard Lee calculated that the !Kung Bushmen spend only 12 to 19 hours a week getting food.[13] Kade (or Gwi) Bushmen, who live in a poorer area to the southeast of the !Kung, have to spend some 32 hours a week collecting edible plants.[14] Still, much leisure time remains for visiting, entertaining, and especially for dancing.

Anthropologists once thought that hunters died young. In fact, the life expectancy at birth of a male Bushman is estimated at thirty-two years, a span not particularly short compared with life expectancies in many agricultural communities that have no access to modern medicine. More impressive is the number of Bushmen who live to at least sixty years; some even reach the Biblical threescore and ten. Although tuberculosis, rheumatic fever, and venereal disease are problems, the people are generally healthy and vigorous. Undernourishment does occur, but not severe malnutrition.

Society is egalitarian. Both men and women go out in search of food, and both take turns caring for the children. Boys and girls can play together because they do not have competitive team games. A basic reason for these egalitarian and nonaggressive traits is the small size of the Bushman band. Not enough people make up each band for the development of sharply differentiated roles, whether based on sex or on age. Affection is openly and sometimes effusively expressed between members of the same sex. Married couples usually stay married for life. Neurological diseases are rare, suicide appears to be unknown, and there is no stealing.[15] Children are greatly loved. Bushmen place a child's health and wishes uppermost in their minds. Contrary to earlier scientific opinion, the old and the senile do receive care, and this despite the strain they put on the resources of a small migratory band.

The Bushman's world is not, of course, easy nor is it all sweetness and light. Although the people do not fear the bush, they are well aware of its numerous dangerous animals, especially snakes, the larger cats, and elephants. Food is scarce from time to time. Disputes arise over the distribution of victuals, but they seldom explode into physical violence. Like the Tasaday and the Semang, the Bushmen feel uncomfortable with the dead, whose spirits they believe may appear as whirlwinds and cause mischief. The !Kung in particular are so fearful that, in contrast to neighboring bands, they abandon the grave immediately after burial. Whenever the !Kung pass near a grave they blow *sasa* (a herb) toward it to ensure their safety.[16] But what stands out about the Bushmen is not their common human failings; rather it is their good manners, gentleness, contentment, and essential fearlessness in a natural setting that is harsh and fickle.

When we look at these four groups of hunter-gatherers we may well ask, What factors account for their exceptional peaceableness, their lack of strife whether this be directed toward nature or other humans?[17] One factor is the natural setting, which need not be luxuriant but must be supportive in the sense of providing a wide variety of food—particularly edible plants—to its inhabitants. At least as important as the character of the physical setting are the following social and cultural traits: an economy in which the people do not impose their wills on the environment but make do with what is available; a social group of small size, which necessitates not merely cooperation but a genuine concern for the welfare of individual members; rootedness in one place. The Mbuti Pygmies have lived in the rain forest for so long that they are biologically adapted to it: their small size is adaptive, as is their skin color, which makes them invisible from a distance of a few yards. The Tasaday believe they have always lived in their part of the Mindanao forest; and although scientific evidence has not yet established this claim, there is no doubt that they are singularly attached to their home ground. The

Semang are an ancient Australoid race; they may well be the oldest inhabitants of Malaya. As for the !Kung Bushmen, they were once thought to be newcomers to the edge of the desert, driven there by the cattle-herding Bantu. Recent evidence suggests, however, that they have lived in the same part of the Kalahari for some 10,000 years. Artifacts of hunter-gatherers dating back to the Late Pleistocene have been found at the same water holes where the modern !Kung set up camp.[18]

5.

Fear of Nature:
Great Hunters and
Pioneer Farmers

Archaic ways of living have survived into the modern era. In the rain forest as also in the desert, small bands of people with keen knowledge of their environment and very modest demands seem able to lead contented lives unshadowed by lacerating fear. Do the habits and livelihood of these primitive groups tell us something about how our remote ancestors lived? Was the long prehistory of the human stock a time of almost constant struggle and anxiety, or was it, on the contrary, one of peace and abundance relative to needs? In the absence of detailed knowledge, these two polarized images tend to dominate our thinking. Which is more nearly correct? To attempt an answer we must separate, first, the long preagricultural period from the much shorter agricultural one; and then recognize the important distinction between two preagricultural economies: one based on unspecialized gathering and hunting in a richly diversified ecological niche, and the other based on specialized skills needed to corner and kill large and swift-footed game.

Without doubt, gathering and scavenging came long before specialized hunting. If we probe the distant past, some two million years ago, we may envisage the following scene: by an African lakeshore or riverbank, in a woodland-savanna environment, small bands of hominids or protohumans forage among the plentiful resources of land, strand, and shallow waters. We can postulate an egalitarian society in which males and females cooperate in the undemanding tasks of collecting edible plants, tracking down small animals, and bringing the more important foods (a carcass or a tuber) back to the home base. A "child-centered" family life may be inferred, for the long dependency of the child was already a trait of these protohumans that distinguished them from the nonhuman primates. The available archaeologic evidence, sparse as it is, supports this calm domestic picture, and from what we know of primitive human foragers of modern times a life unburdened by conflict and the stressful demands of survival is indeed possible.[1]

Moving up the line of evolution to some half a million years ago, we encounter protohumans whom the technical literature dignifies with the genus name of *Homo—Homo erectus.* The best-known representative of this race is Peking man of northern China. Their stone tools showed no marked advance from those of the much earlier African hominids, but they were far more proficient hunters. An extraordinary variety of animals fell prey to their skills: deer, elephant, rhinoceros, bison, water buffalo, horse, camel, wild boar, and even saber-toothed tiger and cave bear. Given the meagerness of their material equipment, their hunting successes must have been based on efficient teamwork, which raises the possibility that they developed a web of consciously maintained social relations and possessed articulate speech. A further evidence of their humanity is that, unlike the African hominids, Peking protohumans made full use of fire. Their hearth was their home; their habits were essentially sedentary. On the other hand, the life span of the Peking-man population was brief by modern standards: 40 percent died before the age of fourteen, and less than 3 percent achieved the sixth decade of life. Moreover, many of these people were cut down early in life by injuries. It would appear that Peking man killed his own kind for flesh, brain, and marrow.[2]

Neanderthal man, who lived some 50,000 years ago, had a brain capacity that compared with our own. Like Peking protohumans, Neanderthals were proficient hunters of big game; but the techniques used showed little change, remaining basically a combination of the wooden spear and the pit trap. However, the Neanderthal people could claim two most striking achievements: adaptation to cold climates, which called for skills in making skin clothing and possibly skin-covered dwellings; and burial, which testified to the uniquely human belief in life after death. On the other hand, Neanderthals may have been little disposed to make ornaments and symbolic objects; evidence for their artistic endeavor, such as the Tata (Hungary) plaque, is scarce.[3] Like Peking protohumans, they practiced cannibalism: at a site in Yugoslavia the bones of a dozen individuals, male and female, young and old, were broken for the purpose of extracting marrow.

The protohumans of tropical Africa foraged among nature's

wealth and, we may presume, led peaceful, unspecialized, un-self-aware, and unstressful lives. That was our distant Eden, if one ever existed. Then the course of human development in the long Paleolithic (preagricultural) period was toward a more antagonistic relationship with nature. This trend culminated in the high achievement of the Upper Paleolithic peoples who flourished in parts of Europe and southwest Asia toward the end of the Ice Age some 35,000 to 12,000 years ago. At that time icecaps still covered much of northern Europe and the high Alps. The landscape, in contrast to the African scenes of a much earlier stage of human evolution, was bleak and the weather inclement and variable. In this demanding milieu, human culture attained a dynamism and sophistication previously unknown. For perhaps the first time humans had established themselves, indisputably, as the dominant species. More efficiently than ever they hunted large and dangerous animals, including mammoth, woolly rhinoceros, bison, and bear. They might indeed have abused their power and contributed to the extinction of certain Late Pleistocene megafauna. The artifacts they left behind, particularly the sculptures and cave paintings, still command admiration. Here we see a paradox. The artworks of the great hunters give evidence of leisure time, an imaginative and confident spirit, and sheer delight in technical mastery over materials. Yet they also suggest anxiety. The content of the art leaves little doubt that it was conceived in the hopes and fears of a people who, despite their competence in the chase and entrapment, were subject to all the tensions of a livelihood that depended on the availability of a few large beasts. Unlike the diets of foragers and fisherfolk in the better-endowed environments, the hunter's diet probably gained little from plants. The small range of dependable foods must have made life seem insecure. Game might move away or fail to reproduce. To an Upper Paleolithic people, neither animal nor human fertility could be taken for granted. Their art, which we so greatly admire, not only satisfied aesthetic impulses but also pressed magic into the service of this uncertain life. Thus to promote fertility, figurines of human females were made to show grotesquely exaggerated breasts and buttocks. And in the deep recesses of limestone caverns, by flickering torchlight, we can imagine how artist-magicians strove to propitiate with etching and paint the spirits of the animals they had killed in order to ensure continued fertility.[4]

We can only guess at the feelings and moods of prehistoric peoples. For those of our contemporaries we are able to speak with greater confidence. In the last chapter, we noted four groups of hunter-gatherers whose unspecialized way of life may be threadbare in material goods but is, on the other hand, free of severe stress. For comparison, it is useful to consider the great hunters of the Arctic, the Eskimos.

Enthusiastic accounts of their way of life often appear in school textbooks, in best-sellers, and in social-scientific treatises. Here is a people we can unstintingly admire because they have adapted with such technical resourcefulness to a harsh environment on the "edge of the world." Eskimos are noted for their intense enjoyment of life. According to Peter Freuchen, "they believe themselves to be the happiest people on earth living in the most beautiful country there is."[5]

Despite their more specialized economy and superior technical culture, Eskimos share with Pygmies and Bushmen certain social traits that add up to an appealing picture of group living. Their society is essentially egalitarian. In theory, the man is master of his household and his word is law. In fact, the woman performs vital economic functions; she has enormous influence, if not formal authority, and is not in the least servile. The basic social unit, centered on the nuclear family, is small. In this respect Eskimos resemble other hunting groups who have to adjust to the migratory habits of game and a general sparsity of resources. Again like unspecialized hunter-gatherers, Eskimos deeply love their children. A man would lose his honor if he hit a child. The father who has a leisure hour with his family is almost certain to spend it playing with his children. Harsh discipline and the deliberate inducement of fear in children, so often practiced among agricultural peoples, must strike the Eskimos as extremely perverse.

There are, however, important differences between the Eskimos and the Semang or the Bushmen—differences that would seem to explain the larger component of fear in the Arctic world. As big-game hunters Eskimos are more migratory; they have to move over far greater distances in search of food than do the inhabitants of the Malayan forest or the Kalahari Desert. As a result, their attachment to place is somewhat weaker than that of the Pygmies or the Tasaday. Eskimos lack the security that comes from being able to identify with a specific, dearly loved, and intimately known home ground. A second important difference is that not only the rain-forest dwellers but the Kalahari Bushmen obtain a large part of their food from edible plants, the variety and availability of which minimize the consequences of drought or dearth of game. Eskimos, on the other hand, are almost entirely dependent on animals for food, animals that roam—not always predictably—the Arctic waters and land. The Eskimos are thus more likely to feast or starve than the forest dwellers or even the Kalahari Bushmen, who can almost always find some edible roots. A third difference is the Eskimos' greater mastery over nature. Sophisticated hunting techniques enable them to survive in an inhospitable environment, but at the same time the exercise of power seems to remind them of their antagonistic relationship with nature. To be aware both of exploiting the animals and of a complete dependence on them creates a sense of guilt and fear.

Although Eskimos may sometimes claim to be "the happiest people on earth," all is not well with them. Both from objective evidence and from what the people themselves say, it can be shown that these successful dwellers in the Arctic lands are often hard-pressed, anxious, and fear-ridden. Objective evidence includes the killing or abandonment of infants, orphans, and old people in times of stress. When twins are born, one may be killed, especially if it is a female. Deformed children are killed. Death is usually imposed at birth but may be postponed until the child is four to six years old.[6] It is the family's duty to take care of orphans, widows, and old folks; in the absence of close relatives the larger community dispenses aid. But when food is scarce they may be abandoned. Orphans are blocked up in snow houses, and old folks (often at their own request) are left behind when the community moves on. Such drastic acts must affect the minds and emotions of their unwilling perpetrators. Eskimos tell stories in which people who abandon their dependents incur ignominious death, and also tales in which the abandoned are miraculously rescued. In addition, there is great fear of the dead person, even one beloved in life. Unless all the prescribed rituals are followed and all precautions taken, the dead can wreak terrible vengeance.[7]

Eskimos are an ingenious and eminently practical people who do not normally seek supernatural causes for natural events. Yet many events of vital concern to them seem so far beyond their comprehension that supernatural powers must be postulated in order to retain a sense of the world as cosmos, not chaos. Why are there no bears? A hunter may reply, "There are no bears because there is no ice, and there is no ice because there is too much wind, and there is too much wind because we have offended the powers." The Eskimo's world is controlled by the personalized forces of nature, by human and nonhuman souls, spirits, and deities. Some of these powers are evil; many have no moral attribute but can nonetheless cause harm simply because they are so severe.[8] Here is Aua, an Iglulik Eskimo, as he declaims a long litany of fears:

> We fear the weather spirit of earth, that we must fight against to wrest our food from land and sea. We fear Sila. We fear dearth and hunger in the cold snow huts. We fear Tákanakapsâluk, the great woman down at the bottom of the sea, that rules over the beasts of the sea. We fear the sickness that we meet with daily all around us; not death, but the suffering. We fear the evil spirits of life, those of the air, of the sea and the earth, that can help wicked shamans to harm their fellow men.

But to Aua, the greatest peril of life lies in the fact that human food consists entirely of souls. What deeper expression of guilt and dread than this?

> All the creatures that we have to kill and eat, all those we have to strike down and destroy to make clothes for ourselves, have souls, like we have, souls that do not perish with the body, and which must therefore be propitiated lest they should revenge themselves on us for taking away their bodies.[9]

Above and beyond the host of minor spirits and souls, Eskimos of the Canadian Arctic believe in three major deities: one is associated with the moon, another with the air, and the third with the sea. Only the moon god is good and well-intentioned toward humans. He is the maintainer of fertility and visits barren women. He is a mighty hunter, willing to share his game with human beings. He has influence with the sea goddess and marine animals—a belief based, apparently, on the Eskimos' observation that the moon affects tidal movements. He protects people from accident, and he comforts those on the point of suicide, calling out to them, "Come, come to me! It is not painful to die. It is only a moment of dizziness. It does not hurt to kill yourself."[10] The god of air is fierce and detests mankind. He hovers over the earth and threatens people with wind, fog, rain, and snowstorm. But the most problematical deity for the Eskimos is the goddess who lives at the bottom of the sea, for she is both mother and mistress of animals, those in the sea as well as those on land. In Aua's litany, she is Tákanakapsâluk, the great woman down at the bottom of the sea. Elsewhere along the Arctic coast, she is known as Nuliajuk. Different versions exist of the story of the sea goddess's origins and why she can barely tolerate human beings. However, through all of them are threaded the themes of betrayal, abandonment, and cruelty under the pressure of extreme hardship. Here is one version:

Once in times long past people left the settlement at Qingmertoq in Sherman Inlet. They were going to cross the water and had made rafts of kayaks tied together. They were many and were in haste to get away to new hunting grounds. And there was not much room on the rafts they tied together. At the village there was a little girl whose name was Nuliajuk. She jumped on the raft, together with the other boys and girls, but no one cared about her, no one was related to her, and so they seized her and threw her into the water. In vain she tried to get hold of the edge of the raft; they cut her fingers off, and lo! as she sank to the bottom the stumps became alive in the water and bobbed up round the raft like seals. That was how the seals came. But Nuliajuk herself sank to the bottom of the sea. There she became a spirit, the sea spirit, and she became the mother of the sea beasts, because the seals had formed out of her fingers that were cut off. And she also became mistress of everything else alive, the land beasts, too, that mankind had to hunt.[11]

Hunting is a high-risk occupation. Even in the nurturing forest of the Pygmies, there are wild pigs and elephants which can turn violent and threatening when cornered. The Eskimos, unlike the Pygmies, are great hunters who must confront large beasts of sea and land. A wounded walrus, whale, or bear can be extremely dangerous. Yet Eskimos do not fear animals. They fear, rather, their absence—their unavailability in times of need —and they fear those natural forces that withhold the animals from them. Among Eskimos and other hunters who must rely on the presence of a few large game animals, uncertainty is a more stressful form of fear than physical dangers that can be circumvented by skill.

In contrast to such hunter-gatherer dependence on the unmodified provisions of nature, farmers try to create a world of their own, a garden in which plants and animals—those favored by humans—can grow under human care and control. Food becomes not only more plentiful but also more reliable. Because it grows within a small, humanly defined space, people no longer have to roam for it. The roots of agriculture reach back more than 12,000 years. Since antiquity, the image of a fertile and restful garden has had an immense appeal to civilized people. But was there ever, in fact, an Eden? Did primitive cultivators live in a world free of worry and fear?

Some scholars believe that the earliest experimentations with agriculture began on the richly diversified peninsulas and islands of southeast Asia. They suggest that progressive fisherfolk took certain plants and animals under their care while still depending on the free provisions of nature for the bulk of their food. Victuals being available from a variety of sources, periods of real scarcity probably did not occur. In time, greater reliance was placed on domesticated plants. These were likely to have been tropical roots and tubers that could be harvested at different times of the year. Again, periods of real stress when food was unavailable would have been infrequent, especially if the people had not altogether lost their skills as gatherers and hunters.

In higher latitudes of greater seasonality, cultivators tended to discard rootstock crops in favor of seed-planted grains and pulses. Agriculture became somewhat more specialized. Though such a change meant greater technical competence and control over nature, it also made the cultivators more vulnerable to unseasonable weather. Harvests, instead of being multiple and staggered throughout the year, occurred at critical times, and when they failed, people were threatened with starvation. Anxiety was the price of progress.[12]

Shifting cultivation—a pioneering form of agriculture in which new clearings are made every few years—still provides a livelihood for more than 150 million people in the tropical and subtropical areas of the world. By observing current practice we gain insight into how the earliest farmers might have viewed, and coped with, their environment. Today, and probably also in the past, the time for disencumbering the land of trees is one of anxiety and stress. Food is short and the work is hard. Burning is a method for removing some of the vegetation, but what if the trees have not had time to dry and will not burn? Yet if the firing is postponed, the cultivators risk being caught by the first rains. The effort at clearing will have been in vain, and food shortage will threaten. With the crops coming up, the cultivators can hardly rest: they have to struggle against invasion by weeds and rhizomes of tree stumps that remain in the field. The crops must be protected against the ravages of ruminants and birds. Nature seems hostile and constant vigilance is necessary to keep it at bay. In Zambia, Pierre Gourou writes,

> Green corn crops attract wild herbivores, and these are frightened away. The Bembas of Zambia keep them off by putting up palings. The flights of birds which dart down on the ears of corn are driven off by shouts or volleys of stones. A network of strings is set up over the crops to enable a watchman perched on a platform to sound clappers to frighten away the birds. . . . The cultivators must often leave their villages and temporarily live near the plantation so as to keep a more effective watch. In these ways the crops are saved, unless they attract the attention of a herd of elephants.[13]

Agriculture marks a great technical advance over the economy of hunter-gatherers, yet it does not ensure a life of relative stability and ease. The paradox of success is vividly exemplified by the way two groups of people—Pygmies and Negroid shifting cultivators—respond to the Congo rain forest. The Pygmies, we have seen, have adapted well: life with them is not a constant struggle, nor is fear a burden. Compared with the Pygmies the Negroid farmers are late-comers to the forest, having moved in during the last four hundred years. They came as superior beings, with the power to alter the environment to an extent undreamed of by the hunter-gatherers. They revel in their superiority and treat their neighbors, the Pygmies, as servants. But despite the cultivators' technical knowledge and power, they have to struggle far harder for a living than do their "servants," the hunter-gatherers. To grow anything at all they must clear a patch of the forest. The task is laborious and time-consuming, for the trees are often twelve feet or more in diameter. Once more or less cleared, the ground has to be worked on repeatedly to prevent its being overgrown by weeds. It is difficult to maintain an artifactitious world in the tropical forest. Whereas Pygmies take only a morning to set up their informal camp, cultivators need months to construct their village. Once completed, the village attracts swarms of flies and mosquitoes that are rarely seen in the depth of the forest. Without the protection of the canopy, temperatures soar into the 90s at midday. The ground, covered with dry choking dust, turns into mud after rain. In three years the forest triumphs over the village, and the cultivators must move to another location and begin again their cycle of labor. Unlike the hunter-gatherers, therefore, the villagers see the forest as their enemy, which they mistrust and fear. As Turnbull put it, "they people the forest with evil spirits, and they fill their lives with magic, witchcraft and a belief in sorcery."[14]

Nature is energetic and unpredictable. One way to make sense of nature is to see it as packed with dangerous spirits that need to be propitiated. Almost without exception spirits haunt the villagers' world, and this is true whether the villagers practice shifting or a more permanent form of traditional agriculture. The spirits may be human or nonhuman in origin; villagers do not trouble themselves to make clear distinctions. Generally speaking, human spirits hover around the settlement and tend to be benevolent or at least harmless, though this is not always the case. Nature deities dominate the encircling bush. Villagers are afraid of the bush, about which they know little.

In different parts of the world, the attitudes of villagers toward their spirit-ridden environments show basic similarities despite significant variations in detail. To illustrate the basic similarities, consider two widely separated groups, the Mende and the Tarongans.

The Mende are an agricultural people of Sierra Leone. Their environment of tropical forest and savanna is fairly benign, but the Mende do not feel particularly secure: they see themselves at the mercy of drought and floods, lightning and squalls, poisonous snakes, bush pigs that threaten their crops, and leopards that carry off their chickens and may kill a human being. Spirits and powers that are potentially dangerous lurk almost everywhere. Their actions, however, are not entirely arbitrary. The Mende learn to interpret them in accordance with a loosely conceived hierarchical system. At the top of the hierarchy is the supreme God. He sends rain to fall on his "wife," the Earth, but otherwise his impact on the affairs of humans is small. Far more important to the Mende are the ancestral spirits. They stand next to God, and mediate between God and human beings. Ancestors are not sharply distinguished from various kinds of nature divinities. Sometimes the nature divinities are simply ancestors who inhabit natural objects such as mountains and trees. Some are tied to particular localities and set specified times to receive formal offerings from communal groups, like those given to ancestors. Others have no ties to place; they are capricious individuals with human tastes and passions, and the Mende must confront them as individuals with the help of human cunning and magic. Of the place-bound spirits, those of the rivers are among the most powerful. Once these river spirits commanded human sacrifices. They are still responsible for the death of people who try to cross a river in a dugout canoe, or try to swim or fish in it. Fear is centered on the rapids, eddies, and deep channels that cut through rock barriers.[15]

The Tarongans are rice farmers. They live in small isolated communities on the northwestern tip of Luzon in the Philippines. Their country is rugged but attractive, consisting of majestic mountains that slope down bamboo-topped ridges and terraced valleys into the sea. Plant life is rich. Many wild fruits, vegetables, and roots are suitable for human consumption. Animal life, by contrast, is sparse except for the omnipresent but harmless lizards. Snakes are rare. In fact, the bush harbors few dangerous animals. Nature seems provident, yet the world of the Tarongans is a troubled one. Spirits manifest themselves in unpleasant ways around dark bushes, at shadowed water holes, under large isolated trees, about the houseyards, and even within the house. Ancestral beings haunt the area of the house; though friendly most of the time, they can also be dangerous. When a spirit of the dead touches a person, he is chilled and develops a headache and fever.

The farther the Tarongans move away from their settlement the more likely they are to meet nature spirits that are maliciously rather than unintentionally harmful. Several kinds exist. The least dangerous are mischievous, humanlike creatures who live in thickly wooded places. A greater threat are the "black ones," malevolent beings who dwell in large isolated trees far from human habitation. Even more powerful and threatening are the *sa'ero,* whose habitat is again large trees and dark brushy places. The *sa'ero* are invariably evil-intentioned; they will go so far as to lure people from their houses to do them injury. Fortunately, the *sa'ero* are not numerous. The largest class of supernatural beings and therefore the ones most likely to be met with are known under the elastic term of "nonhumans." These spirits can cause illness, accident, and death. They are omnipresent at night and follow the dark as it closes in on the house. For this reason, say William and Corinne Hydegger,

> Tarongans fasten their shutters and stay indoors if possible; when they must go out, they carry a light and stay close to the house unless they are part of a safely large group. Only on full-moon nights, when additional light is almost superfluous, is it safe for Tarongans to gather in the yard to boil peanuts, chat, or practice dueling with long, hardwood swords.[16]

Why do villagers live in such possessed worlds? The Mende, it is true, face a number of real dangers, including poisonous snakes and bush pigs. But what have the Tarongans to fear from their beneficent environment? Illness, accident, and premature death do occur, but these griefs are the inescapable fate of all mortals and cannot in themselves explain the prevalence of malignant spirits. As a general answer, we may say simply this. Villagers everywhere create a humanized landscape out of an original wilderness, knowing that they can maintain their creation only through sweat and constant vigilance. Despite a surface appearance of calm, village life can be full of uncertainty and stress, exacerbated (perhaps) by a sense of transgression against nature. Under such circumstances, the imagination is quick to populate space with lurking evil spirits.

6.

Natural Calamities and Famines

Although organization is power, power over the natural environment does not automatically produce a sense of security: subsistence farmers do not usually feel more secure than do primitive hunter-gatherers. Likewise, the move from village to state, from culture to civilization, does not necessarily result in any significant abatement of fear. What may indeed change is the character and frequency of dread. Villagers, for example, are haunted by local nature spirits who require frequent propitiation; by contrast, the subjects and rulers of a state fear the breakdown of cosmic order and the unleashing of violent natural forces that can devastate whole regions.

A notable fact about archaic civilizations is that they evince a persistent lack of confidence in the cosmos as a going concern. The movement of the sun, the cycle of the seasons, and the orderly procedure of society itself cannot be taken for granted. Why did the ancients feel so vulnerable when, wherever they looked, they saw cities, monuments, and irrigation works that testified to human achievement and control? One reason may have been that the threat of famine remained ever present and had especially devastating implications for city dwellers who neither caught nor raised their own food. Transportation was too primitive to bring relief from distant provinces, and the evacuation of masses of hungry people was rarely feasible. Even in the countryside, dependence on only one or two staple crops meant that when the harvests failed, people lacked other foods with which to feed themselves. Moreover, farmers in archaic civilizations had lost the skills to live comfortably off wild nature. Let us look at a few cases.

Egypt was blessed with a dependable natural environment:

the sun made its predictable trajectory across the sky, and the Nile, thanks to its broad net of headwaters in sub-Saharan Africa, flooded regularly. Hence the sun and the Nile were the two supreme deities of ancient Egypt. Dependability is, however, a relative term. The sun gives life but its intense heat can kill. It can also destroy life by withdrawing and sending chill and darkness over the land. Moreover, as the Egyptians saw it, light and warmth were not guaranteed, for every night the sun on his journey through the underworld had to do battle with Apophis, the snake of darkness. This struggle became especially intense on the first morning of the new year, when human ritual had to supplement the sun's power were the sun to rise again. As for that other great source of life, the Nile, its dependability was also relative. The Nile was more reliable than the Mesopotamian rivers and the Huang Ho, but water levels did fluctuate over both short and long periods, and either extreme—too little or too much water—could bring disaster to Egypt.

A primary duty of a pharaoh or a nomarch to his people was to mitigate the effects of a natural disaster. He had an obligation to relieve famine. Thus Ameni, the nomarch of Oryx-Nome, boasted: "When the years of famine came I plowed all the fields of Oryx-Nome, preserving its people alive. Then followed great Niles, rich in grain and all things, but I did not collect the arrears of the field."[1]

Cosmic order seemed more tenuous in Mesopotamia than it did in Egypt. Compared with the Nile valley, nature in the land of the Tigris and Euphrates was capricious indeed. There were, of course, the great diurnal and seasonal periodicities; but unpredictable violences such as thunderstorms (described by the Mesopotamians as "dreadful flares of light") and floods disrupted them.

> The rampant flood which no man can oppose
> Which shakes the heavens and causes earth to tremble,
> In an appalling blanket folds mother and child,
> Beats down the canebrake's full luxuriant greenery,
> And drowns the harvest in its time of ripeness.[2]

All peoples yearn for life, but the Sumerians' longing had a special pathos because they did not believe in a paradisiac afterworld. Security even in this world proved elusive. Fear, said the Orientalist S. N. Kramer, darkly stained the life of the Sumerian. "From birth to death he had cause at times to fear his parents, his teachers, his friends and fellow citizens, his superiors and rulers, the foreign enemy, the violence of nature, wild animals, vicious monsters and demons, sickness, death, and oblivion."³

To the archaic mind, a major fear was that the cosmos itself might momentarily collapse. Even the great cycles of nature could fail unless they were maintained by rituals and sacrifices, including human sacrifice. In Babylon during the first millennium B.C., for eleven days every spring the thoughts of the entire population were riveted on the ceremonies of the New Year Festival. The ceremonies were meant to reassure every Mesopotamian who felt that the cosmos might revert to chaos and that the fate of the country depended on the judgment of the gods. Nothing short of such an elaborate ritual loaded with magical virtues could solve this unavoidable crisis of faith and put an end to the terrible uncertainty that overwhelmed the whole people.⁴ At one point in the festival a priest would cut off the head of a ram, rub its blood on the temple walls, and then throw both head and body into the river. Could a human being—perhaps the king himself—once have served this role as a scapegoat for the transgressions of the past year? The Babylonian historian Berossus, writing in the third century B.C., suggested the possibility of a royal sacrifice in remote times. What the extant texts do record is the public humiliation of the king: he was struck on the cheek until the tears flowed.

The ancient Chinese, particularly during the Shang dynasty (c. 1500–1030 B.C.), believed that human sacrifices were necessary to promote the fertility of the earth. "One gains the impression," Wolfram Eberhard writes, "that many [Shang] wars were conducted not as wars of conquest but only for the purpose of capturing prisoners." These prisoners were killed and offered to the gods. The custom of using human victims to sustain fertility extended far beyond the places of high ritual. In some regions men lurked near springs awaiting travelers from other villages, and slew them for sacrificial purposes. Portions of the victims' flesh were then distributed to the owners of nearby fields, who buried them.

Although by Confucian times (sixth century B.C.) all ritual murder was prohibited, the practice was reported in the central regions of China down to the eleventh century and later. The famous boat festival of southern China, held yearly in the spring, had once been a device for offering human victims to the deities of fertility.⁵ In the feudal courts of the Early Chou dynasty (c. 1030–722 B.C.) an exorcist danced to inaugurate the New Year, and the ceremony ended with the quartering of human victims at the four gates of the principal city. Even at the time of Confucius, the Chinese still thought that in order to inaugurate a new reign and disperse the miasma of the old order, it was well to kill a man and fling his members to the four gates of the city. When a great drought gripped the land, witches were required to dance in the fields until exhausted, and then they were burned. However, by the Earlier Han dynasty (202 B.C.–A.D. 9), priests and officials made only symbolic sacrificial gestures to maintain the correct alternation of the seasons. At an appropriate time, images of a male and a female spirit of drought were thrown into the water; or a household of plowmen in effigy might be immolated.[6]

The sacrificial killing of human beings reached an apogee in the Aztec civilization in the Valley of Mexico. At the capital city of Tenochtitlán, which had a population of 300,000, some 15,000 people were sacrificed annually. Most of the victims were prisoners of war. Indeed, a primary purpose of war was to ensure the necessary supply of victims. Here was a robust people who, from modest beginnings, had created a high urban culture and an empire in less than two hundred years. Yet the world seemed to them most insecure. The Aztecs believed that other ages had existed before their own and that each had ended amid cataclysms during which humankind was wiped out. Even while their world flourished they could see that it was built on the ruins of another high culture, the Toltec, which had vanished. Nature's most predictable rhythms failed to assuage the Aztecs' disposition to be anxious. The sun rose every morning, but could it do so without its food, human blood? To nourish "our mother and our father, the earth and the sun" was the first duty of man. To shirk such a duty was not only to betray the gods but all humankind. Men were offered to the sun and killed on top of a pyramid. Women were dedicated to the goddesses of the earth: while they danced, pretending to be unaware of their fate, their heads were lopped off. Children were drowned as an offering to the rain god Tlaloc.[7]

Ancient states and empires such as the Chinese and the Aztec had the knowledge and organization to build monuments and cities, but they remained at nature's mercy. Splendid artifacts could not persuade the people that they lived in a predictable world. Stars, like the monuments that were built to conform with celestial coordinates, seemed permanent. Yet the people knew only too well that, so far as their livelihood was concerned, these guarantors of permanence had little or no effect. Nature's behavior close to earth was wayward. No one could prognosticate the weather with certainty and presage whether next year the people would prosper or starve. Under such circumstances, stability must have seemed an illusion and chaos a constant threat. It is not rash to say that, except for a small elite class, almost every adult in premodern society knew the threat and often the reality of hunger. Crops shriveled by the sun, submerged under floodwaters, or ravaged by pests were a common sight.

To alleviate the anxiety of the people and prevent mass starvation, enlightened rulers established food reserves in granaries. The Book of Genesis tells the story of Joseph, who helped the pharaoh build storehouses in Egypt in anticipation of the predicted "seven lean years." With the stored grain Joseph could feed both the Egyptians and natives from other countries, for "famine was sore in all lands." By the Han dynasty, China at least recognized the need for granaries. As Chia Yi (200–168 B.C.), the able adviser to Emperor Wu, asked his master, "In case of a famine in a territory of two or three thousand *li,* where could relief be procured?"[8]

In ancient Mexico, a major task of any government was to forestall severe natural disasters by accumulating grain in the storehouses. The Aztec emperor, known traditionally as "the father and mother of his people," was obligated to struggle for them against famine. The emperors took their duties seriously. Motecuhzoma I distributed food and clothing to the entire population; Auitzotl shared out 200,000 loads of maize among the victims of flood. The Chinese emperor, likewise the "father of his people," mediated between heaven and earth. When harvests were poor, he demonstrated his paternal concern by remitting taxes in the afflicted areas and by opening up government granaries. Should a natural calamity persist, the emperor had to intercede with heaven. Imperial decrees of 1832 and 1878 show that in the Ch'ing dynasty the Chinese ruler still subscribed to the ancient belief that his own transgressions might bring on cosmic disorder and that it was his duty to fast and offer sacrifices in atonement. The petition of 1832 reads in part:

> This year the drought is most unusual. Summer is past, and no rain has fallen. Not only do agriculture and human beings feel the dire calamity, but also beasts and insects, herbs and trees. I, the minister of Heaven, am placed over mankind, and am responsible for keeping the world in order and calming the people. Some days ago I fasted, and offered rich sacrifices on the altars of the gods of the land and grain, and had to be thankful for gathering clouds and slight showers, but not enough to cause gladness. Prostrate I beg Heaven to pardon my ignorance and stupidity, and to grant me self-renovation; for myriads of innocent people are involved by me, the One man. My sins are so

numerous it is difficult to escape from them. Summer is past and autumn arrived; to wait longer will really be impossible. I humbly supplicate Heaven to hasten and confer gracious deliverance —a speedy and divinely beneficial rain, to save the people's lives and in some degree redeem my iniquities. Oh, alas! imperial Heaven, observe these things. Oh, alas! imperial Heaven, be gracious to them. I am inexpressibly grieved, alarmed, and frightened.[9]

Food shortages and starvation threatened premodern agricultural peoples almost everywhere, but nowhere on such a scale as in India and China. By A.D. 2 both countries supported large populations. China had some 50 million people, mostly concentrated in the subhumid valleys and plains of the Huang Ho basin; the Indian subcontinent's population was almost twice that size. These two largest and densest assemblages of human beings in the world depended (and still depend) on the timely arrival and retreat of the monsoon rains. When they came too late or withdrew too soon, famine threatened hundreds of thousands, sometimes even millions, of peasants. In India, one of the worst calamities of all time occurred in 1770, the result of two years of poor crops followed by the complete failure of the rains in the third year. Some 30 million people in West Bengal and Bihar suffered, and perhaps as many as 10 million of them died of starvation and disease. In Orissa and along much of the east coast of India, the drought of 1865–1866, followed by torrential rains in 1867 and bungling government policy, caused some 10 million people to perish from disease and lack of food.[10] In China, practically no rain fell on the densely settled northern provinces between 1876 and 1879; the famine and ensuing outbreaks of violence took a toll of between 9 and 13 million people. Famines induced by drought recurred in the years 1892–1894, 1900, 1920–1921, and 1928: the number of people who died during and soon after each disaster ranged from half a million to 3 million.

Drought was the greatest but not the only natural calamity. In China, floods came a close second, followed by pestilence and earthquakes. The flooding of the Yangtze River in 1931 affected more than 12 million people. Some 14 million were dislodged from their homes when the same river went on a rampage in 1935. The total number of deaths from that disaster remains unknown, but it must have been extremely high: one unprepared county in Hupei province lost 220,000 of its total population of 290,000. The flooding of the Huang Ho between 1938 and 1946 probably took half a million lives.[11] In India, the densely populated Ganges delta stands only a few feet above sea level and is easily submerged during the cyclone season. Every year or so thousands of Bengalese peasants may die in quite ordinary storms. Exceptional storms drown rice crops and can trigger food shortages and starvation over a broad region. Officials estimated 1.5 million deaths in the Bengal famine of 1943, although the actual number may have been more than twice as great.[12] Half a million people perished when a hurricane struck East Bengal in November 1970.

A bare recitation of major calamities leaves out the large number of minor droughts and floods that plague an area, and it omits the actual experiences of suffering and fear. Nature's oscillations need not induce widespread famine to cast a pall of dread if they recur often and unpredictably. We lack reliable data for the less dramatic events even in a country as well documented historically as China. Ping-ti Ho, however, has been able to make an estimate of the number and frequency of disasters that affected Hupei province during the 267 years of the Ch'ing dynasty (1644–1911). Through this entire period, droughts occurred in 92 years and floods in 190 years. The Hupei records indicate that natural calamities struck an average of 7 counties out of a total of 71 every year; in other words, about one-tenth of the province was hit annually by one or another type of misfortune. Other parts of China, particularly those in the north and in the Huai River basin, might have fared worse—far worse—because they lacked Hupei province's stable climate and diversified environments.[13]

Historical records rarely depict scenes of famine in all their desolation and horror. Officials who witnessed the disasters wrote in a formal style and appear to have suppressed their feelings, perhaps because they themselves had enough to eat as they tried to help the dying who swarmed about them. The afflicted, when they survived, lacked the literacy to record the depth of their anguish. However, a few vivid accounts do exist. Kashmir's drought in 917–918 was described in Kalhana's *Rājataranġini* (A Chronicle of the Kings of Kashmir). Kalhana (fl. 1148) wrote:

> One could scarcely see water in the Vitasta (Jehlum), entirely covered as the river was with corpses soaked and swollen by the water in which they had long been lying. The land became densely covered with bones in all directions, until it was like one great burial-ground, causing terror to all beings. Meanwhile the king's ministers and the Tantrins (guards) became wealthy by selling stores of rice at high prices.[14]

In China, an imperial commissioner for the relief of famine in Shansi reported what that province was like in the winter of 1877:

> From my inspectional tours which have covered some 3,000 *li* all that my eyes could see were those thin and emaciated human figures and all that my ears could hear were the howls of males and screams of females. Sometimes my cart had to detour in order to avoid rolling over human skeletons which piled up on the highways. Many of those still alive fell flat on the ground after calling for help.[15]

The China Famine Relief Committee described the perils of laboring among starving people thus:

> Barrenness and want were seen on every side, and apart from the danger, by coming in contact with such sights as were everywhere met with, and breathing the pestilential air of the neighborhood, the whole was only fitted to shock every feeling of humanity, and excite the deepest sense, at once, of pity and disgust.[16]

Another prolonged drought devastated much of North China between the years 1941 and 1943, when China was at war with Japan. The reporter Jack Belden wrote vividly of the scene.

> In Honan, the roads to the Taihang Mountains were soon filled with corpses. In the spring of 1942, the buds of all trees were eaten. The bark was stripped from every tree so that the trunks presented a strange white appearance like people stripped of clothes. In some places, people ate the feces of silkworms; in other places, they ate a queer white earth. . . . Women exchanged their babies, saying: "You eat mine, I'll eat yours."[17]

In 1962, a villager in Yenan recalled his personal experience of the famine of 1928 and 1929, when he was a small child.

> We went about begging. We had nothing to eat. Father went to Chaochuan to gather firewood and beg food, but he didn't get any. He was carrying elm leaves and firewood when he fell by the roadside. We waited for him all night. In the morning, when he hadn't come, Mother said: "Now let's go and see what's happened to him." Then Mother and Uncle and I walked along the road towards Chaochuan. I was the one who saw him first. He was lying on his face and was dead. The elm leaves and firewood were still there beside him. No one had touched a thing. The elm leaves were for us to eat. He wasn't ill; he had just starved to death.[18]

Governments had the power and organization to collect taxes and draft men for war against human enemies. Why couldn't they have fought against nature and at least mitigated the distress it caused? Some rulers lacked the will; indeed, Kalhana's account of the Kashmir famines (917–918 and 1099–1100) suggests that kings and ministers might blatantly seek personal profit from natural disasters. Some governments lacked the necessary organization even if they had the will. In the early part of the seventeenth century, when the Mogul Empire in India was at the height of its splendor, it still could do nothing to avert a major calamity like the Gujarat famine of 1632.[19] Indian princes, unlike those in China, did not see it as their duty to provide public granaries in those parts of the country likely to be afflicted. Local granaries, in any case, could provide only temporary relief to swelling masses of starving people. When a drought persisted, food had to be brought in from outside. The solution sounds simple, but in reality it was not. A prime reason for the high death toll in stricken areas was the primitive state of communications. This fact has long been recognized. Inland cities were especially vulnerable to shortages and famine. As Gregory Nazianzen, a fourth-century divine, put it:

> The city [of Caesarea in central Asia Minor] languished but there was no help from any part, no remedy for the calamity. Cities on the sea coast easily endure a shortage of this kind, importing by sea the things of which they are short. But we who live far from the sea . . . are able neither to export what we have nor import what we lack.[20]

When drought struck the densely populated interior provinces of China, isolation from outside help led to death by the millions. During the famine of 1876–1879, months passed before news of distress even reached the capital and coastal ports. Peasants were already dying in large numbers before any concerted effort was made to bring in food. After the desperate conditions had become widely known, the problem of transporting the needed quantity of grain over distances of hundreds of miles on narrow dirt roads proved almost insurmountable. The resulting horror was vividly depicted in an official report:

> During the winter and spring of 1877–78, the most frightful disorder reigned supreme along the route to Shansi. Fugitives, beggars, and thieves absolutely swarmed. The officials were powerless to create any sort of order among the mountains. The track was completely worn out. Camels, oxen, mules, and donkeys were hurried along in the wildest confusion. . . . Night traveling

was out of the question. The way was marked by the carcasses or skeletons of men and beasts, and the wolves, dogs, and foxes soon put an end to the sufferings of any wretch who lay down to recover from or die of his sickness. Broken carts, scattered grain bags, dying men and animals so frequently stopped the way, that it was often necessary to prevent for days together the entry of convoys on the one side, in order to let the trains from the other come over.[21]

Droughts and floods, starvation and death, are grisly though familiar tales out of China and India. In comparison, Europe is a favored continent where nature seems mild. Weather oscillates but on a minor scale, and European rivers are small and well behaved compared with those in the Orient. Yet famines and starvation induced by the vagaries of nature were very much a part of European history until modern times. Terrible and widespread famines visited the continent in the early decades of the eleventh century. In the twelfth century the opening up of new arable land eased the demographic pressure, although here and there irregular harvests resulted in scarcities, and hordes of hungry people in search of food periodically besieged monasteries and city gates. The fact was that even in a good period lean years followed fat years, and even in the best seasons many people had to be content to live from hand to mouth in springtime and in the weeks before the harvest.

After 1300 an age of catastrophic shortages began. Climate deteriorated markedly: pack ice in the Arctic Ocean moved south so that the shipping route from Norway to Greenland had to be shifted. A succession of wet seasons made the difficulties of chronic poor harvests much more acute, and provoked in 1309, in the south and west of Germany, a crisis in the supply of wheat which then spread to the rest of Western Europe. During the worst period, from 1315 to 1317, crop failures were reported from Ireland to Hungary. In 1316, the records of Ypres in Flanders show that between May and October some 2,800 bodies, or roughly a tenth of the population, were buried at public expense. Villages, especially in Germany, were abandoned wholesale, and many of them were never resettled.[22] Famines of comparable severity were a recurrent threat to towns in late medieval Europe. From the archives of Toulouse seven famines can be traced between 1334 and the middle of the fifteenth century. The problems of food supply became everywhere a permanent and acutely felt burden on all municipal bodies—in Italy as well as in Languedoc and Germany.[23]

We would expect people in medieval times, isolated in their

villages, towns, and feudatories, to have been backward, lacking the organizational and technical means to combat the tough exigencies of nature. Yet when we turn to seventeenth-century France, we find that the subjects of the Great King were not much better off. Nature was still all-powerful. France's economy relied heavily on cereal crops, which were most sensitive to unseasonable weather, particularly cool summers and excessive rain, and these appeared with abnormal frequency throughout the seventeenth century. When crops failed in one area, poor transportation made swift relief impossible. On the other hand, rumors of famine could and did spread rapidly, and their effect was to make the price of grain soar in the markets. From time to time people starved to death, not because food was absolutely unavailable, but because it cost too much.

Food shortages, famines, and periods of relative well-being followed one another with demoralizing regularity. Bad weather and poor harvests brought on the widespread famine of 1661–1662. Beggars from rural areas flocked to city gates and charitable institutions, demanding bread. All over the country citizens formed militias to drive them back. A spell of favorable weather produced good harvests in 1663, and that year marked the beginning of a decade of relative prosperity. From 1674 onward, however, the times were once more "out of joint." A wet summer curtailed the harvest of 1674 in many places; those of 1677, 1678, and 1679 fared worse. Yields were poor in 1681 and catastrophic in some regions in 1684. The price of food shot up. Between 1679 and 1684 the death toll began to rise throughout France. Weather was good again from 1684 to 1689. Magnificent harvests made for cheap grain, and the people were adequately fed. Then came the great famine of 1693–1694, the culmination of a series of cold and wet years. The majority of people in France, and many in other countries as well, were threatened with, suffered, or actually died from starvation. In April 1693, a minor official of the bishopric of Beauvais observed

> an infinite number of poor souls, weak from hunger and wretchedness and dying from want and lack of bread in the streets and squares, in the towns and countryside because, having no work or occupation, they lack the money to buy bread. Seeking to prolong their lives a little, these poor folk eat such unclean things as cats and flesh of horses flayed and cast on to dung heaps. ... Others will grub up the beans and seed corn which were sown in the spring.[24]

Was starvation a serious problem in Tudor and Stuart England? The record seems to point that way. Peter Laslett suggests at least the possibility that the very high death rate in Colyton, Devonshire, in 1645 was caused by local famine. The villagers at Hartland, fifty miles to the west, had enough to eat but no surplus, it would seem, to help their distressed neighbors.[25] Andrew Appleby argues that the high death rates in the northwestern counties of Cumberland and Westmorland were induced by famine rather than by epidemic disease, as had been thought previously. People died from lack of food in northern England in 1587–1588, 1597, and 1623. The dismal sequence was a wet summer, followed by harvest failure, the soaring of food prices beyond the reach of the poor, and starvation. Such a sequence might be repeated over a number of years before a good harvest brought relief.

> A citizen of Newcastle wrote, in 1597, of "sundry starving and dying in our streets and in the fields for lack of bread." Newcastle's corporate records confirm the distress: in September and October of 1597, 25 "poore folkes who died for want in the streets" were buried at the town's expense. A dismal picture—yet Newcastle seems to have been better off than other areas in the north, thanks to the importation of foreign grain. But for these grain shipments, thousands would have died of starvation, the Dean of Durham wrote to Robert Cecil.[26]

In the seventeenth century, life was insecure not only for farm laborers, small farmers, and the poor in general, but also for people of superior economic means. Although we lack quantitative data to support this statement, a detailed case study such as Alan Macfarlane's portrait of an English clergyman nevertheless conveys, forcefully, an impression of life's precariousness. Ralph Josselin (1617–1683) had three major sources of annual income: his living as vicar of Earls Colne in Essex, profits from farming and leasing land, and fees from teaching at a school. Josselin kept a diary, densely packed with facts and observations, over a period of more than forty years. What were this clergyman and family man's worries and concerns? Religious meditations occupy much space in his diary, but almost as much is taken up by references to the weather and the progress of the harvest. Weather appears on most pages; dozens of entries record the amount of rain, the degree of warmth, and the excesses of wind. Josselin spoke of drought on several occasions, but without doubt felt most threatened by the wet years and floods. A typical entry for 1648 notes: "This weeke was very wett, the season very sad both in reference to corne and unto fallowes, very few lands being fitt to be sowne upon; some say that divers catle that feed in the meadowes dye, their bowells being eaten out with gravel & durt." The weather affected Josselin's food supply, the amount of money he was able to save and spend on his children, and the amount he had to spend on fuel. However, even in the worst years, the late 1640s, Josselin and his family did not starve, unlike the poor who crowded the streets of Earls Colne.[27]

In the eighteenth century, life grew notably more secure in Western Europe. Famine and starvation, recurrent threats in rural France in the seventeenth century, were no longer a common event. Thanks to more clement weather conditions, to a more effective royal government, and to a more efficient national distribution of supplies, local calamities gave way to something better—in a rather desperate sense—namely, a generalized pattern of chronic distress. The end of severe famine made it possible for the poor people of France to multiply. A starving population could not reproduce itself, but a merely undernourished one had no difficulty increasing. Ironically, with improved conditions, there were more poor people than ever, and hunger could never have been far from their minds. Even more than in the past, hunger threatened because, following a meager harvest, profiteering by local traders and city merchants quickly raised the cost of food and put it beyond reach. People seem to have lived in a state of nagging anxiety; any family not producing enough to feed itself must have wondered whether it could afford to purchase food when there was a shortage. Fear lurked in the background even though on the surface people might have appeared calm and gay. "Communities and individuals alike lived on their nerves," writes Olwen Hufton. People with very little dreaded falling to the level of those who had nothing at all. "In times of dearth . . . fears multiplied and others were added, not least the fear of calculating outsiders intent upon removing grain from a community to push up prices and the fear of village for town and of small town for large town, each suspicious that someone was enjoying better conditions and lower prices."[28]

Natural calamities, obviously, did not affect all strata of society to the same extent. Those who toiled on the land and the poor in general suffered most. Statistical data on mortality rates, contemporary reports, and government documents make it possible for us to envisage the horrors of famine; but the victims themselves—the thousands and (in the case of India or China) even millions who succumbed to each major disaster—left no personal record of their fears, anguish, and suffering. Indeed, to be a victim was to be unheard: the cries that pierced the air were quickly absorbed by it. When an ancient text preserves a people's fears, we consider the preserved account a fortunate happenstance. From such a text we can imagine, for instance, how the Sumerians saw the rampant flood "which shakes the heavens and causes earth to tremble" and "in an appalling blanket folds mother and child." Job, as he lamented God's indifference, was surely also expressing the people's anguish and bafflement: "When a sudden flood brings death, he mocks the plight of the innocent" (Job 9:23). The *Tao Teh Ching* says: "Heaven-and-Earth is not sentimental; it treats all things like straw-dogs."[29] Here too is folk wisdom, recorded in a Chinese classic.

Nature's ways and moods fluctuated unpredictably. That inconsistency was a constant source of fear from ancient times to the beginning of the modern age. Floods, earthquakes, and swarms of locusts appeared with little or no warning. The response to them was alarm—a sickening sense of the dissolution of the known world. Drought, by contrast, appeared gradually. As the sun blazed day after day, people became increasingly anxious and searched the sky for every portent of rain. Perhaps the following account of the heat and drought in the Punjab before the burst of the monsoon gives us an idea of how peasant farmers might feel as they waited for the moist winds:

> Man and beast languish and gasp for air, while even in the house the thermometer stands day and night between 95° and 115°. Almost all green things wither; the grass seems burnt up to the roots; bushes and trees seem moribund; the ground is seamed with cracks; and the whole landscape wears an aspect of barrenness and sadness. At length, in June, the hot winds cease to blow, and are followed by a calm; and now indeed the heat is truly fearful; grass screens avail naught; all things pine for rain; but no rain, not even a shower can one hope for, till the south and east winds shall have set in.[30]

But what if the calm persists and the southeast winds do not come? Before modern irrigation networks were built in the upper Indus and Ganges valleys, this was a life-or-death question to hundreds of thousands of peasants, and one that plagued them every year.

Human beings cannot bear to live in a permanent state of anxiety. They need to retain a sense of control, however illusory this might be. Granaries, wells, and dikes provided a measure of assurance in the past, but only a measure: nothing could shield the populace from major disasters. Until modern technology gave human beings their feeling of mastery over nature, they could not rely on their own handiworks; these had to be supplemented by magical rites and ceremonies. With the Aztecs the ceremonies required so much thought, organizational effort, and toil that we may wonder why they did not use their resources and energies for more practical ends, such as building grain stores and improving methods of water control. But the Aztecs believed that the cosmos itself was threatened and the sun might not rise. No human work could prop up the cosmos, and only human blood could give the sun the strength to move on its course. Bloody human sacrifice, a horror to our sensibilities, was to the Aztecs a means to mitigate anxious dread. Even the victims' fear may not have been as intense as we now imagine, for high ritual could make one's own death seem not only appropriate and dignified but distant and impersonal.

Natural disasters were seen as departures from nature's essential harmony, which could be restored by human ritual. Ritual has this in common with scientific procedure or effective practical action: it follows definite and predictable rules. In times of uncertainty, the performance of set gestures can be reassuring in itself; and the sense of assurance is greatly increased when the gestures individually and together are believed to transmit supernatural power. Human sacrifices undertaken to promote fertility or ward off disaster were always part of a ceremony. In the course of time, animal victims took the place of human beings and animals made of straw were substituted for live ones. Only the gestures were retained. Ethnographic literature documents the numerous kinds of ritual that existed and probably still exist in different parts of the world. The Indians of the American Southwest continue to perform the rain dance. In rural churches, as the people stand or kneel, prayers are still offered for timely showers and a good harvest.

Ritual is a public act and an expression of faith in the world's orderly processes. When life and livelihood seem uncertain—for either natural or man-made reasons—another, more individual response is possible, and this is gambling. The Chinese are widely known for their propensity to gamble. Could indulgence in games of chance be a response to the precariousness of life? We don't know. However, several scholars have suggested that in the subhumid and semiarid lands of Alberta, Kansas, and New Mexico, farmers have developed a gambling attitude toward their enterprise in the face of highly variable rainfall. Dry farmers often have pessimistic moods and yet maintain enough confidence in their luck to keep on trying. They say, "It's good luck when we hit and bad luck when we don't"; or, "We're betting our labor, our seed, and our fuel against whether we make anything." In New Mexico, the Spanish-American farmers are more resigned. They believe in absolute chance, chance that cannot be outguessed—*sea lo que sea* (what will be, will be).[31] This is fatalism. To be fatalistic is to view the natural world as so immutable or so arbitrary and powerful in its ways that human initiatives must often end in failure. To a weary and frightened people, fatalism does offer the consolation of lethargic peace.

On the other hand, violence driven by fear is a common human response to food shortages and to noncatastrophic famines. Since anger cannot reasonably be directed against nature, it has been aimed at other human beings such as ruthless or irresponsible officials, traders who profited by adversity, and fellow sufferers who competed for vanishing supplies of food. In China during the T'ang dynasty (A.D. 618–907), for instance, natural disasters played a role in 22 out of a recorded total of 39 "minor agrarian riots." (A minor agrarian riot is a spontaneous uprising undertaken by peasants without the support of a political-military leader or an articulated ideology.) In the *Tzu Chih T'ung Chien,* a history written in 1084, such incidents as the following are recorded:

> In November 621, three thousand hungry people with a few hundred carts left Iu Chou for grain, which had been promised them. They rioted because the warlord in Yen Chou did not keep his promise. . . . A serious flood occurred in September of 811 in western Hu-nan. The local officials forced the peasants to repair the embankment. The peasants objected and started a riot which lasted several days.

Natural disasters caused hardship, but not necessarily rioting if the government was perceived as just and concerned. Chinese peasants knew better than to rebel against the decrees of Heaven. However, when natural disaster was added to the burden of a corrupt and irresponsible government, the people's anger and frustration might well erupt in acts of violence.[32] The result was a tottering world in which all known harmonies threatened to dissolve—those of nature, those of society both at the level of formal governance and at that of intimate human relationships, and those of body and mind.

Anger and alarm still signal life. Toward the end, as starvation proceeds, these sensations yield to cold despair. A landscape of dying men, women, and children with barely the energy to stir and cry may have aroused feelings of the utmost horror in passers-by, but as to how the victims themselves felt the record is silent.

7.

Fear in the Medieval World

An external nature that seemed all-powerful and hard to predict was one major cause of human insecurity and fear in prehistoric times, in archaic civilizations, and in tribal and traditional societies. Another was and is human nature, its fickleness, its potential for violence and cruelty. We have noted the adult's often harsh attempts to domesticate childish nature. In subsequent chapters, we shall examine the fear of evil and chaos in human individuals and groups. The forces that threaten humankind from without and within can thus be explored one by one. There is need, however, to see how all of them appear to dovetail with and even merge into one another in a particular culture. To satisfy this need, we shall explore medieval Europe. A good reason for selecting Europe is, of course, its historical role in generating the beliefs and attitudes of the modern age. Our own kind of mentality, with its curious excesses and fervors, has its roots in the past. What were the superstitious fears which prevailed in that past?

Europeans in the Middle Ages were insecure to a degree that it is hard for us now to envisage. Eighteenth- and nineteenth-century medievalism (from which we are not wholly free) tended to romanticize this bygone age, detecting in it a colorfulness, an intensity, and a range of feeling, a scope for the imagination, that shrank and faded with the appearance of modern industrial life. But if the people of the Middle Ages feasted on color and beauty in their churches and festivities, they saw also utter drabness and filth in their daily surroundings; if they knew ecstasy and caught glimpses of heaven, they were far more familiar with toil and danger, acedia and fear.

The emotional tone of the Middle Ages had material causes.

Premature deaths, epidemics, and violence gave life a special quality of excitement and stress. Modern writers of history, with their broad perspective on time, may see A.D. 1250 as the culminating point of medieval culture; they observe impressive progress in art, technology, and the institutions of government, particularly from 1100 onward. But to people who lived in those times, much more evident were month-to-month, year-to-year events, which included civil and religious strife, wars, epidemics and famines. Poor health, bad food, and bad eating habits no doubt played tricks on the imagination, making it easier for a person to hallucinate, have nightmares, and see visions. Overeating among the rich and undernourishment among the poor surely militated against a balanced view of life.[1]

The supernatural was intimately present to the medieval person. Angels and demons occupied the same space as he, and accompanied him in all his activities. An important reason for this strong sense of the supernatural was that it played a key role in resolving social conflicts. Peter Brown notes that prior to the twelfth century the primary unit of society was the extended kin group: safety lay in having kinsfolk and dependents in small, tightly knit clusters. Because the coercive power of the state was so weak, only in an appeal to supramundane authority was there a chance to resolve conflicts peacefully, because only such authority was recognized as rising above the subjectivity of the contending parties. In a trial by ordeal, the accused was pronounced innocent if he or she sank in consecrated water. The theatricality of the ordeal made it into an instrument of consensus—a powerful device for containing potentially disruptive conflicts. At the same time it drew people's attention to the actuality of the supernatural. Society, in other words, required the miraculous and took steps to highlight it.[2]

Belief in angels, demons, and spirits is deep-seated in the human mentality. People everywhere, past and present, have an awareness of the preternatural, however faint and infrequent. The number of people who believe in spiritual agents and order their life's priorities accordingly has varied, of course, from culture to culture, and has diminished over the world as a whole with the progressive dominance of the scientific world-view. Today, belief in and communications with poltergeists and other suprasensible beings thrusts a person to the fringe of respectable cultivated society. In the early medieval world, such a person would have moved at its center. It was Saint Jerome, not an ignorant peasant, who proclaimed that "compared to the multitude of supernal and angelic beings, the mass of humanity is as nothing"—a view reaffirmed by Isidore, bishop of Seville, a couple of centuries later.[3] What made the world ominous to a medieval person was the large number of demons among the spirits. No less than a tenth and perhaps as many as a third of all the hosts of heaven fell with Satan. For this reason, one human individual could be tormented by a host of demons.[4] We are troubled today by the multitudes of people crowding the earth. To a medieval person it was not human beings but spirits both good and bad who packed space.

By the twelfth century, there were signs that the chimerical world of pseudo-nature was beginning to lose its grip on some people's imaginations. In theology, scholars showed increasing concern to distinguish between preternatural events, which were dramatic and miraculous, and the supernatural order of grace, which did not traffic with marvels. In art, the designers of monstrous symbolic bestiaries began to make way for naturalistic sculptors who created little scenes of plant, animal, or human life on cathedral façades. Side-by-side with gargoyles, chimeras, and other legendary beasts might appear fine carvings of oak leaves and hawthorn sprays, faithfully copied and tenderly arranged.[5] Deeply held ideas do not, however, change overnight. Even sophisticated medieval thought still differed markedly from our own. Consider the divergent meanings given to "corporeality," "life," and "sight."

To the modern person, the corporeal is the real, and what is tangibly present has a higher ontological status than the products of fantasy. To the medieval theologian, by contrast, corporeality was not the norm of existence but a sign of inferiority on the scale of creation: corporeality was a measure of distance from God and of the inability to contemplate him. The invisible hosts were more "real" than embodied human beings.

To the modern person, "life" is defined by sentience and reproductive capacity. In medieval thought, life was an essential quality of existence shared by stones, water, and fire as surely as it was by trees and angels. All creation was therefore alive. Even Copernicus retained a measure of this belief. When he described the sun as occupying "a throne in the middle of all things," from where "it could throw light on everything at once," he attributed to the sun the nature of a divine body that was able to see all and hence had the power to navigate the universe. Medieval people showed a tendency to animate even human-made objects; they christened ships, swords, and bells as though these things possessed unique powers and personalities. Pealing church bells frightened demons, calmed storms, and fended off lightning.

The church building at Glastonbury was so mighty, wrote William of Malmesbury, that "if any person erected a building in its vicinity, which by its shade obstructed the light of the church, it forthwith became a ruin."[6]

Lastly, the primary human faculty of sight was as much valued in the past as it is today, but for different reasons. To us, sight is precious because it enables us to live and act confidently in the world. To the medieval scholar, the utility of sight lay less in its survival value than in its ability to beget philosophy. Sight was the instrument of understanding: with it humans could penetrate crude reality and apprehend its ultimate meaning. Nothing, to the medieval scholar, was what it superficially seemed. Colors had symbolic value, social ranks carried religious import, and nature revealed the divine.[7]

Sophisticated medieval thought encouraged the acceptance of a reality that transcended the world perceived by the senses. Below this level, superstition was rife: humanity's natural predilection for the marvelous received every support. However, the difference in understanding between the unlettered and the learned was often minor. In stormy skies people saw phantom armies passing by. Armies of the dead, said the populace. Armies of deceitful demons, the learned might assert, much less inclined to deny these visions than to find for them a quasi-orthodox interpretation.

The supremacy and omnipotence of the Creator-God was recognized by everyone in the Middle Ages. But as with many preliterate peoples, God was remote and lived in the sky. On earth human beings suffered all kinds of misfortune; rather than try to reconcile them to the will of God, it was easier to explain them as the consequences of perpetual strife among numerous minor powers, good and bad. "Who does not know," wrote the priest Helmold, "that the wars, the mighty tempests, the pestilences, all the ills, indeed, which afflict the human race, occur through the agency of demons?"[8] We have noted that in late medieval churches, sensitive representations of nature shared space with sculptures of strange beasts. An even more vivid conflict could be seen: on one side the triune God, on the other the grimacing faces of evil—a fantastic display of demonic imagery. "The atmosphere of formal worship," a modern medievalist writes, "was not one of divine victory but of an uneasy truce between the powers of light and darkness. Here the dark side of the enchanted world—its fear of unknown yet powerful incorporeal beings—fused with the theology of evil. Together they underscored the sense of arbitrary tragedy that loomed so large in the medieval period."[9] The antitheses of day and night, summer and winter, reinforced the sense of the dualistic nature of the universe. Jehovah seemed only the God of spring and summer. Winter, a time of privation even for those who lived in castles, belonged to Satan. The regions of cold and bad weather were his especially. The devil lived in the north, as we see in Jeremiah 1:14, in Saint Augustine, and in Chaucer's "Friar's Tale."[10]

Uncertainty in life goaded medieval people to grasp at every sign that promised to foretell the future and raise such time-centered questions as: Would the crop survive the frost? Would there be war, famine, and pestilential visitations? People looked heavenward for portents. The brilliance of the night sky in those times was undimmed by city lights. Normally philosophers and scholars contemplated it with pleasure and awe, for there lay the calm of the heavenly spheres. But for that reason any disturbance in the sky—an eclipse of the sun or moon, the appearance of a comet, or an unusual display of the aurora borealis—signaled disaster. The Venerable Bede described "the great terror" that struck all beholders when two comets appeared around the sun in the year 729: "One of them preceded the sun as it rose in the east in the morning and the other followed it as it set in the west in the evening, as if to herald disaster in both east and west. . . . They appeared in the month of January and remained for nearly two weeks. At this time a terrible plague of Saracens wasted Gaul with cruel bloodshed."[11] It was the custom then to animalize the heavenly bodies. Bede's comets had "long hair ablaze with flames." In 793, Symeon of Durham saw "fearful prodigies," "horrible lightnings," and "dragons" flying to and fro. In 664, an eclipse of the sun led the people in Essex to desert the Christian church and rebuild the ruined pagan temples. By contrast, a similar portent in the late Middle Ages served to strengthen the faith. Brother Salimbene of Parma reported:

> In the year of our Lord 1239 there was an eclipse of the sun, wherein the light of day was horribly and terribly darkened, and the stars appeared. And it seemed as though night had come, and all men and women had sore fear, and went about as if bereft of their wits, with great sorrow and trembling. And many, smitten with terror, came to confession, and made penitence for their sins, and those who were at discord made peace with each other.[12]

Judgment Day was another temporal fear. When would it come? Even in our time, fringe religious groups believe in it enough to plan their lives around it. Today in Western culture, however, the fear of an impending nuclear holocaust or of a world-wide population disaster may more closely approximate the medieval fear of Judgment Day. Several Illinois scientists have even calculated precisely when the population doomsday will occur: Friday, November 23, A.D. 2026.[13]

Doomsday fever was no doubt far more virulent in medieval Europe. As the year 1000 approached, pious souls girded themselves in preparation for the imminent arrival of the Kingdom of God. Every wicked prince could be the Antichrist; every calamity foretold the end of time. Priests sounded the alarm in their pulpits. Why then did not the masses throughout Europe become hysterical on the eve of the year 1000? Possibly people in the medieval period, unused to thinking in figures computed precisely on a universal basis, only felt vaguely that a dreaded date was approaching. They may not have identified that date with a precise moment in the steady passage of time.

Although all Europe did not tremble in unison with fear toward the end of the first millennium, what happened was bad enough: waves of fear swept from one region to the next, subsiding in one place only to rise again elsewhere. Marc Bloch described this occurrence:

> Sometimes a vision started the panic, or perhaps a great historic calamity like the destruction of the Holy Sepulchre in 1009, or again perhaps merely a violent tempest. Another time, it was caused by some computation of the liturgists, which spread from educated circles to the common people. "The rumour spread through almost the whole world that the End would come when the Annunciation coincided with Good Friday," wrote the Abbot of Fleury a little before the year 1000.[14]

The heavenly spheres stretched beyond the orbit of the moon, beneath which the air, no less than the earth, was tainted by sin. Above the moon's orbit the people of the Middle Ages saw the serene and constant movement of the stars; below it, the turbulences of air, storms, thunder, and lightning. In the Middle Ages bad weather was associated with Satan and the witches. The Pauline passage in Ephesians 2:2 about "the prince of the powers of the air" might have encouraged this association. Chaucer, we have seen, made the north country Satan's home—north being the place of bad weather. John Milton in *Paradise Regained* made Satan claim the air as "our old conquest."[15] It was common enough, in the medieval period, to believe that devils rode the storm that unroofed the monks' cloister, or that they sent the fire from the air that struck the steeple and burned the church to the ground. The *Malleus maleficarum [Hammer of Witches]*, a treatise first published in 1486, notes the appropriateness of assigning bad angels to the aerial domain.

> By nature [angels] belong to the empyrean of heaven, through sin to the lower hell, but by reason of the duty assigned to them—as ministers of punishment to the wicked and trial to the good, their place is in the clouds of the air. For they do not dwell here with us on the earth lest they should plague us too much, but in the air and around the fiery sphere they can so bring together the active and passive agents that, when God permits, they can bring down fire and lightning from heaven.[16]

The authors of the *Malleus maleficarum,* Heinrich Kramer and James Sprenger, were two inquisitors who enjoyed the patronage of Innocent VIII. In this work they accumulated numerous cases of how witches caused meteorologic turmoil. The inquisitors raised the question of remedies against hailstorms, some of which they judged superstitious and others not. To the modern mind their way of mixing logic and faith is as strange as the thought patterns of the most inaccessible primitive tribe. What is the proper procedure for dealing with hailstorms and tempests?

> Three of the hailstones are thrown into the fire with an invocation of the Most Holy Trinity, and the Lord's Prayer. . . . [Then] the sign of the Cross is made in every direction towards each quarter of the world. . . . And suddenly, if the tempest is due to witchcraft, it will cease. This is most true and need not be regarded with any suspicion. For if the hailstones were thrown into the fire without the invocation of the Divine Name, then it would be considered superstitious.[17]

Mountains are places of turbulent weather. It is not surprising that they were once regarded as the habitat of witches, demons, and dragons. In Europe the tendency for people living on the plains to see the mountains as haunted by demonic beings was strengthened by two additional factors. One was the difference in social organization between plainsfolk, who participated in mainstream feudal culture, and mountain dwellers, who lived outside the culture of the manor house. The other factor was that two heretical groups, the Albigensians of Languedoc and the Vaudois of the Alps, withdrew to their mountain redoubts in times of persecution. Witch-craze was endemic in the Pyrenees and the Alps. It prevailed there for two centuries before 1490—that is, before the time when a positive doctrine of witchcraft took its final form and the witch-craze began to ravage the more densely peopled plains. Naturally, where one found witches one also found demons who commanded them; and although in time witches invaded the richest lowlands their special niche remained the storm-wrapped peaks.[18]

The Alps are the greatest mountain bastion in Europe. Hannibal's heroic crossing of them could have been viewed as a conquest of nature. Evidently the feat failed to make any such impression on the European mind, for the idea endured until well into the sixteenth century that the Alps were a fearful region to be avoided or traversed only under the pressure of necessity. Apart from the physical difficulties of the mountain barrier, certain ancient superstitions also discouraged people from exploring and enjoying the Alps. For instance, the folks held the curious belief that the spirit of Pontius Pilate caused frightful storms there. Pilate's body—the story went—was thrown into the lake on Mount Pilatus near Lucerne. His ghost, after it was exorcised, agreed to remain quietly in the lake except on Good Friday and on those occasions when passers-by threw things into the water. To forestall the possibility of provoking Pilate the government of Lucerne forbade people to go near the mountain lake. The story was not finally discredited until 1585, when Johann Müller of Lucerne deliberately threw stones into the lake and no meteorologic disaster ensued. By this time, hardy hikers were already crossing the Alps for pleasure. Yet a certain apprehensiveness persisted until much later, and even the belief in monsters lingered. Take, for example, Johann Jacob Scheuchzer of Zurich, a great Alpine explorer. He crossed the mountains many times from 1702 to 1711, and studied their plants, minerals, and ice movements as a scientist. On the other hand, he also produced a reasoned catalogue of Swiss dragons. The best dragons lived in the Grisons, the largest and most sparsely settled of the Swiss cantons. As he put it, "That land is so mountainous and well provided with caves, that it would be odd not to find dragons there."[19]

Mountains came under the category of willful and uncontrollable nature beyond the human domain and even, in a sense, beyond God's purview. Likewise, wild animals and dark forests. The root meanings of the word "wilderness" are suggestive: the adjective "wild" comes from "willed," and *dēor* is Old English for "animal." Wilderness is thus the region of wild animals over which human beings have no control. Wild beasts in northern Europe lived in forests. As a scene or environment "wilderness" is a forest, and indeed the word "wild" may have another root, *weald* or *woeld,* the Old English word for forest.[20] Cultivated fields are the familiar and humanized world. By contrast, the forest surrounding it seems alien, a place of possibly dangerous strangers. (Note that the words "forest" and "foreigner" share the meaning of *foranus,* "situated on the outside.") The forest is a maze through which wayfarers venture at risk. Wayfarers can literally lose their way, but lostness also carries the sense of moral disorientation and of disorderly conduct. The forest is infested with outlaws—wild animals, robbers, witches, and demons.

Negative images of the forest are old and enduring. In time, they migrated from Europe to the New World, where as late as 1707 Cotton Mather could write about "dragons," "droves of Devils," and "fiery flying serpents" in New England's primeval forest.[21] On the other hand, we know that by the late medieval period lords as well as peasant farmers valued their adjacent woods and made good use of them: the lords took to the hunt and returned with supplies of fresh meat; the peasants benefitted from the herbs and acorns—food for men and swine. The medieval European's attitude to the forest was, in fact, a mixture of dread and appreciation. Some of this ambivalence is reflected in the following passage from the encyclopedia composed by Bartholomaeus Anglicus, an English Franciscan friar, in the middle of the thirteenth century:

> Woods be wild places, waste and desolate, that many trees grow in without fruit, and also few having fruit. In these woods be oft wild beasts and fowls, therein grow herbs, grass leas, and pasture, and namely medicinal herbs in woods be found.... In woods is place of deceit and hunting. Fore therein wild beasts are hunted. . . . There is place of hiding and of lurking, for oft in woods thieves are hid, and oft in their awaits and deceits passing men come, and are spoiled and robbed, and oft slain.[22]

Forests aroused fear partly because of their wild animals, which pressed close to the settlements throughout the medieval period and beyond. In *Beowulf* the homeland of Grendel is depicted as one of "wolf-haunted valleys." A biography of Saint Sturm, written about the year 820, provides vivid impressions of the wildness of the German countryside at that time. Saint Sturm is described as alone in a place near Mainz among "gloomy woods, seeing nought but beasts (whereof there was an innumerable multitude in the forest) and birds and vast trees and wild solitary glades."[23] By the late Middle Ages wild animals were less of a threat to wayfarers, but they remained a terror to peasant farmers and even to city dwellers in times of famine. On the plains of Lombardy, Brother Salimbene observed in 1233: "There was so great snow and frost throughout the month of January that the vines and all fruit-trees were frostbitten. And wolves came into the cities by night; and by day many were taken and hanged in the public streets." In another passage, Salimbene described the suffering caused by prolonged wars between the party of the pope and that of the emperor:

> And evils were multiplied on the earth; and the wild beasts and fowls multiplied and increased beyond all measure. . . . [Finding no sheep or lambs in the villages to eat] the wolves gathered together in mighty multitudes round the city moats, howling dismally for exceeding anguish of hunger; and they crept into the cities by night and devoured men and women and children who slept under the porticoes or in waggons. Nay, at times they would even break through the house-walls and strangle the children in their cradles.[24]

Danger from wild animals persisted into the modern era. In 1420, packs of wolves entered Paris through a breach in the ramparts and through unguarded gates. They appeared again in September 1438, attacking people this time outside the town, between Montmartre and the Saint-Antoine gate.[25] In 1493, the Flemings petitioned Maximilian, their Hapsburg overlord, for some remedy against harassment by wild animals. Earlier, civil strife and revolt in Flanders had created conditions in which wolves and boars had so multiplied that the countryfolk no longer dared to till their lands for fear of these beasts, which daily devoured their cows, calves, and sheep. In 1573, the ravages of wolves around Ypres were so excessive that a high tariff was put on their heads. In 1765, wolves caused such havoc in the Gevaudan district of France that the people believed it to be the work of a supernatural monster. In some French districts the threat from wild beasts continued until the Revolution, thanks in large part to the nobility, who for better hunting protected the beasts from the populace.[26]

A kindly sentiment toward wild animals was most rare in the Middle Ages. We can think of the Irish saints, remarkable for their warm sympathy toward the animals which they must have frequently encountered on their distant journeys. And of course, there was Saint Francis's unusual love of nature—unusual even for Franciscans, for by 1260 the General Chapter of Narbonne had forbidden the brothers to keep animals other than cats and certain birds useful for the removal of unclean things in the monastery.[27]

It seemed natural to attribute evil to animals. The devil himself was often depicted with claws, beak, and tail. Even today we may call a cruel person "bestial." In the Middle Ages people could believe that not only snakes and wolves but even harmless creatures were demons in disguise. When Saint Guthlac came to Croyland in the Fens, he constantly heard demons "booming like bitterns" in the dark. Moreover, he sometimes heard them speak in the Celtic tongue, which he himself had learned when he lived in the West. As a young man Saint Edmund Rich saw at sunset a flight of black crows: these he recognized at once as a swarm of devils come to fetch the soul of a local usurer at Abingdon. An extraordinarily cruel story is attached to Saint Dominic. The saint's studies were disturbed by a sparrow fluttering about his lamp. He immediately saw that it was the devil, caught it, plucked it alive, and while it screamed in pain the saint rejoiced in his own victory over the powers of darkness.[28]

The medieval mind could not decide where to draw the line between animals and humans. Were animals an altogether lower category, or did they possess certain human powers and sensibilities? Birds clearly had no souls, but souls could appear as birds. Animals might be punished for impiety, like the fly that dropped dead after hovering near a chalice. And they could appeal to the saints, like the bird that called on Saint Thomas of Canterbury when it was seized by a hawk, and was miraculously released.[29]

These bizarre tales were not simply conjured up by clerics, or by the heated literary imagination. Because animals and insect pests posed a real threat to crops and livelihood, people in medieval times saw nothing strange in labeling them criminals and demons. Offending wolves and caterpillars were tried in courts, given sentences, and executed. One of the earliest recorded animal trials took place in 824, when moles were prosecuted in the valley of Aosta; one of the most recent was in 1906 when a dog drew the sentence of death in Switzerland.[30] Animal prosecution reached a peak in the sixteenth century, that is, at a time when more and more witches were burned at the stake. The worst offenders, no doubt possessed by the devil, could only be disciplined by the Church's power of anathema. A celebrated legist argued in 1531:

> We know that excommunications are in fact effective. We know that they can destroy eels in a lake, or the sparrows that infest

a church. Since, therefore, caterpillars and other rural pests would simply laugh at a condemnatory sentence from the ordinary civil courts, let us use the weapon of Canon Law; let us strike them "with the pain of anathema," for which they have greater fear, as creatures obedient to the God who made them.[31]

Categories that we keep distinct medieval people often fused: tempests, animals, human beings, and demons assumed each other's forms in the literal sense as well as allegorically. The modern habit of saying "This is real, that is mere fantasy" did not much occupy the medieval mind; or if it did, at least the distinctions were drawn along different lines. To us, dreams occur only in the imagination, and we try to impress on young children that the monsters which haunt them in sleep are mere shadows projected by their drowsy brains. Among tribal peoples, however, dream events tend to be treated as real occurrences. Europeans in the Middle Ages probably held the same view. Ernest Jones observed that both the Christian Church and secular society had from early times periodically lent their support to the idea that nightmares involving devils, werewolves, or witches represented actual visits by such creatures. In the sixteenth century, the Church was seriously concerned with the attitudes of dreamers toward their nighttime visitors, taking note of whether a dreamer had submitted to the incubus, in order to assess guilt.[32]

Just as dreams and nightmares were not mere fantasies, so visions yielded real knowledge about heaven and hell. Visions appeared under different circumstances. Usually the person had to enter a state of trance. A major role of the shaman in many primitive cultures was to go into a trance and visit the upper and nether regions. He then returned with a knowledge of their geographies and cures for the sick. From the viewpoint of the medieval Church, a defect of the canonical Bible was that it lacked concrete depictions of heaven and hell. Church fathers remedied this lack by making use of inspired revelations to support their doctrines. Gregory the Great (540–604) drew on such visions for his doctrine of purgatory. Through Gregory and other church fathers, vivid images of the future life passed into the works of local historians, such as Bede in England. Homilies, commentaries, and ecclesiastical histories, alive with visionary accounts of the terrors of the underworld, multiplied in the medieval period. Popular preachers propagated these visions among the people, further inflaming the susceptible imagination of those times.[33]

Christian visions of hell drew on rather meager Judaic sources as well as on Buddhist and Zoroastrian beliefs. Four aspects are repeatedly mentioned. Souls, after being torn and mangled beyond the possibility of recognition, again take on their original shape in order to undergo renewed torment. Hell is fire and ice; torture alternates between the extremes of heat and cold. Hell is filth and stench. And lastly, hell is packed with frightful monsters.

In 1149, Tundale, a wealthy landowner in Ireland, fell into a trance while trying to extract payment from a tenant. His vision became one of the most influential in the late Middle Ages. Tundale saw

> [a] dark valley, filled with foul stench, the ground strewn with glowing coals, over which is spread a sheet of iron, which the flames penetrate. Murderers are placed hereon, and are molten like wax. In this state they trickle through the iron, after which they again resume their shape, only to endure the same torment again. Great mountain full of smoke and fire on one side; ice, frost, snow and wind, on the other. Thieves and robbers are tossed alternately from one to the other. Frozen lake, in the centre of which is a great beast, with terrible black wings. His mouth is full of fire. Into it the souls of unrighteous men of religion are hurled, and when almost wasted away by the heat, they are plunged into the frozen lake.[34]

Tundale himself, in his visionary journey, was exposed to all kinds of danger. Eventually, he emerged from hell, passed through a forest and a plain bright with flowers, and entered paradise. Tundale's vision, in its factual content, reminds modern scholars of Dante's *Divine Comedy*. It also bears a certain resemblance to children's fairy tales, in which the hero must pass through a dark forest filled with perils before reaching the king's castle. Visionary literature is largely devoted to the horrors of hell and has little to say about heaven. Fairy tales expatiate on danger but leave blank the happy life ever after. A reality that is supremely good and capable of surmounting the sorrows of earth and the tortures of hell can be evoked successfully only by a poet of genius.

Medieval people lived close to nature, and we tend to think of them as having intense joys and feelings that are largely lost to us. We may also think of them as dwelling in a calm and stable world in which the years and decades—unlike our own—succeeded one another with little change. To the father of a family living in the Middle Ages, this is not necessarily how the world would have appeared. Change and instability must have seemed at times the dominant features of his life: he experienced, if not the ravages of a battle or epidemic, then the recurrent threat of bad weather, poor harvest, and the accidents of workplace and home. Salvation itself was not assured. In one twelfth-century account of a visionary journey through hell, tormented souls complain that, though all men sin, God chooses to save only a few of them without regard for their good deeds.

Still, we know that human beings are eminently adaptable. Despite the harshness of life, medieval men and women almost surely did not live in constant fear and trembling. In William Fitz Stephen's twelfth-century description of London, for instance, we catch a glimpse of a vigorous people at play:

> When the great marsh that washes the Northern walls of the City is frozen, dense throngs of youths go forth to disport themselves upon the ice. Some gathering speed by a run, glide sidelong, with feet set well apart, over a vast space of ice. Others make themselves seats of ice like millstones and are dragged along by a number who run before them holding hands.[35]

After the long siege of winter came the delightful spring. Between wars and epidemics were interludes of peace and contentment, all the more precious for their transiency.

8.

Fear of Disease

Signs of life are all around us, but so, if we choose to look, are signs of decay and disease: moldering leaves and rotting tree trunks; wounded, sick, dead, and dying animals. Yet, despite the common claim that human beings are a part of nature and therefore must adapt or submit to its rules, nowhere in the world do people accept sickness and death as perfectly natural and thus in no need of special notice or explanation. Night follows day, winter follows summer. People take these great rhythms of nature as given, but not the alternations of sickness and health, not death as the inevitable goal of life.

We are biased in favor of life, particularly as it is manifested in the health of our own body. The body's integrity is the foundation for our sense of order and wholeness. When we sicken, so it seems does the world. When we close our eyes and die, the world too enters oblivion. The body is our most intimate cosmos, a system whose harmony is felt rather than merely perceived with the mind. Threaten the body, and our whole being revolts. Why does the pain persist? Why do I feel nausea? Before medical science had achieved a degree of precision, the answer to such questions was seldom confined to specific material causes. Only the stomach hurts; yet to explain why it hurts might require the healer to look for perturbations in human society, in the world of spirits, and among the stars. We shall see that fear of disease is closely linked to fear of many other phenomena, including defects in the self, tainted or bewitched objects, evil persons, demonic spirits, and a malfunctioning cosmos.

Sickness forcefully directs a people's attention to the world's hostility. What can be done? Human beings have sought answers in nature, studying its properties and processes in the hope of finding cures. With the exception of a few primitive groups, such as the Tasaday, most human societies have acquired some knowledge of the medicinal virtues of natural substances. They also often show a profound understanding of how a person's physical well-being is affected by his or her mental state. A complex civilization such as the Chinese boasts a sophisticated medical tradition of its own, whose lore and pragmatic discoveries complement and supplement those of Western science.

An inspiring story can thus be told of this line of human endeavor. But before the rise of modern society and hygiene, the successes in combatting disease were so limited in scope and available to so few sufferers that they did little to assuage a people's general sense of helplessness. The origin and cure of many diseases were simply unknown. Why was one person struck down with swollen veins while another remained sound of body? Epidemics appeared as sudden and incomprehensible scourges over which people had little control. What evil air could make the population of an entire village burn with fever? Had some taboo been broken? Were the gods angry? What did a comet or an unusual conjunction of stars forebode? It is clear that as we study the fear of sickness in various cultures, we shall also be made aware of a far greater range of anxieties that plague humankind.

Because the etiology of a disease is often complex, it should not be surprising that nonliterate peoples in different parts of the world seldom agree on the origin of any particular form of illness. Nevertheless, primitive views tend to fall under two broad categories. Under one, the cause is perceived as external: a person suffers because he or she is invaded by an external agent— a malefic object or spirit—in the environment. Under the other, the source of illness is internal: a person becomes sick because he or she has broken a taboo and offended the gods. To remain healthy and whole an individual must guard against external threats, and in some cultures must also be sure that he or she is not knowingly or unknowingly the actual source of disharmony.[1]

Harmful intrusions, in primitive thought, are of three types. One is the alien object. Disease is attributed to the presence in the body of a bit of bone, a hair, a pebble, a splinter of wood, or even small animals—worms and insects, for example. These things, which obviously do not belong in the body, induce sickness. Yet not all people holding such a concept insist that the bone or splinter of wood is itself pathogenic; rather, they see the object as containing a spiritual essence which is the true instigator of disorder. The primitive mind seems to treat the disease-causing object as spirit in tangible form. Cure is effected by extracting it.

Another type of threat comes from evil spirits, ghosts or demons. Spirit intrusion is not always bad. A person may become possessed by a divine being, behave erratically, fall into a trance, and utter words that are oracular. A possessed person, not being sick in the ordinary sense, commands respect rather than commiseration. The one danger is that he or she may become insane —"drunk with god." On the other hand, a demon-possessed person is sick, and cure comes with successful exorcism.

The third type of danger is from sorcery and witchcraft. Malevolent human beings, endowed with magic or power over supernatural forces, cast spells over their victims, causing sickness or death. In the Old World there is also the ancient and widespread belief in the evil eye. How the evil eye works is seldom described with any precision. The look itself appears to have the power to injure.[2] In the European Middle Ages, medical science thought that the eye could even transmit the deadly plague.

A person may also fall ill through the loss of soul. Ghosts and sorcerers have the power to extract a person's soul; or the soul, when it leaves the sleeping body and goes on its nocturnal ramblings, meets with some mishap which prevents its return. The remedy, in such cases, is to find it and restore it to the body. Lastly, breach of taboo is a cause of sickness. The breach may be quite unintentional and yet anger the gods, who send down disease as punishment. This explanation presupposes the existence of a complex system of religious tenets tied to social practice. The ancient Near East, Polynesia, and the more advanced cultural hearths of the New World were major centers for the idea of taboo. That breaking a taboo can bring on sickness is probably a much more recent belief than the notion that sickness is caused by object intrusion or sorcery.[3]

How does a large and sophisticated society like China cope with disease? At a practical level, China has coped by accumulating a rich store of materia medica, which have been tested through centuries of use. These substances still serve the people and command the respect of modern science. Much Chinese medical lore, however, is derived from concepts that have been strongly influenced by the great religious and philosophical traditions of Taoism, Buddhism, and Confucianism. Were it our task to survey Chinese medical science, we would do well to follow its development through the intertwined paths of practice and theory. But our purpose here is to describe the fear of disease in China, and how the Chinese have responded to this element of uncertainty in their lives. To fulfill this purpose, we will do well to distinguish between an elitist and a folk view of why diseases occur.

To the scholar-official, illness signified an imbalance between an afflicted organism and cosmic forces; cure lay in restoring the balance. Disease was seen as fundamentally no different from other natural and human-made disasters such as flood, drought, war, and rebellion, all of which were departures from cosmic harmony. To the common folk, the cause of disease was more specific and personalized: it was attributed to a neglected ancestor, ghost, demon, or fox spirit; and cure required either acts of propitiation or the use of magical powers to overcome evil. Between the educated and the uneducated, however, the explanation of personal misfortune differed largely in the level of linguistic abstraction. Thus scholars spoke of the polarized universal principles of Yin and Yang, whereas the peasant understood personal, social, and natural disorders in terms of struggles between the good spirits (*shen,* on the side of Yang) and bad spirits (*kuei,* on the side of Yin).[4]

The most important text of Chinese medicine was the *Huang Ti Nei Ching* (The Inner Classic of the Yellow Sovereign). This collection took shape between 450 and 350 B.C., which makes it a contemporary of the Hippocratic corpus. The coherence of the work rested on the concept of Yin and Yang, the five elements, and the elaborate system of correspondences so characteristic of the Chinese world-view. On the whole, practical advice was slighted. The author of the *Nei Ching* showed more concern with guiding the patient back to the Tao. Why did the people in ancient times live to be a hundred and retain their health? Answer: They understood the Tao, patterned themselves upon Yin and Yang, and lived in harmony with the arts of divination. The human body contained Yin and Yang regions, which were to be harmonized with these polarized principles in the cosmos. Yang was the warm air of the south, which gave rise to fever and inflammation. The clammy excess of Yin, on the other hand, was responsible for the chills of the north. Geographical location affected the nature of sickness. "The people of the regions of the East eat fish and crave salt. . . . Fish causes people to thirst, and the eating of salt injures the blood. Their diseases are ulcers, which are most properly treated with acupuncture." The laws of the seasons had to be obeyed. "Those who disobey the laws of

Spring will be punished with an injury to the liver. For them the following summer will bring chills. Those who disobey the laws of Summer will be punished with an injury to the heart. For them the Fall will bring intermittent fevers."

In Chinese philosophical and religious thought, much emphasis was placed on the harmonious ties between nature and human beings. Medical texts, which relied on this system of thought, differed from belles-lettres and philosophical works in their harsh diagnosis of the nature of the harmonious bond. Failure to obey natural laws meant punishment in the form of fevers. Cosmic forces were portrayed as great powers—not necessarily benign—before which human beings felt vulnerable. Just how vulnerable is made clear in the Chinese attitude to wind: only by remaining quiet and, as it were, unobtrusive might the people be safe. The *Nei Ching* says: "Wind is the cause of a hundred diseases." The skin protected a person against an evil wind, but the skin had pores and could be penetrated. "If one perspires while physically weary, one is susceptible to (evil) winds, which cause eruptions of the skin. . . . When people are quiet and clear, their skin and flesh is closed and protected. Even a heavy storm, afflictions, or poison cannot injure those people who live in accord with the natural order."[5]

As distinct from elitist speculation, that of the common folk was concrete and dramatic. Events, not abstract cosmic principles, were the favored mode of explanation. The peasants were likely to conceive of Yin and Yang (if those terms were used), not as universal entities acting in mutuality and in opposition, but as forces engaged in an eternal struggle, their standing at any time being manifest in the alternations of day and night, warmth and cold, summer and winter. Even more commonly in folk thought, *shen* (god) was substituted for the idea of Yang, and *kuei* (ghost or demon) took the place of Yin. Evil spirits could be appeased by offerings of burnt paper money, food, and drink; or they could be fought against. The peasants felt so helpless before the multiplicity of powers affecting their lives that they much preferred to propitiate them than to fight. They wanted to be on good terms with the gods as well as with the demons, because the gods could also be offended even by innocent acts and might send down misfortune, including sickness, as punishment. In fact, the peasants often failed to distinguish between gods and demons, and sometimes even personalized the "five elements" of the cosmos as specters of disease.

The Sinologist De Groot noted that in the nineteenth century, many cheap handbooks containing the characteristics of diseases and their cure were printed for the use of semiliterates and illiterates. An edition printed in Fu-chien province provided thirty prescriptions, one for each day of the month. A typical prescription stated that if anyone caught fever combined with headache on the day for which it was written, he could be certain that a spirit of a stated class had been offended; either the spirit would inflict the illness directly, or it would send a specter to do the job. The prescriptions mentioned not only the ghosts and demons but also the "domestic *shen* of the soil," the "*shen* of the earth which wander in the streets," the "murderous influences of the earth," and the *shen* of wood, metal, fire, and water. In other words, besides the aberrant elements of nature, its fundamental constituents—earth, wood, metal, fire, and water—could turn malignant.[6]

Although the normal method of averting misfortune was to placate the offended spirits, people would occasionally put up a fight. There is a rich lore on how to deal with animal-demons which could cause disorder of all kinds, including that of the mind, or insanity. Among animal-demons, fox spirits were believed to be the most active and malicious; for this reason people would, from time to time, go on a binge of fox slaughter among the old graves and city moats. Not all demons were embodied. To expel disembodied specters, fireworks, noise, light, and fire were used. In South China, during the hot season when cholera or some other epidemic was rife, an orgy of firecracker explosions would burst forth between sundown and midnight. Soldiers might blow on long trumpets to expel the devils of pestilence; torchlight and lantern processions meandered through the streets for the same purpose.[7]

In the Western world, ideas on the cause and cure of disease have a long and involved history. Some ancient ideas eventually became a part of modern medical doctrine, while others remain as relict folk beliefs. Among the latter, two have shown remarkable persistence: that illness is in one way or another associated with the world's spiritual powers, and that it has its ultimate origin in the stars.

The association of sickness with spirits and demons has taken many forms. E. R. Dodds is emphatic that the Archaic Age of Greece was haunted by an oppressive sense of evil, which to a poet might seem the will of Zeus working itself out through an inexorable moral law, but which to the peasant signified the ubiquity of demons in the universe.[8] The demon might be a "hero." "Heroes," in Greek folklore, were a special class of ancestors whose authority transcended that of the immediate kin. They were generally helpful, but unless propitiated, they could cause all kinds of harm, including sickness.[9] Blaming the pains of the body on malignant spirits is, of course, commonplace. We have seen that the medieval world was dense with the minions of Satan, whose existence helped to explain the numerous ills of premodern humans. That the devil might be the direct cause of fever was put colorfully by Cotton Mather in 1693: "And when the Devil has raised those Arsenical Fumes which become Venomous quivers full of Terrible Arrows, how easily can he shoot the deleterious Miasma into those Juices or Bowels of Men's Bodies, which shall soon Enflame them with a Mortal Fire."[10]

Where disease is endemic it can seem such an implacable power that the disease itself is deified and becomes an awesome supernatural being that must be appeased. Ancient peoples, including the Greeks, spoke of famine and pestilence as "gods"; and some modern Athenians still believe a certain cleft in the Hill of the Nymphs to be inhabited by three demons whose names are Cholera, Smallpox, and Plague.[11] In ancient Rome, malaria was so virulent that temples were built and dedicated to the goddess Febris. She was worshipped on the Palatine Hill and was thought to govern both the tertian and quartan fevers. A modern scholar describes "the great, the mighty, the holy" Dea Febris, goddess of fevers, as "a hairless old hag with prominent belly and swollen veins."[12]

When a disease strikes suddenly, as in an epidemic, it is as though the gods or a righteous God were angry and the people were being punished for their transgressions. Coupling disease with sin and punishment is, in fact, a prominent feature of Hebraic-Christian faith. The ten plagues of Egypt are a well-known example from the Bible. In Exodus 9:3 God bids Moses to warn Pharaoh: "Behold my hand shall be upon thy fields; and a very grievous murrain upon thy horses and asses, and camels and oxen, and sheep." Several verses later God extends his punishment to human beings, saying, "for there shall be boils and swelling blains both in men and in beasts in the whole land of Egypt" (Exodus 9:9). During the Middle Ages this link between sin and disease was not only accepted but precisely calibrated, many writers equating the cardinal sins with particular disorders. Transgression brought on bodily woes, but it was the devil who tempted man to transgress, and ultimately it was God who permitted the devil to act. Dramatic misfortunes were thus signs of God's righteous anger, which must be placated by repentance.

The timeless practice of offering public prayers to mitigate disaster has endured to modern times. In response to the cholera epidemic of 1832 the British government announced a day of fasting and humiliation during which the nation acknowledged its sins and pleaded with God to remove the punishment.[13] America's response to the cholera epidemic of the 1830s was typically moralistic. Pious people pointed out that those countries with the fewest Christians had suffered the most. Cholera was not the scourge of mankind but of the unrepentant sinner. It was a punishment, in particular, for the sins of dirty habits and of intemperance. On July 18, 1832, one observer wrote: "The disease is now, more than before, rioting in the haunts of infamy and pollution. . . . But the business parts of our population, in general, appear to be in perfect health and security."[14] Cholera was first reported in New York City on June 26. On June 29, numerous congregations in the city prayed and fasted. Devout citizens urged President Andrew Jackson to declare a day of national fasting. They argued that England was able to soften the blow by her day of national prayer, whereas the severity of the epidemic in France could be attributed to her atheism. Jackson refused to comply on constitutional grounds. In 1849, when cholera revisited the United States, President Zachary Taylor did not hesitate to recommend a day of national prayer, fasting, and humiliation.[15]

The second of the popular folk beliefs still with us is that our fate and the ultimate source of our illnesses lie with the stars. From Babylonian times to the present, astrology has maintained its grip on the human imagination. The tiniest mishap on earth has its ultimate cause in the remote regions of the sky. Such belief rests on the idea that all things are related, but also on the pathetic assumption that the fate of ephemeral lives is tied to the grand events of the cosmos. An ancient Greek follower of Hippocrates might note the condition of the weather and of the stars as he wrote down the clinical history of his patient.[16] He could see that the spreading of infection downward from a head wound might be related to the time when the wound was inflicted, which was as the Pleiades began to set. Aristotle believed that the phases of the moon influenced the course of illnesses. In the sixteenth and the early seventeenth century physicians taught that the period of the full moon was fraught with special risks for the sick. The moon was "refrigerant, humectant, and excitant," according to Francis Bacon.[17]

Unusual events in the sky presaged calamities on earth. At the time of the great plague in 1348, extraordinary meteors were reported at many places in Europe. People viewed them nervously. Other weird phenomena included a pillar of fire, which on December 20, 1348, remained for an hour at sunrise over the pope's palace in Avignon; and a fireball, which in August of the same year was seen at sunset over Paris.[18] When plague devastated London in 1665, it was heralded by portents in the heavens and in the air. London citizens sat up to watch a new blazing comet in December 1664, and talk buzzed excitedly in the city as to what it could mean. In a week or two it was gone, but letters arrived from Vienna which described the sighting of a bright comet with "the appearance of a Coffin, which causes great anxiety of thought amongst the people." From other parts of Europe came reports of terrible apparitions and of strange noises in the air like the sounds of cannon and musket shot.[19]

Yellow fever struck Philadelphia in August 1793, one of the worst disasters ever to have overtaken an American city. Earlier that year people had been made uneasy by all kinds of unusual events: in July, out of the blue sky lightning struck and split a noble old oak into eleven pieces; a sudden hailstorm cut down fields of grain and flax and broke thousands of windows, while less than three miles all around the day remained dry and calm.[20] In the winter of 1831–1832, people began to see omens in the sky once they learned that cholera was threatening America. One Washingtonian said, "The Sun Rised and Set Red . . . and two Black Spots could be discovered disstint *(sic)* in the Sun."[21]

Pestilence was believed to have its origin in the venomous quality of the air. But what made the air venomous? In 1348, learned doctors on the faculty of the University of Paris were anxious to link general with particular causes, the stars with the air. They looked into the sky for explanations rather than for portents. The conjunction of Jupiter and Mars foreboded ill because, as the Paris doctors explained, Jupiter, being a warm and humid planet, drew up evil vapors from earth and water, and Mars, being excessively hot and dry, set fire to those vapors; whence the flashes of lightning, lights, noxious vapors, and fires. This account, which was taken up all over Europe, re-emerged in 1665 as an explanation for the epidemic that swept London. A pamphlet of the time distinguished between the special causes of the corruption of the air—unburied corpses, stinking ditches and drains—and the general cause, which derived mainly from "influences, aspects, conjunctions and oppositions of ill planets."[22]

By the middle of the nineteenth century, medical science had largely dissociated itself from spirits, demons, and the cruder elements of astrology. Among general ideas on disease causation prevalent in ancient times and still held by isolated folks, one idea remains potent in modern thinking, and that is the influence of environment. "Environment" is a broad term that includes the stars at one end of the scale and specific geographic localities at the other. In ancient times, distant stars as well as terrestrial environments were thought to influence human well-being. Even in our day, the "stars" still retain a role—at least, if we believe the eminent cosmologist Sir Fred Hoyle, who has recently suggested that comets from outer space may introduce viruses and bacteria to earth and cause epidemics.[23] However, most modern medical scientists, insofar as they trace a disease to the physical environment, look not to heaven but to earth—to pollutants in the air and water. The view that corrupted vapors in the lower atmosphere cause disease is ancient. Grounded in Hippocratic teaching, it was elaborated by a host of later thinkers and writers, including Varro (116–27 B.C.), Vitruvius (late first century B.C.), Columella (ca. 3 B.C.–A.D. 65), Galen (129–199), and Avicenna (980–1037), the outstanding Arab physician.

When the plague reached Italy in January 1347, doctors in Paris offered an interpretation of its origin and spread that remained essentially unaltered until the second half of the nineteenth century.

> In India and about the Great Sea, constellations, combating the rays of the sun, struggled violently with the waters of the sea, which rose in vapor and fell again for twenty-eight days. At last the greater part of them were drawn up as vapors, those which were left being so corrupted that the fish within them died. The corrupted vapors which had been drawn out could not be consumed by the sun, nor could they be converted into wholesome water like hail and dew, but spread abroad through the air. This had happened in Arabia, India, Crete, Macedonia, Hungary, Albania, and Sicily, and if it should reach Sardinia no one would survive; the danger would continue in which this air had access so long as the sun was in the sign of the lion.[24]

Note, in this account, the role given to the stars, the idea of putrefaction, and the notion of a poisoned air that moved from place to place, killing all that lay in its inexorable path. Air is our pervasive environment; if it is poisoned, no one can escape agonizing death. During the First World War, the news that poison gas might be used on crowded cities excited understandable terror. We can imagine how medieval and later populations felt when they heard rumors of spreading lethal fumes.

There was no lack of literature to stimulate the imagination. Numerous theories emerged to account for the contamination of

the air. Among nonorganic theories, one pointed to "subterranean fumes" as the culprit. In the fourteenth century, some people believed that the earthquakes of 1347 enabled the fatal gases
of the earth's inner parts to escape and infect the surface air.
J. F. C. Hecker, a nineteenth-century historian of medieval epidemics, found reason to subscribe to this subterranean thesis. He
thought that the scientific observations of his day demonstrated
that volcanic eruptions could contaminate the atmosphere, giving people headaches and rendering them stuporous or uncon-
scious.[25] When the cholera epidemic raged in 1832, English
physicians, noting a resemblance between the symptoms of
cholera and those of arsenic poisoning, wondered whether the
disease itself might be caused by a similar though unknown
compound. The favorite culprit, however, was portentously
called the "electric fluid," or the "miasmatic electric effluvium."
One doctor argued that just as a thunderstorm turned milk sour,
so electricity in the atmosphere could make the body fluids acid
and thereby produce cholera.[26]

To certain writers of the 1830s, inorganic compounds or electricity seemed a nobler agent of infection than "mere animal
contagion." They were reacting to the traditional and widely
accepted doctrine that swamps, stagnant waters, and decaying
organic matter were the main sources of pathogens. Traditional-
ists (or miasmatists) expatiated learnedly on noxious clouds,
putrid fumes, and toxic miasmas, but they were vague as to the
nature of the toxin and how it was carried to human beings.[27]
They sought reassurance in jargon and spoke of "aeriform poison," "choleraic distemperature," and "uncontrollable atmo-
spheric peculiarity." Vague and conflicting medical opinions
contributed to a sense of unease and fear: almost any foul odor,
it was believed, could cause death. In 1848, miasmatists in London blamed the cholera infection in Millbank prison on the
"effluvia" from the bone-boiling works on the other side of the
Thames in Lambeth. They also asserted that the smell from an
artificial manure factory was the cause of cholera and other
diseases in the Christchurch workhouse in Whitechapel. As
proof, miasmatists pointed out that the unfortunate boys whose
wards faced the factory always suffered heavily, whereas the
girls on the other side of the building escaped.[28]

The odor of poorly buried corpses was regarded as a major
organic source of infection. This belief had the authoritative
support of Avicenna and was popular from the late Middle Ages
onward. During the great plague of 1348, and again in 1665, so
many people died so quickly that interment was often haphaz-

ard: bodies were piled one on top of another in church graveyards within the city, and when these could not possibly accommodate more, large trenches were dug on open land for mass
disposal. Burial grounds were evil-smelling and horrendous
places: it was only natural that people should look upon them as
sources of poisonous fumes. The idea continued to find supporters in modern times. A physician writing in 1891 was convinced
that the dead poisoned the air. He believed that the origin of the
Black Death could be traced to the mounds of corpses left unburied by the successive disasters that overtook China. He invoked cadaveric poisoning as the reason for the high death rate
among priests and monks in Europe. Priests lived near the village churchyards, while within the monastery walls were buried generations of monks as well as the bodies of princes and of
notables from the surrounding country.[29]

Human beings depend absolutely on air; they are almost as
dependent on other human beings. When a deadly epidemic
strikes, both become immediately suspect. Not only cadavers but
the live victims of disease can sully the atmosphere. In the Middle Ages, lepers were the most suspect of afflicted people. Their
asylums were built outside cities and located downwind wherever possible.[30] In the nineteenth century, European colonists
broadened this fear of a pariah race to include native populations who, in their crowded and fetid quarters, were liable to be
host to all kinds of pathogens. British medical and military authorities in India believed that the "foul air" drifting in from
native towns could endanger the health of Europeans. Colonists
were advised to settle in hill stations well above the putrid
miasma of the lowlands, and also to avoid locations downwind
from the malodorous Indian towns.[31]

At the height of the Black Death, fear of the plague victims
stimulated the revival of an ancient belief in the evil eye. Guy
of Chauliac, a distinguished surgeon and Pope Clement VI's physician in 1348, thought that the plague was so contagious, especially when accompanied by the spitting of blood, "that not only
by staying together, but even by looking at one another, people
caught it." The physician of Montpellier, in a tractate of May
1349, endorsed the idea. He spoke of a deadly "aerial spirit going
out of the eyes of the sick" and striking "the eyes of the well
standing near and looking at the sick, especially when they are
in agony."[32] Nonetheless, the orthodox view was that the disease
was passed primarily through the breath, which contaminated
the air as did the other fumes of decay.

The plague made everyone both suspicious and suspect. Strangers, intimate neighbors, and close kin could all be carriers of death. Fear of infection was such that those who had to pass through the streets moved in corkscrew fashion, crossing from side to side to avoid contact with other pedestrians. Awareness and dread of contagion increased after the plague's first onslaught on the European mainland in 1348. Cities tried to defend themselves by isolating the sick. A regulation promulgated in 1374 required that every victim "be taken out of the city into the fields, there to die or to recover." An increasingly common practice was to barricade the sick and their families inside their houses, where for lack of care and food not only the sick but the well perished.[33]

When a deadly epidemic hit a town, the almost instinctual response of its inhabitants was to flee. But where could they go? Whether sick or not, they were regarded by other people as tainted with the disease and presenting a threat more specific but no less ominous than the onslaught of a "poisoned cloud." In October 1347, Genoese galleys brought the plague to Messina, Sicily. Its extraordinary virulence forced the inhabitants to abandon their homes. They scattered over Sicily and into Calabria, but the places where they sought shelter would not receive them. They were forced to camp out among the weeds and vines.[34]

Stories of this kind, varying only in scale and degree of gruesomeness, could be repeated over and over again for the successive pestilential visitations. In June 1665, Londoners began to abandon their city. By July the houses left empty and forsaken were more numerous than those marked by a red cross to show where the plague had entered. The exodus was checked at last by the Lord Mayor's refusal to sign more papers certifying the health of those who fled, and by the opposition of the neighboring townships, which in self-defense placed armed guards on their roads.[35]

During the cholera epidemic of 1830, authorities in Russia established *cordons sanitaires* around the major areas of infection. The military and the police were charged with maintaining barriers on the land routes leading out of the infected areas, and were allowed to shoot anyone they caught trying to leave. Moscow was to be protected, but for the quarantine to work the neighboring provinces had to cooperate. The military governor of Moscow asked officials in Tula, Riazan, Vladimir, and Tver to destroy bridges and block water traffic to prevent their people from entering the metropolis.[36]

In Spain, authorities established triple cordons and proclaimed it a capital offense to leave an infected town. Prussia posted soldiers along its frontiers as though it were defending itself against an invading army. In the United States, fear of a cholera epidemic in 1832 resulted in stringent quarantines and local violence. "In Chester, Pennsylvania," Charles Rosenberg writes, "several persons suspected of carrying the pestilence were reportedly murdered, along with the man who had sheltered them. Armed Rhode Islanders turned back New Yorkers fleeing across Long Island Sound. At Ypsilanti, the local militia fired upon the mail stage from cholera-infected Detroit."[37]

News of the approach of pestilence aroused at first curiosity, later a feeling of unease, and then—as invasion seemed inevitable—a rising tide of panic. New Yorkers felt mildly perturbed when they heard that cholera had reached England, then seriously alarmed when told that the disease had jumped the natural *cordon sanitaire* of the Atlantic Ocean and was reported in Montreal. For a time there were comforting rumors that it was spreading west rather than south, but such snippets of good news did not deter New Yorkers from abandoning their city in large numbers.

Moscow was likewise gripped by fear as cholera spread toward it in 1830. The government published daily reports on the disease's movements up the Volga River during the months of August and September. Alarm diffused quickly among the educated as they corresponded with one another. On September 5, Ferdinand Christine wrote to inform Countess S. A. Bobrinska that people were dying at the rate of fifty a day in Astrakhan, that the situation at Saratov was almost as bad, and that the quarantine lines had failed to hold the cholera, for "one man died on the road, and another at the very gates of Moscow." An oppressive air hung over the city. Inhabitants remembered and exaggerated the effects of earlier epidemics, particularly that of 1771, and became neurotically suspicious of every symptom of illness. By September 11, the government could no longer control the panic. Neither physicians nor the police could persuade the people to stay in Moscow. They fled from pestilence as they had fled from Napoleon's armies in 1812.[38]

What were the methods used to prevent or combat epidemic diseases? In the nineteenth century the emphasis was placed on personal and public hygiene and on segregating the sick. These were sensible measures. In earlier ages, although people were aware of the need for quarantine and for cleanliness, this knowledge was offset by other beliefs, of which some were quaint and relatively harmless, while others added to the discomfort and horror of pestilence.

In the Middle Ages, for instance, attempts at personal hygiene were hampered by the notion that a hot bath, and indeed any sort of bath, tended to open up the pores and thus expose the body to corrupt air. The air being the villain, medieval physicians advised people to combat it by burning scented woods, juniper, ash, or rosemary. The house was to be filled, whenever possible, with pleasant-smelling plants and flowers and the floors sprinkled with vinegar and rose-water.

Another school of thought believed that "bad drove out bad." Far from avoiding certain kinds of foul odors, such as those that emanated from latrines, one should imbibe them.[39] In the seventeenth century, people came to hold that the fumes of saltpeter were a powerful disinfectant and so they tried to flash gunpowder in pans. Poor folk burned old shoes and odd scraps of leather and horn to get the desired smell. Fire, which had been used to fight corrupt air since the time of Hippocrates, remained a popular device. A pamphlet published in London in 1665 recommended that people light fires daily and heap a dozen or so different pungent substances on them, "for there is a marvelous great vertue and strength in fire, to purge, correct and amend the rottenness and corruption of the ayre."[40] Fires were lit in London streets in early September. Night and day their smoke and stench added foulness to so much that was already foul and horrible. After dark, the coals glowed red and flames flickered in a city wherein few residents could be seen.

Chinese peasants held that the noise from firecrackers and guns might dispel the demons of disease. Londoners in 1665 thought likewise. Through the three months of June, July, and August, they could be observed firing their guns out of windows in the hope that the explosions would blow away the lethal air that had gathered around their houses. London's College of Physicians endorsed the frequent firing of guns.[41] Even skeptics approved the practice on the grounds that "configurations of particules in the ether might be radically changed by such detonations." In 1831 the British medical journal *Lancet* reported, somewhat condescendingly, how a city in Persia had tried to frighten cholera away. "A singular sanatory measure is recorded to have been practiced here in an attempt to turn aside the current of calamity. Salvoes of artillery and peals of musketry roared from the rising to the setting sun; loud shouts were raised by united thousands, and gongs and trumpets increased the horrid commotion."[42] Yet when the disease reached London in 1832, many public-spirited citizens volunteered advice to the authorities, and the advisers with the largest following favored the use of explosives. In a public letter to the Lord President of the Council, a certain William Hunt urged that twenty-two pieces of cannon be distributed around London and that they "be discharged singly at intervals of an hour each beginning at sunrise and ending at sunset" for the purpose of "disinfecting the atmosphere by the destruction of the presumed animalculae."[43]

How did a city devastated by pestilence look? Chaos, ubiquitous death, and the desolation of abandonment all in their different ways augmented the atmosphere of horror. Thucydides, an eyewitness to the typhus epidemic that ravaged Athens in 430 B.C., stressed the breakdown of social order.

> An aggravation of the existing calamity was the influx from the country into the city, and this was especially felt by the new arrivals. As there were no houses to receive them, they had to be lodged at the hot season of the year in stifling cabins, where the mortality raged without restraint. The bodies of dying men lay one upon another, and half-dead creatures reeled about the streets and gathered round all the fountains in their longing for water. The sacred places also in which they had quartered themselves were full of corpses . . . for as the disaster passed all bounds, men, not knowing what was to become of them, became utterly careless of everything whether sacred or profane.[44]

The chronicles of Henry Knighton depict scenes of desolation, rural and urban, in plague-struck fourteenth-century England. Outside London, so many sheep died of the plague that in a single pasture one could count 5,000 bodies, and "they rotted so much that neither bird nor beast would touch them." Abandonment was widespread. Knighton observed: "After the pestilence many buildings both great and small in all cities, boroughs and vills fell into ruins for lack of inhabitants, and in the same way many villages and hamlets were depopulated, and there were no houses left in them, all who had lived therein being dead."[45] As human beings left or died the empty buildings decayed: the effect was as if the disease could corrupt even the inanimate features of the landscape.

London's epidemic of 1665 created ghastly scenes. To envisage them, we need to remember the numerous and conjoint circumstances that made for fear. The modern writer Walter George Bell draws our attention to the relentless tolling of bells from one or another of a hundred church steeples, each toll announcing yet another death and putting one more burden on strained nerves. What the ears heard the eyes confirmed. None could go into the streets without encountering people carrying coffins. There were few passers-by, but of those that one could see, many had sores on them. Others limped painfully from the effects of sores not wholly healed. In silent streets, the red cross flamed upon doors, the few dwellings not so marked being left tenantless and open to the winds. At night one could hear the dead-cart rumbling noisily over the cobblestones and the melancholy call of the bearers, "Bring out your dead!" Churchyards bulged with hastily buried corpses. Samuel Pepys wrote of passing by such a place, "It frightened me more than I thought it could have done." Even into the twentieth century, churchyards in the City of London stood high, dismal reminders of pestilential might.[46]

Public measures that were used to cope with pestilence and public response to its attack changed little from the Middle Ages to the first part of the nineteenth century. A town struggling to survive under the cholera epidemic of the 1830s looked much the same as a medieval settlement gripped by the plague. A local resident of Cromarty on the Moray Firth described his beleaguered town late in 1832:

> The disease went creeping about the streets and lanes for weeks after.... Pitch and tar were kept burning during the night in the opening of the infected lanes; and the unsteady light flickered with ghastly effect on house and wall, and the flitting figures of the watchers. By day, the frequent coffins borne to the grave by but a few bearers and the frequent smoke that rose outside the place from fires kindled to consume the clothes of the infected had their sad and startling effect.[47]

Faced with disaster or its impending onslaught, the human response is often a combination of good sense and superstitious fear. Diseases of pandemic proportion, more than other natural calamities, tended to produce such effects, partly because their origins were less well known, and partly because their courses seemed more erratic. A disease might appear suddenly and as suddenly disappear. It could strike one neighborhood and then leap over much of the city to hit another. In the past, although many steps taken to combat disease were reasonable, quite as often they went far beyond the bounds of reason. It made sense to purify the air, but not by burning old shoes. Quarantine was a sound precaution, but locking the family in with its sick members and leaving them without food or care was extraordinary cruelty explicable only by panic. Harsh measures and treatments frequently created a terror of their own exceeding that of the disease itself.

In a natural disaster such as flood, authorities and populace fought against a common external enemy. In an epidemic, human beings themselves were a major cause of fear. People feared the sick as well as those suspected of being sick. And they dreaded the vastly expanded power of the authorities, who could impound them in filthy hospitals that were in reality death traps or shoot them when they sought to enter a barricaded area.

An outbreak of cholera or plague threatened a whole people. Terror of contagion could so derange reason that to those sound in body the sick seemed not only the victims of evil but its perpetrators. It does not, however, take an epidemic to generate an atmosphere of panic and suspicion. In communities that are close-knit and labor under unacknowledged social strain, sickness may arouse feelings of deepest enmity even when it claims only a few victims. When one person or family falls sick and not another, conditions are ripe for acquaintances and even relatives to accuse each other of sorcery and witchcraft.

9.

Fear of Human Nature: Witches

It is reasonable to fear the wilder manifestations of nature. We still see the need to protect ourselves against flood, lightning, and the rattlesnake. What we do not see from the safety of our built environment is the horror these natural elements once inspired because they also stood for *human* maliciousness. People the world over have shown a tendency to anthropomorphize the forces of nature. We cannot, in fact, feel strongly about any object, animate or inanimate, without endowing it with human attributes. But the physical environment of dark nights and mountaintops acquires an extra dimension of ominousness, beyond the threat of natural forces and spirits, when it is identified with human evil of a supernatural order, that of witches or ghosts.

A witch is a person who inflicts injury through the exercise of exceptional powers. These powers may be regarded as supernatural because they operate in a manner that cannot be detected; the cause is recognizable only in the damage that comes to light. Belief in witches in some form is universal. The importance of witches in the scheme of things varies greatly, however, from culture to culture.

Witches are necessary to explain individual rather than communal misfortune. When drought afflicts the entire community, perhaps the gods are angry and a communal rain dance is called for to restore the harmony of the universe. But if lightning should strike one man's livestock and not those of other herders, or if only one man's son should fall sick while other people's children remain healthy, how is the afflicted individual to assuage his anguish? He does so by finding a cause or answer for the personal disaster. Four types of answer are possible: it is fate, the working of a mysterious order that all mortals must accept; it is truly an accident which only a statistical law can explain; it is a just punishment for an individual's faults, such as failure to observe certain rites; it is caused by a malicious and envious being—a witch. Without a philosophical acceptance of fate or statistical sophistication, only the last two answers are viable, and of them it is easier to favor the idea that another person rather than oneself is to blame.

The witch looks like an ordinary human being. He or she may be my next-door neighbor or even a close relative—one can seldom tell. The person I see every day, who smiles so ingratiatingly, may, at night, be casting spells that will make me break a leg or lose a child. Witches are incognito enemies within: that is why they arouse so much unease. Consider the Amba, an agricultural people of western Uganda. The 30,000 or so Amba are divided among numerous small settlements, most of which used to be independent political entities that made war against one another from time to time. Villagers in a different part of Amba territory are actual or potential enemies. Intercourse with them is utilitarian during the peaceful interludes and violent when the tensions of a blood feud build up. These other villagers, however, are not witches. Witches are a problem only where people live close together and recognize communal ties. It is among members of the same settlement—Amba who claim descent from a common ancestor—that suspicions of witchcraft are rife. Despite emphasis on the ideal of harmony within the village, the Amba are keenly aware of the fragility of their social bond.[1]

Witches are a plague of the local community. Yet the people in one village may overlook their own social tensions and point to other villages as especially witch-possessed. This happens when the relationship between different settlements, unlike that of the Amba, is not one of open hostility but one of wariness and suspicion. The attitude then becomes: these other villagers are like us and we have dealings with them, but somehow they are also not quite like us. In the American Southwest, for example, the Navaho Indians at Ramah believe that the Canyon de Chelly and Cañoncito are two witch-infested areas. They tend to feel that their fellow tribesmen there are in some sense aliens, "Navahos who are not quite Navaho." Subtle differences do in fact exist, as the anthropologist Clyde Kluckhohn has pointed out. Unlike the Ramah Navahos, those who live in the Canyon de Chelly have a high proportion of Pueblo blood, and those in the Cañoncito area are mostly descendants of tribesmen who came strongly under the influence of the Spanish missions during the eighteenth century.[2]

Misfortunes occur unpredictably. Why? One answer is that there are witches. Quite ordinary-looking people may, in dark and secret places, subvert society's most deeply held beliefs. The antisocial traits of witches the world over are much alike, because in all viable communities the basic social values are much the same. Foremost among them are the respect for life, for property, and for the rules of sexual behavior. Witches not only maim, kill, and destroy but they appear to be indiscriminate in their choice of victim, who may be a stranger, a neighbor, or a sibling. Witches are lustful and incestuous, they consort with corpses and demons, they have no control over their impulses.[3] Witches are a force for total chaos, and they are closely associated with other forces or manifestations of chaos such as dark nights, wild animals, wild bush country, mountains, and stormy weather.

Dark nights curtail human vision. People lose their ability to manipulate the environment, and feel vulnerable. As daylight withdraws, so does their world. Nefarious powers take over. Witches and ghosts figure prominently in the lore of the Western world. The ancient Greeks believed in them and in Hecate, their chief goddess who was also Goddess of the Dark of the Moon—the black nights when the moon was hidden. On such nights, Hecate appeared at the crossroads, invisible to human beings but visible to dogs, which howled terrifyingly. Offerings were placed at these crossroads each month to propitiate the goddess and her cohorts. In medieval times good Christian folk also avoided crossroads during the dark hours; where Hecate had once reigned, witches and ghouls of hell now congregated under the aegis of the devil himself. Night covered evil activities and symbolized evil; it seemed proper to medieval people that witches should gather then. In inquisitors' manuals, confessions of the following kind are common:

> Françoise Secretain added that she used always to go to the Sabbath at about midnight. . . . But always it is a condition of these devilish assemblies at night, that as soon as the cock crows everything disappears. . . . Some have said that the sound of the cock is deadly to Satan, just as it is feared by lions.[4]

Before the age of electric lighting, people everywhere retreated to their homes after dark. "It is better at home, for it is dangerous outdoors" is an old Greek saying, found in Hesiod and in the Homeric Hymn to Hermes. Such advice still makes sense to people in isolated communities as yet unpenetrated by modern ideas and technology. The ethnographic literature on Africa provides a wealth of examples. The Gusii, who inhabit the fertile highlands of southwestern Kenya, state openly that it is dangerous to walk about at night. Children learn at an early age to fear the darkness outside the hut. When they are small and cry, their mothers threaten to throw them out to the witches and hyenas unless they stop. Adults express uneasiness about venturing forth after sundown. Gusii men carry lanterns to calm their fears. Women are even more reluctant to go out. Married women, who walk miles away from home by themselves in daylight, are at night too apprehensive to go unaccompanied twenty yards to another house in the homestead. Their fear of the dark encompasses many things but particularly the likelihood of encountering witches at work. This danger is real to the Gusii because their friends and neighbors claim to have seen witches, or to know of someone who has. Youths, including those taught at mission schools, give eyewitness accounts. They say they have seen the eerie light of a witch's torch as it flickered in the distance. Witches are supposed to run naked at night carrying firepots which burn herbs or grasses.[5] Belief in witches is reinforced each time a Gusii encounters a burnt area. Fear of the dark is even more extreme among the Kaguru of east central Tanzania. Chiefly because of their fear of witches, Kaguru homes have shuttered peephole windows, and some prefer to defecate or urinate in their huts rather than venture outside after dark.[6]

Witches and wild animals, both of which defy human control, are closely associated in occult lore. European witches fly to their sabbats on the backs of goats and horses. Although the goat and the horse are domesticated animals, they can evoke not the farmstead but wildness. The goat is a denizen of mountain crags, an outlaw of society (the scapegoat) tainted by a reputation for lecherousness. The symbolism of the horse is extremely complex: it stands for intense desires and instincts; it is the oppressive nightmare of dreams; and it is an omen of war and death. The horse suitably evokes the witches' inordinate appetites, their nocturnal and death-dealing activities. In Africa, hyenas are the most common ally of witches and their chief means of transport. Witches race through the sky clinging onto the bellies of their hyenas. They travel upside down, thus typically inverting normal human behavior. Most of the wild animals in the bush are regarded by one people or another as the witch's associates. These animals are characteristically black, disgusting, dangerous, or active at nighttime. To the Lugbara of western Uganda, associates include the toad, snake, lizard, frog, jackal, leopard, bat, owl, and a kind of monkey that screeches at night.[7] To the Kaguru, they are the hyena, lion, and snake; to the Dinka of southern Sudan, the hyena and the black cobra, which is the most dangerous snake in Africa.[8] The distinction between animal and human becomes even fuzzier in the many reports of witches that appear dressed in animal skins: they are were-animals. Navaho witches roam about at great speed in the skins of wolves and coyotes. In a Swiss town, five witches were burned in 1604 for having pounced on a child in the guise of wolves. As late as the nineteenth century, witches in Scotland and Wales were believed capable of transforming themselves into hares to suck cows' udders for milk.[9]

Witches track down their victims individually and as a rule carry out their crimes alone. They are not, however, wholly antisocial; they have their own gatherings, their orgiastic sabbats. These are frequently held in remote and wild places such as mountaintops, caves, forests, and springs. A Navaho reports: "Witches meet at night. The meeting place is usually in the mountain or in a big hollow rock. They [undress]. They sing and paint up at the meeting place. They make noises like coyotes and owls."[10] In Africa, witches congregate in abandoned or wild bush country. The Kaguru say they assemble in deserted huts and hold dances at night on mountaintops.

When the European witch-craze was at its height, roughly between 1580 and 1630, every country could claim hundreds of sabbats. In Lorraine alone, no less than eight hundred meeting places were thought to exist. Hugh Trevor-Roper even speaks of national and international centers for the congregation of witches, giving as examples "the Blocksberg or Brocken in the Harz Mountains of Germany, the 'delicate large meadow' called Blakulla in Sweden and the great resort of La Hendaye in southwest France where no less than 12,000 witches would assemble."[11]

There seems little doubt that witches were seen as favoring the highlands. In the popular mind, they endured longest there. The great European witch-hunts focused on the Alps, the Jura, the Vosges, and the Pyrenees. In the Basque region's wilder areas, even in the early part of our century peasants and shepherds still spoke of a mountain spirit who presided over the witches and had the power to create storms. Personalized forces of nature and witches, in their minds, were barely distinguishable.[12]

Blaming evil persons for bad weather was especially common in Europe, though not limited to that continent. Witches worked in a variety of ways and on different scales. To ruin the crops of a particular district, a witch might conjure a hailstorm by moistening her broom in some dark liquid, pointing it at the sky and then at the condemned field. In 1610, it was thought that the witches of Zugarramurdi in the western Pyrenees raised storms to wreck the ships that entered or left the harbor at Saint-Jean-de-Luz. Turbulent air and violent meteorologic phenomena could be the joint work of a witch and the devil. Nicholas Remy, the author of *Demonology* (1595) and the inquisitor who boasted of having burned nine hundred people in fifteen years, insisted that when trees and houses were struck by lightning they showed the marks of a demon's claws, and that "a most foul smell of sulphur" was released.[13]

In Africa, the Shona of Zimbabwe believe that lightning is the witch's favorite tool of nature. A European doctor reported that at Harare Hospital many Shona patients diagnosed lightning as the cause of their illness. Since few people live after being struck by a powerful electric discharge, we must assume that a witch's lightning is of a psychic kind—one that may, for instance, hit victims in their sleep. The Shona sometimes envisage lightning as a bird that lays its eggs where it strikes. The sending of the lightning-bird is no more difficult for a witch than the dispatch of any other animal associate.[14]

How can people, then, protect themselves against witches and other forces of evil? Europeans possessed treatises and manuals in which methods to ward off the devil and his minions were clearly specified. The simplest way and among the most popular was to use the names of the Savior, the Virgin Mary, the Evangelists, or the words of Saint John, "The Word was made Flesh." These lexical talismans could be attached to vulnerable places, objects, animals, and human beings.[15] The sign of the cross was and still is regarded as effective. In our century, when Basque herders and travelers approached the cliffs at Ozquia or Arkaitz, they took care to collect pebbles and make with them the sign of the cross to repel witches and other demonic powers.[16]

Navaho Indians use gall medicine—a concoction made from the gall of eagle, mountain lion, and skunk—as the antidote against the "corpse poison" of witches. Corpse poison is produced from the flesh of corpses, those of children being the best. Witches grind the poison to a fine powder which they can drop through the smokehole into a hogan, place in the nose or mouth of a sleeping victim, or blow from sticks into the face of someone in a crowd. Conservative Navahos carry the gall medicine with them if they anticipate entering a large crowd, when they travel away from home, and especially when they plan to pass through a witch-infested region such as the Canyon de Chelly or Cañoncito.[17]

Medicine or a talisman provides one form of protection against the designs of malevolent powers. Another is to acquire the technique for reading omens, which will enable a person to avoid inauspicious times and places, or to postpone an enterprise if the signs are not good. The ancient Greeks, the Romans, and the Chinese put great faith in omens. In certain areas of twentieth-century Africa, skill in omen interpretation is necessary to one's basic sense of security where witches and other evil spirits abound. Take the witch-possessed Zande of southwestern Sudan, who attribute anything unusual or the slightest mishap to witches. These people become very much afraid when they see an object they associate with witchcraft. Security lies in possessing an oracle board, which the Zande carry about with them so that it can be consulted at any moment. They use it to decide on every type of undertaking, a proposed journey, a hunting expedition, marriage, or whatever. A man who is away from home may be advised by his rubbing-board oracle to leave his host's village at an unusual time, or to take a roundabout route so as to avoid the witchcraft that is lying in wait for him. He dodges witchcraft almost as though it were a natural danger or a human trap laid at a fixed place. A Zande feels in control if he can approximately determine the time and location of a threat. Despite all precautions, misfortunes still befall individuals, and at such times the Zande ascribe almost invincible cunning to witches.[18]

Belief in witchcraft modifies behavior. One stays home after dark; one avoids certain places; one extends hospitality even to uncouth people and strangers because they are likely to be endowed with witchlike powers. In Africa, the size and spacing of settlements may reflect the fear of witches: a village splits and a branch is established elsewhere to avoid the tensions of witchcraft.[19] Even social behavior while eating is affected by precautions against daytime witchcraft. The Wambugwe, a Bantu people located at the southern end of Lake Manyara in Tanzania, believe that daytime witches can induce sickness by casting an evil eye on the victim's food. For this reason the Wambugwe take extraordinary steps to ensure privacy during meals, which are consumed inside the house even in the hottest weather. The anthropologist Robert Gray comments at length on the neurotic suspiciousness of the Wambugwe. Members of a person's own matrilineage are regarded as safe, but not those of his or her spouse's matrilineage; hence, even relatives do not often come for meals. When the men are away from home, hunting or clearing bush, they cannot retire into their houses for meals; even then precautions against the evil eye cannot be relaxed. "Unless the men should all be lineage-mates, they disperse at mealtime, and each man eats in seclusion behind a bush or tree. If it is a large group and cover is sparse, each man goes off a little distance and covers himself completely with his cloth while he eats."[20]

10.

Fear of Human Nature: Ghosts

Ghosts are dead persons who, in some sense, are still alive. They may be known only by their effects, such as a creaking door or sudden illness. They may appear as an ectoplasmic shadow or mist. They may have a recognizable human form and expression but lack the full materiality of a live human being. They may look misleadingly normal and solid like the person sitting next to you. Or they may be zombies, the walking dead.

Fear of ghosts is rooted in the human apprehension of the unknown and the bizarre. Specters haunt people in essentially the same way as do other mysterious forces in the environment. To the premodern mind, no sharp distinction is drawn between nature deities and ancestors, ancestors and ghosts, ghosts and witches, witches and murderers, murderers and burglars, burglars and wild animals. Where the forces of nature are benevolent and predictable, people acknowledge them as divinities. Where they are fierce and erratic, people call them demons. The spirits of the dead can be a force for good; if such is the belief, then they are worshipped as ancestors. If malicious will is attributed to them, then they are ghosts to be propitiated. An ancestor or a dead human hero is almost a god; likewise, a ghost that causes injury is readily confused with a nature demon. Ghosts, like witches, are an intermediary concept from which one moves, in one direction, to the supernatural realm of gods and demons, and in another, to the natural and human realm of wild beasts, murderers, and burglars.

Our feelings toward fellow human beings are often ambivalent. We need them and like them, but there are times when they threaten us just as beasts, monsters, and witches do. We need the company of others, but have also secretly wished for their absence. Such ambiguity is intensified in our attitude to the dead, and particularly to the corpse. Is the corpse a beloved person, a decaying body, an ancestor, or a potential demon? When someone close to us dies we may be genuinely overcome with grief, and yet we are not happy with the thought of his or her return in the form of a spirit or walking corpse trailing odors of the grave. A perceptive missionary made this comment on the very mixed feelings of mourners in Gabon in west Africa:

> The outcry of affection, pleading with the dead to return to life, is sincere, the survivor desiring the return to life to be complete; but almost simultaneously with that cry comes a fear that the dead may indeed return, not as the accustomed embodied spirit, helpful and companionable, but as a disembodied spirit, invisible, estranged, perhaps inimical, and surrounded by an atmosphere of dread imparted by the unknown and the unseen.[1]

Europeans and Americans are deluded if they think that ordinary human affection can conquer the revulsion from death and the dissolution of the body. The chilling effect of W. W. Jacobs' well-known tale "The Monkey's Paw" derives from the reader's sudden awareness of the inadequacy of human love. The story depicts an old man and his wife who possess a shriveled monkey's paw that has the power to grant three wishes. Their first wish is for money. A stranger soon comes to deliver it, but informs the couple that the money is his company's token of regret for an accident in which their son was badly mangled by a machine and died. After recovering from the shock the old couple see to the burial of their son in a cemetery a short distance away. Then they return to their lonely home and try to carry on as best they can. About a week later, in the middle of the night, the woman suddenly remembers that the monkey's paw can still grant two more wishes. She picks it up and requests that her dead son return to her. At first, nothing happens. Half an hour later, however, in the time it would take a person to walk two miles, the couple hear a loud and insistent knock at the door. The woman runs downstairs to open it. Her husband tries to stop her, but she cries, "It's our son, Herbert! Are you afraid of your own son?" As the woman fumbles with the heavy bolt, her husband quickly picks up the monkey's paw and makes the third wish, which is that the decayed corpse of their son should remain in the grave and not return to test a mother's love. The door is flung open, cold air rushes in, but all the couple can see outside is the street lamp, its light flickering on the quiet and deserted road.

Human love between close kin and neighbors is insecure if it fails to recognize its own shadows. Belief in witches and ghosts is evidence of weaknesses in human bonds that are not acknowledged forthrightly because to do so would generate an awareness that would undermine the idealized image of good will on which the rules of acceptable behavior depend. A witch is a neighbor or a relative we dislike and distrust. Our distrust, we claim, rests on objective evidence when the root cause may in fact lie in our own repressed feelings of hostility. A ghost is frequently a dead kinsman for whom we feel resentment or guilt.

In societies where both witches and ghosts exist, the distinction between them is not finely drawn. Witches are closely associated with death, the dead, and the spirits of the dead. Bad weather, desolate hills, lonely roads, and abandoned houses are ambiences of both witches and ghosts. Places of burial are their familiar haunts. Both witches and ghosts can take the shape of wild animals.

To the Navaho, ghosts are the witches of the world of the dead. The lack of any sharp boundary between these two sorts of evil being is suggested by the Navaho's attitude toward the aged. White-haired people are respected but also feared. They are suspected of being witches—why is not clear. Perhaps the Navahos see the aged as an economic liability, persons who resent their loss of power, who are close to death and hence less amenable to social control. Navahos are uncomfortable with very old men and women for another reason: they are "almost ghosts." The very old, being near death, partake of death's repelling attributes.[2] On the other hand, when they do die they are not expected to return as specters, the assumption being that they have already lived fully their allotted span on earth.

In other parts of the world, we find a similar tendency to commingle witches and ghosts. The Kaguru of Tanzania, for example, believe that both witches and zombies dance at night on mountaintops.[3] In Zimbabwe, the Shona recognize a category of ghosts known as the *ngozi,* which include the vengeful spirits of murdered people as well as grudge-bearing ancestors. Because of their special malevolence, the *ngozi* are the handy tools of witches.[4]

By definition, witches are evil. The spirits of the dead, in contrast, may be evil or benevolent. Wherever witches exist they are feared; the dead, on the other hand, are not everywhere feared. Their spirits, especially those of one's own ancestors, can be forces for good. A strong evidence that people do not always fear the dead is the custom of burying the dead or preserving portions of them in the houses in which they once lived. This custom was known in Greece during Mycenaean times and in ancient Italy. Ethnographers have encountered it in widely different parts of the world, notably in Africa, South America, and Micronesia. The Gilbert Islanders, a Micronesian people in the Pacific, may be taken as an example of such fearlessness. When an Islander died, a grave was dug in the floor of the house. A near relative would then make a bed close to the grave and open it from time to time to look on the beloved's remains. The skull might be removed and kept in a box. The widow or child of the deceased was privileged to sleep and eat beside it, carry it about on all excursions, and anoint it with coconut oil. Gilbert Islanders expected the ghosts of dead kinsfolk to help them in life's practical affairs; they wanted to keep the remains and reminders of the dead close at hand.[5]

At the opposite extreme are the Navaho people. Their abhorrence of death and everything connected with it is total. Observers of Navahos have commented at length on their morbid fear of corpses. The anthropologists Kluckhohn and Leighton noted that to the Navaho, "even to look upon the bodies of dead animals, except those killed for food, is a peril. Dead humans are buried as soon as possible, and with such elaborate precautions that one of the greatest favors which a white person can do for Navahos is to undertake this abhorrent responsibility."[6] A house in which a person has died is burned, or else the roof beams are allowed to fall in, indicating that the place should be avoided. A Navaho would risk freezing rather than seek shelter in such a house or make a fire with its wood.[7]

Navahos shun corpses because they are likely to turn into ghosts. In some ways ghosts are more terrible than witches; witches can be captured and killed but the spirits of the dead are beyond normal human power. Only those who die in infancy or old age do not become specters. Otherwise, any dead person, no matter how affectionate he or she may have been when living, is a potential source of danger. Ghosts pervade the Navaho's world after dark. They appear in human form and as coyotes, owls, mice, whirlwinds, spots of fire, or indefinite dark objects. They make noises of movement—whistling sounds—and noises that resemble the calls of birds and other animals. All sorts of night shapes and sounds arouse dread. After sunset, fear of ghosts and witches keeps the Navahos inside their hogans.[8]

In most cultures, attitudes toward the dead and the spirits of the dead are more ambivalent and complex than those of Gilbert Islanders and Navaho Indians. The Mende of Sierra Leone assign an important role to ancestral spirits. Mende ancestors re-

tain their ordinary appetites and passions. They are willing to
help their descendants most of the time but can be angered by
evidences of misconduct; and since they are capable of feeling
hunger and thirst they turn vindictive if neglected. Mende ancestral spirits are not, however, truly frightening. They reveal
their displeasure rather tamely in dreams or by making the
culprit sick.[9] Ancestral spirits also play a major part in the lives
of the Shona of Zimbabwe. They are known as the *vadzimu* to
distinguish them from the *ngozi,* who are ghosts. The Shona
regard with special affection the *vadzimu* of parents and grandparents, and the spirits in their turn promote the welfare of the
lineage. Yet when a *vadzimu* is offended it can change into a
vengeful *ngozi.*[10]

In the Western Highlands of New Guinea, the Kyaka horticul-
turists tend to view the spirits of the dead as inimical. Ghosts
haunt trees and burial grounds. They come to the aid of kinsfolk,
but they can also be full of spite. They are known to have hurled
people into trees, leaving them hanging there helplessly, their
eyes and ears smeared in excrement. They have the power to
inflict blindness, leprosy, yaws, and internal swellings, and they
can cause insanity.[11] The Mae, who also live in the Western
Highlands, see ghosts either as wholly malignant or at best neu-
tral. Most injuries, illnesses, and deaths are attributed to them.
Family relations among the Mae are tense. Perhaps for this reason the ghosts to be feared most are those of close blood relatives
—father, mother, siblings, and offspring who die unmarried.[12]

Among the ancient Greeks ambivalence toward the dead was
evident in their attitude toward heroes. Like many primitive
peoples, the Greeks felt that their world contained more gods
and spirits than it did human beings; the Greek landscape was
cluttered with holy spots and shrines. Shrines to heroes made up
a large part of this landscape of worship, and some of them could
be fearful places, as Pausanias, a geographer of the second century A.D., tells us.[13]

Who was a hero? A hero was a brave man. When alive he
protected his kinsfolk and friends. Once he was dead his power
became more impersonal and reached beyond the bounds of his
own people.[14] Heroes were not clearly distinguishable from
ancestors. Both had protective functions, but both could also do
harm. Fearsome stories circulated among the peasants. There
was the evil hero Actaeon, who devastated the fields of the Boeo-
tians until, on the advice of his oracle, his statue was chained to
a rock. There was the hero of Temesa, to whom the most beautiful virgin of the town had to be sacrificed until the boxer Eu-

thymus drove him out; and the hero Orestes, whom the Athenians did not like to meet at night because he was apt to tear off their clothes and give them a thrashing. Heroes might cause sickness. They frightened the peasants not only as disembodied spirits but also as corporeal revenants who inflicted injury like bandits.[15]

Devising such categories as gods, ancestors, ghosts, and witches enables peasants or small traders in any society to live comfortably with the often unpredictable forces in their universe. Folk beliefs, however, lack logical consistency, and the categories often overlap. In ancient Greece, as we have noted, an ancestor could have authority over a larger group than his kins-folk and be worshipped as a hero. A similar idea existed in China. The Chinese did not ascribe much power to their ancestors, who as a rule could affect only the fortunes of their descendants. Nevertheless, a forebear who had become a scholar-official in his lifetime might upon death be elevated to the status of a minor god with jurisdiction over the people of a whole district. Gods, ancestors, and heroes were interchangeable. Today an educated peasant or small-time trader in modern Taiwan may be heard to deny the supernatural standing of gods, claiming that the numerous temples dedicated to them are no more than shrines for heroes. "A local god is a kind of hero, like your Lincoln," one said to an inquiring American.[16]

The Chinese are well known for their devotion to ancestral spirits. Officially, these spirits are always benevolent, their chief concern being the welfare of their progeny. The living, on their part, have definite obligations to their forebears for the gift of life and for support during childhood. Dead ascendants require the respect and attention of the living if they are to be happy in the other world. They have the power to demand, if need be, the care they require. This element of threat, which maintains the social hierarchy of the living, continues in the relationship between the living and the dead. The Chinese are most reluctant to admit that ancestors can be mean-spirited, but as misfortunes recur people are sometimes forced to entertain this extremity. They then say that ancestors are capable of inflicting harm just because they have a "bad heart," and that even when people make regular offerings to their forebears, they cannot rest assured that these will not return and cause trouble.[17]

An elder who dies does not immediately become an ancestor; he or she is for a time a corpse. The part of the death ritual the Chinese feel most uneasy with is the short period before coffining, when the living are directly exposed to the dead body. The exposed corpse is feared because it is in an indeterminate state between a living elder and a buried ancestor. In such a state the corpse's behavior is unpredictable: it may even change into a raging monster. For this reason, anyone present at the coffining, whether a relative or not, should receive ritual protection against injury. One act in the ritual is called "cutting." At some stage in the coffining process, one end of a rope is tied to the corpse and the rest of its length is given to the mourners to hold. The rope is then cut, the purpose being to prevent the dead from coming back and troubling their descendants later on.[18]

Once in the grave, the dead person is transformed into an ancestor, whose behavior can be predicted. The living members of the family, on their part, now know how to act toward the dead. Nevertheless, Chinese villagers do not feel entirely comfortable at places of burial. The grave is located at the margin of or outside the village. It lies at the fringe of the Yang world of the living; it is the gateway to the Yin world of the dead. The living have little sense of control over access to this gateway, where inimical ghosts may gather. By contrast, villagers interact confidently with ancestral spirits in the ancestral hall, which is located within the settlement. When villagers visit the grave they approach the unknown Yin world. On the other hand, when the souls of ancestors visit the hall they rejoin the Yang world of the living, and the living know just how to relate to them as familiar forebears.[19]

To be an ancestor one must have male progeny. But many people die before marriage, and many of those who survive to marry fail to produce male heirs. The status of these beings falls between that of ancestors and that of ghosts (or *kuei*—with the connotation of evil). People who die as dependents of the agnatic line but have no offspring of their own to worship them are treated as "almost ancestors," and their tablets are placed on the right of the family altar. People who have contributed to the line but are not members of it are treated as "almost ghosts," and their tablets are placed in a corner of the kitchen or in a hallway.

Infants and small children who die become ghosts. The souls of one's own children, if they die young enough, thus join the souls of malefactors—bandits and murderers—as ghosts who loiter dangerously in the world. Shrines are built outside the house and in the fields to propitiate them. The spirits of strangers and of malefactors must also be appeased in the same way and for the same reason that one treats live strangers warily and buys off bandits. A further complication is this: just as my relatives are strangers from your point of view, so my ancestors might appear to you as ghosts with the will and power to cause you injury.[20]

Like other folk, the Chinese suspect and fear whatever is alien and unknown. Originally, the word for ghost, *kuei,* meant a bizarre simian creature—a wild animal. Its meaning was then extended to cover alien races and, finally, spectral beings who did not belong to the known and respectable world of family, officials, ancestors, and gods.[21]

Even in modern times, in countries of high culture, rural folk have continued to carry a heavy load of ancient fears that their city cousins have more or less learned to discard. In a country like China, the urban-rural dichotomy remained sharp up to at least the time of the Second World War: while college students discussed Einstein's theory of relativity, just beyond the city walls villagers still used magic to dispel epidemics and demons.

In 1934, the sociologist Wolfram Eberhard analyzed folktales he had collected in China's Chê-chiang province, and found the following characteristic beliefs concerning ghosts and demons. Corpses in coffins that have not yet been buried, or have not been buried correctly, become ghosts. Human beings whose lives have been truncated do not rest in peace. Thus murder victims and people who have been forced by circumstance to hang themselves (usually young women) may return as ghosts.

A revenant, in Chinese folktales, terrifies because of its grotesque appearance. Horror is augmented by surprise: a revenant may at first assume the shape of a beautiful person; but just as people begin to accept the metempsychosis, it is transformed into a monster with long hair, a long tongue, claws, and blood dripping down its white dress.[22]

We do not know how ghosts fare in the People's Republic. We do know that in the Taiwanese countryside they remained strong in folk awareness at least through the late 1950s, as the ghost lore of the village of Peihotien shows. The village is located on the Tamsui River and was at that time an hour by train and foot from metropolitan Taipei. After water had been withdrawn from the Tamsui for irrigation projects, the river had shrunk to the size of a stream. Yet village parents still forbade their children to swim in or play near it. The reason for their fear was this: in the old days, many people had been drowned when ferries capsized while crossing the river. The villagers believed that the souls of those who drowned remained in the water as unhappy souls until they succeeded in pulling in other victims to take their place.

Peihotien's ghosts were not confined to the river. Margery

Wolf, in her study of the village, reported that several apparitions were observed near a bamboo grove, and that another had repeatedly been seen combing her long hair in the ruins of a pigpen. "A quite comfortable room in a house near the village is rarely rented and then only to outsiders because of the unpleasant habits of the ghost of its former owner."[23]

Almost everywhere, the dead are suspected of resenting their condition: they yearn to return and visit the places and people they once knew. Such specters, potential forces of chaos, hover just beyond the world of the living and are a recurrent threat to it. People deal with such threats by defining their own space, erecting barriers around it, and cleansing it ritually from time to time. The diligent scholar Sir James Frazer collected evidence from all parts of the world to show how the living try to sever links with the dead and guard against their nefarious influence.[24]

The Arunta of central Australia believed that after a man's death his ghost should be allowed to roam freely for a period of twelve to eighteen months; thereafter the restless spirit had to be confined within narrower bounds. Because a ghost—any ghost— was known to like to return to the burnt and deserted camp where his death had occurred, on a certain day a band of men and women would go to the camp, dance around its charred remains, shout, and beat the air with their weapons and hands to drive the spirit from the spot he loved too well. When the dance was over the whole party proceeded to chase the ghost back to the grave, where he presumably would remain.[25]

A custom broadly diffused among American Indians was to destroy a dead man's property, or to refuse to make use of it, for fear of the possessiveness of the ghost. The Ahts of Vancouver Island showed a variant of this custom. When a man died his personal effects were buried with him, but not valuable items such as canoes, house-planks, and fishing gear, which the eldest son inherited. Among the more superstitious Ahts, however, the dead man's house and all its contents were burned. The descendants were thus deprived of an opportunity to accumulate wealth through inheritance.

A more sensible practice, which likewise discouraged a ghost's return, was to remove all the materials on a dead man's property and use them to build a house elsewhere.[26] Alexander von Humboldt has this to say about Indian tribes in the valley of the Orinoco River:

Some tribes, for instance the Tamanaca, are accustomed to lay waste the fields of a deceased relative, and cut down the trees he has planted. They say that "the sight of objects which belonged to their relation makes them sad." They prefer to efface than to preserve remembrances. These effects of Indian sensibility are very detrimental to agriculture, and the monks oppose such superstitious practices with energy.[27]

James Frazer thought, however, that the true motivation was fear of the dead, a fear that the Tamanaca were reluctant to admit to Humboldt.[28]

Ghosts, it would seem, can be discouraged by the simplest material barriers. The Kpelle of Liberia held the view that two posts planted in the ground with wattlework stretched between them sufficed to prevent the ghosts from the graveyard from molesting villagers. In India, it was an ancient custom that when the mourners left the cremation ground the officiating priest would raise a barrier of stones between the dead and the living. The hill tribes of northern India adopted and retained this custom until well into the twentieth century. In Europe, peasant farmers seemed to think water an effective protection against the restless spirits of the dead. In Transylvania late in the nineteenth century, the procession returning from a funeral might go a mile or two out of its way to avoid all bridges and seek a stream of running water to cross, thus making sure that the vagrant soul of the deceased would not be able to follow the mourners home. In parts of Germany as well as in modern Greece and Cyprus, a more economical version of this is to pour water behind the corpse as it is being carried from the house; the idea is that if the ghost returns it cannot step over the water. Ghosts can be kept out of dwellings by shutting all apertures. In England and Savoy, householders along the route of a funeral procession made sure that their doors and windows were properly closed.[29]

Ghosts can be prevented from entering a house, or be driven out of it, by simple physical means. In Madagascar, people believed that the spirits of the dead hovered around settlements, seeking an opportune moment to re-enter their former homes. In times of flood or torrential rains, men and women beat the sides of their shelters violently in an effort to push back the *angatra,* or specters, which would try to get in with the water.

The Germans once sought to rid their houses of ghosts by waving towels about, or by sweeping them out with a broom.[30] The ancient Roman practice was more refined and elaborate. The father of the house rose at midnight and after purification took black beans and cast them over his shoulder without looking back, saying at the same time, "With these beans I redeem myself and my family." Nine times he repeated the spell, while the ghosts came behind him and gathered up the beans. Once more the head of the house washed himself and clanged brass vessels. Nine times he repeated the formula, "Ghosts of my fathers, depart," and then the purification was complete.[31]

If even those relatives who died a natural death might not rest in peace, to the superstitious mind people who had been murdered were much more likely to return as ghosts. Measures could, however, be taken against that eventuality. A story told about Yang Chien, founder of China's Sui dynasty (A.D. 581–618), illustrates this type of belief. After the emperor had moved to his newly built capital of Ta-hsing, he flooded the palaces of the old capital, Ch'ang-an, so that the ghosts of the princes he had murdered in his rise to power would not be able to come back and trouble him.[32]

Wherever ghosts are acknowledged as regular visitants, people develop standard methods of response. At the communal level, they may build shrines so that ghosts can be formally propitiated. At the individual level, a person who runs into a spirit in a lonely field will know how to fend it off with sacred words and ritual gestures; and if a specter should persist in haunting a person's house, the occupant can appeal to the aid of a priest. Human beings learn to take precautions against attacks by demons and phantoms as they would against attacks by bandits. Here is a typical illustration taken from late medieval England.

During the reign of Richard II, a monk in Yorkshire recorded a number of encounters between the people of his neighborhood and ghosts. In one of the reports, a ghost pestered a tailor named Snowball. The apparition assumed different forms: a raven, a peat stack, a dog with a chain collar, a she-goat, and finally "the likeness of a man of great stature, horrible and thin." With each encounter, Snowball defended himself by some religious gesture such as making the sign of the cross, carrying the cross-shaped hilt of his sword ahead of him, or uttering the names of the Trinity. At the last meeting, which was prearranged, Snowball took exceptional precautions: he wore on his person the four Gospels and other holy words; he made a great circle with a cross; he stood at the center of the circle and placed within it reliquaries in cruciform. Why, the monk asked, did God permit the ghost to harass the tailor? Answer: The tailor had neglected to attend mass. What was the ghost seeking? He sought to be relieved of his terrible suffering as an excommunicant. He asked Snowball to find a priest who could absolve him. He also requested that the "full number of nine times twenty masses" be celebrated on his behalf.[33]

From this tale, we see that ghosts were regarded in medieval England as dangerous and bizarre creatures. On the other hand, both the Church and the ordinary individual seem to have known exactly how to behave toward them. Spirits of all kinds were so much an accepted part of medieval culture that the awe they excited may not have been as intense as that a modern person might feel in the face of the wholly inexplicable. It may well be that the most frightening encounters with specters have occurred since the eighteenth century, a time when belief in them, while diminishing, has not by any means disappeared. This much is clear: supernatural tales that owe the special quality of their terror to deep psychological insight are a product of the modern sensibility.

In the English-speaking world, when we think of ghosts and haunted houses we turn perforce to the mother country. Spectral lore was particularly rich in the Victorian era, but the taste for tales of the uncanny persists to the present.[34] Antiquarian societies, local historians, and folklorists keep on collecting ghost stories and adding new ones as they appear. In Wiltshire alone, a folklorist in 1973 gathered 275 separate accounts, and the list is far from complete.[35] Widespread literacy, even in England, has been a feature of life for less than two hundred years. In the absence of books that opened up the world, men and women were intensely involved in local events and in stories of their own neighborhood, passed on orally with embellishments and additions from one generation to the next. Of such stories, those of a spectral nature seem to have left the deepest impression.

Ghost stories alone could have only fleeting entertainment value without the support of other superstitious beliefs and practices, and these were many in nineteenth-century England. Village lore included all sorts of omens for death. As death approached, owls hooted, dogs howled, and cats left the house. A guttering candle that sent down a cascade of melting wax foreshadowed the winding sheet. Countryfolk distrusted the dead and were reluctant to enter churchyards by night. They disliked the idea of keeping the body in the dwelling. A hearse aroused unease. Ghosts intruded on life's ongoing activities, and not just in stories. A century ago, it was not unusual to ask the local clergyman to quelch their obnoxious behavior. At Wyke House in Trowbridge, a ghost gave so much trouble that no less than twelve Anglican priests came to expel it.[36]

Ghosts can be pathetic as well as frightening. There is an inexpressible air of sadness and unfulfillment in the way they haunt specific localities. They appear at the same place and at the same time again and again. In England, many old or abandoned houses, inns, and monasteries are rumored to have visitors from beyond the grave. The dead return to these constructed places for many reasons. A common one is that their remains have been disturbed or that they are dissatisfied with the way they were buried. This theme may well be the prototype of the haunted-house story in the Western world. An early version is that of the younger Pliny who noted how a ghost kept appearing in an Athenian house until the skeleton of a man was discovered in the courtyard, dug up, and ceremonially reinterred.[37]

In modern England, tales like the following are told. Two children staying at a house in Lacock were frightened by an "ugly little man" who walked through their room. Many years later a skeleton was found under the bedroom wall. A woman who slept in an old manor house at Sutton Veny thought she felt a child's head resting on her shoulder for two consecutive nights. Later, when a wing of the building was pulled down, workers discovered the skeletons of five children.[38] Of course, only in a long-settled country might a house in the course of construction incorporate the skeletal remains of the place's former inhabitants.

Two other types of ghost story further illustrate the English person's strong sense of the continuity of place and of the people who live in it. One type hinges on the belief that a visitant may appear in a house which has, in some sense, been violated: for example, the ancestral home of an old family that is taken over by the newly rich, or a priory that has been converted into a youth hostel. Such visitants are usually harmless and not particularly frightening. At night, one may see the shape of a cowled monk disappearing through a wall which, several centuries ago, had a door leading to a wine cellar. The phantom monk returns because the house, however much it has been altered, was and still is its home. The second type of yarn focuses on the dwelling itself. A characteristic story goes like this. A cyclist is caught in a sudden shower on a rural road. She sees a cottage by the wayside, enters it for shelter, and is made welcome by a taciturn old man. When the rain stops, the cyclist continues on her way into town, where an astonished friend tells her that there is no such cottage along that particular stretch of road; there is only the ruin of a dwelling abandoned fifty years before. This type of story suggests that people are reluctant to admit that houses and other deeply human objects can, like the mortals who made them, disappear forever from the scene.

On a lonely moor, a shepherd might report that he had met strange soldiers wearing skirts and marching up a nonexistent path, or a hearse, with a crown on top of the coffin, drawn by black horses. A historian would nod and say, "Yes, there was a road across that moor and Roman soldiers might well have marched on it," or "In medieval times royal corteges could have passed that way." How could an illiterate shepherd living in Britain at the turn of the century have known such facts? He might, of course, have seen pictures of Roman soldiers. Whatever the origin of the story, the significant point is that it was told and remembered: people who lived in an age of trains and horseless carriages found it easily acceptable.

Ghosts are the last of the suprasensible beings to lose their grip on the landscapes of Europe. Nature gods and goddesses departed first. In England, the River Ribble was once the home of a goddess to whom sacrifices were made at regular intervals. It is now the home of a ghost called Peg O'Nell, who demands a life every seven years. In the River Swale, Hoggett's Hole probably owes its reputation as a haunted place to another forgotten river spirit. The hole now takes its name from Tom Hoggett, a highwayman of coaching days, who drowned in the river while trying to cross it and escape arrest. It is said that no one who falls into it ever comes out alive, no matter how strong a swimmer he or she is. The Wild Hunt of the Germanic god Woden may have been the predecessor of "the phantom coach," which is the spectral world's favorite vehicle. "There is scarcely an old road in England along which the Coach has not trundled at some time or another," writes Christina Hole. "Sometimes it comes to fetch away the dying; sometimes the already dead use it in their perambulations along the roads and fields of their old home."[39]

Ghosts fade slowly from the imagination. Modern machinery does not necessarily destroy them. An abandoned factory no less than an old mill is a suitable site for apparitions. Phantom motorcars have displaced phantom coaches. On the remaining lonely roads of Britain, motorists can still pick up spectral hitchhikers. Stories of haunted houses still circulate and can affect rents. "A house which is reputed to be haunted is often difficult to let, so difficult in fact that legal action has been frequently taken against those who spread the tale . . . and so depreciated the value of the property."[40]

The United States of America would seem to be the country in the world least hospitable to ghosts. It does not believe in the sanctity of the past. Ancestor worship plays no role in its religions. Thomas Jefferson once said, "The dead have no rights. They are nothing. . . . Our creator made the earth for the use of the living and not of the dead." A new nation, America lacks the favored haunts of ghosts: old houses that belong to families with blood-stained histories, old inns, and abandoned monasteries. The nation has its face to the future, and it projects a public image of bustling cities, lush cornfields, and superhighways. This image is, of course, misleading. The American landscape has a time dimension. Drive off the hardtop road in Tennessee, Kentucky, or the Ozark Hills, and in a matter of minutes you enter another world of closely knit communities that retain many of the superstitions and customs of Old Europe. In the isolated hollows, ghosts and witches are as much a part of living tradition as dying in one's own home and maintaining the family graveyard. A country lane or covered bridge, so picturesque to the passing tourist on a sunny day, can seem ominous to the old-timer trudging home before the shadow deepens.

In the backwoods life can be cozy, but also insecure. Death is omnipresent rather than a distant abstraction. Reminders of death are everywhere. If a Kentucky hillman sees a cloud shaped like a coffin or if he hears a cow bawling at night, then someone he knows will soon die. If the oldest person at the table sneezes during breakfast on Sunday morning, he will hear of a death before the week is over. A door that opens without apparent cause forebodes death. Dreaming of muddy water is prognostic of death. Almost anything that happens unexpectedly and is therefore beyond a person's control is an ill omen.[41]

Intimate human ties compensate somewhat for this pervasive sense of life's precariousness. But they can also generate repressed feelings of hostility which may be projected into the world beyond death. The help or injury that one person receives from another does not terminate with the cessation of life; the spirits of relatives and neighbors remain close at hand and continue to be concerned with the affairs of the living. Some old folk in the Ozarks pretend to lay a ghost by putting little stones on the dead person's grave. Vance Randolph, writing in 1947, said that he had seen graves that were conspicuous for their gravelly cover, and that he had witnessed adults tossing pebbles on them with an apologetic air.[42] The ghost of even the closest blood relation may not be welcome. In the mid-1930s, a man of Wayne County in Kentucky said:

> I always kept a horseshoe over my door to keep the evil spirits
> away. We live very close to the graveyard. And my boy, Ed,
> said he had been seeing his brother, Charlie, in his room
> every night. If he was livin' right he would not be seein'
> Charlie every night. Charlie never bothers me! He was my boy
> that died and is buried in this graveyard above our house.[43]

All evil beings, ghosts included, are denizens of the dark.
Countryfolk in the South used to say that roving at night was a
sin; respectable people stayed indoors. When families visited
one another or went to the store they made sure to get there "by
the edge of the dark." Ozark housewives seldom swept their
cabins after nightfall and never swept anything out their front
doors, since ghosts stood around the cabins at night and it was
dangerous to offend them by throwing dirt in their faces.[44]

The dead of long ago are known to visit contemporary America; though, predictably, calls by historic personages are less
often reported in the United States than in Europe. One ghost-
haunted place of historic interest was Breadtray Mountain in
Stone County, Missouri. Hill people carefully avoided the land-
mark, believing that Spaniards, centuries ago, had buried a
great store of gold on Breadtray Mountain just before they were
all killed by Indians. Travelers who passed close to the mountain
at night claimed they could hear the sobs, groans, and smothered
screams of the murdered soldiers.[45]

Ghosts in backwoods America, as in Europe, most frequently
visit man-made features: in the United States these include old
or abandoned houses, old mills, covered bridges, and country
roads. Ghosts also appear in natural settings such as hills, hollows, and woods. Wherever a ghost is reported, that place acquires a numinous cast; it is set aside from the ordinary world.
A landscape, to stay haunted, must be maintained by the art of
storytelling, which until the Second World War was a popular
pastime in many homes and country stores. To people who
disapproved of dancing or cardplaying, swapping supernatural
tales was almost the sole form of social entertainment.

Do rural folk really believe in the stories they so fondly tell?
Quite possibly they do: the psychology of embracing as real the
phantasms of one's own imagination through repeated telling is
well known. Evidence of such credulity and self-persuasion
comes as well from ethnographic surveys. For example, the people of a Tennessee community near Nashville, as in some other

parts of the South, produce corn whiskey illegally. They try to protect their distilling equipment in two ways: by posting sentries and through the circulation of scary ghost stories. Several stills are actually built in the vicinity of isolated family graveyards on the assumption that no one would dare venture near them after sundown. Although the moonshiners attempt to take advantage of other people's superstitiousness, they themselves do not wholly rise above it. They are victimized by their own tales.[46] They work the stills at night with a forced jocularity that barely hides their own nervousness.

So much of human fear is of other people who sustain our world but also threaten it. Destructive natural forces and diseases wear human masks, and in witches and ghosts the fear of human evil takes on a supernatural dimension. Where can one hide? The home, though a haven from external threats, is not exempt from conflicts that are all the more intense for taking place between family members who feel strongly toward each other. In modern times, the typical setting for murder is not the street but the private residence. Along with the home, the countryside projects an image of peace. But we shall see how misleading this image can be. Violence and fear have been regular components of the rural scene. Feuds, wars, banditry, and personal vendettas in country towns and villages erupted periodically to destroy the countryside's superficial air of calm. The city is humankind's most ambitious attempt to create physical and human order. However, success was and is mixed. The congregation of people that can lead to great achievement also provides the opportunity for violence and chaos. In order to forestall violence and prevent chaos, powerful rulers and governments have created fearsome landscapes of punishment.

11.

Violence and Fear in the Countryside

A sign of efficient, if not necessarily good, government is peace in the open countryside as well as in the city. Early in the fourth century, a Roman governor of Britain (Pacatianus, for instance) could well have boasted to a visitor: "You have traveled the whole day in comfort, and have nowhere been robbed, or molested, or threatened. You have seen the natives peacefully gathering in their corn. You have passed villa after villa standing alone in the open country, with no fortification, and with no protection save that which the owner's slaves would render without fail in case of need."[1]

The rulers of T'ang-dynasty China, even in its declining years, would have been justified in making similar claims. Although the evidence for this assertion is indirect, it is persuasive. A Japanese monk, Ennin, was in China between the years 838 and 847. During this period he traveled extensively by boat on rivers and canals and on foot on the highways and side roads of the country. From the entries in Ennin's diary a detailed picture of the T'ang empire emerges. Edwin Reischauer comments: "Perhaps the most surprising aspect of this composite picture is something that is missing from it entirely. Not once during his months of wandering between the major cities of the land through remote and sparsely populated mountain and coastal areas was Ennin in danger from bandits or brigands of any type."[2] The Japanese monk and his companions more than once crossed an area that had recently suffered from famine, each time in complete safety and without fear that anything unpleasant would happen. When the government was efficient and trusted, even famine did not necessarily result in violence.

Generally speaking, prosperity and peace went together.

Europe has known periods of prosperity in the countryside and probably of safety as well. Brunetto Latini (d. 1294?) spoke of the open manor houses of the Île de France, surrounded by gardens, orchards, and rural peace. Froissart in the next century depicted the rich Cotentin region with evident admiration. French and German literature of the time made fun of prosperous peasants who had the means though not quite the savoir-faire to imitate their betters effectively.[3]

There were indeed times when "the countryside was fat and full of good things" (Froissart), but such times did not last. The rich Cotentin was soon desolated by war. Periods of tranquillity and order in the countryside were brief interludes in the history of nations and empires. Quite apart from wars, epidemics, and famines, violence was endemic in villages no less than it was in cities. Since the Romantic era, literate Westerners have been disposed to forget all the factionalism and gore in country places and have come to see them not only as safe but as inherently wholesome and good. Reading about murder in a country vicarage sends a special thrill through us, because the juxtaposition of violence with rose gardens and cow pastures seems so incongruous. On modern highways and country roads motorists are not in the least afraid of being waylaid by gangsters. It is only as they drive into the decaying urban core that they nervously lock their car doors for fear of being molested at the traffic light.

However, taking a broader swath of time, we are quickly forced to discard this image of rural peace and urban turmoil. It is true that in some places in certain historical periods—sixteenth-century Spain, for instance—the bitterness of strife within cities did make the countryside seem calm.[4] In others, our information, though seldom conclusive, points the other way. Consider the proverb *Stadtluft macht frei*—"City air makes one free"—of the late Middle Ages. It expressed the civil and political freedom a citizen enjoyed in comparison with the constrained life of a serf, but it affirmed as well the citizen's greater security of possession and person. The town dweller behind the city walls had less to fear from the ravages of bandits and armies than did the isolated and unprotected peasant. This was true of Germany even in the seventeenth century, at the time of the Thirty Years' War.

Historians have portrayed medieval Europeans as emotionally unstable, given to impulsive acts and to outbursts of rage followed by extravagant displays of contrition. To one scholar, the most vivid characteristic of Londoners in the thirteenth century was their "capacity for reckless violence." To another, society in the rural Midlands at the end of the same century was one in which "expectation of life was short, death in all its forms was always present," and where "violence, bribery and corruption were normal means of settling issues which arose between men."[5] James Given has made an attempt to calculate the homicide rates of that time in several English counties by using the records of visiting royal justices empowered to try all crimes. He concludes that in the thirteenth century, homicide rates could be as high as 28 per 100,000 population per year in such essentially rural counties as Bedford and Kent. Rural Warwick had an overall homicide rate of 19 per 100,000 per annum for a twenty-five-year period. Norfolk had the lowest average rate, 9 per 100,000 per annum for the twenty-three years covered by the visitations. Homicide was noticeably less common in urban areas. The rate for Bristol in 1227 and 1248 was only 4 per 100,000; in London, it was 8 per 100,000 in 1227, and 15 per 100,000 in 1276. How shocking these figures are becomes plain when we compare them with those of modern Britain, which has hovered around 0.4 per 100,000 since 1930, or even with that of the United States in 1974, which was 9.7 per 100,000.[6]

In the late Middle Ages, the greatest threat to life, limb, and property came from other people in the local neighborhood, whether urban or rural. Violence and crime were endemic to community. The horrors of home, however, tended to be taken for granted. People were more conscious of danger when they traveled. For one thing, they had highway robbers to contend with. Although just about any roadside ditch or thick coppice could spell danger, certain localities and roads were known to be especially threatening. The wooded defile at Trimpley on the edge of Wye forest was frequented by a gang that specialized in robbing traveling merchants. The place where the three counties of Lincolnshire, Leicestershire, and Rutland joined was also a favorite haunt of robbers. From the criminal's viewpoint it had two advantages: several roads ran nearby, and the shire boundaries were so ill-defined that sheriffs were reluctant to assume responsibility. Since merchants were a major quarry, highwaymen operated repeatedly on roads that linked important fairs and market towns. For instance, Alton pass, on the busy road between London and Southampton, was notorious for its robberies and murders.[7]

The need to deprive robbers of their hiding places was recognized in 1285 in the Statute of Winchester. Edward I ordered that the edges of highways be cleared for a distance of two hundred feet on both sides, in such a manner that evildoers could not hide in coppice, brushwood, hollow, or ditch. Only large trees such as oaks might remain. Responsibility for clearing the land was left to its proprietor; if he neglected his duty he could be fined severely for crimes committed on his grounds. Where the road crossed a park, it was the noble owner's obligation to border it with a thick hedge or a ditch so wide and deep that robbers could not easily cross it or hide in it before or after their attacks.[8]

The appeal to the lord was somewhat ironic because noblemen were among the worst offenders against social order in the countryside, especially in the fourteenth and fifteenth centuries. Acts of criminal violence were not restricted to any social rank. The nobility and the gentry committed felonies quite as often as did their inferiors. The very idea of a criminal class, different from law-abiding citizens, was not clearly held by the people of the late Middle Ages; a person might break the law for profit or revenge when an opportunity arose and then revert, quite unselfconsciously, to upholding the law.

Local magnates provided leadership and livery to roaming brigands: the two classes sometimes found it convenient to join forces. A magnate surrounded by his liveried partisans believed himself to be above the law. He waged battles against his rivals, and in a showdown could marshal as many as several thousand supporters. A magnate's followers might act on their own and plunder the country, kill, maim, and rape under the cover of their lord's colors. Compared with the ordinary highwaymen, the liveried gangs were better organized, more open in their sorties, and far more destructive. An enduring testimony to such turbulence is the large number of castles built from the eleventh century onward. The ruins of these bastions are now seen through a romantic haze. We forget that their discomfort and inconvenience were the price that the magnates and their followers had to pay for security in a landscape of violence. By the fourteenth century, castles dotted the face of England, some forty of them in Kent alone.[9]

Medieval England was widely known in Europe for its high rate of crime. This ill repute persisted through the Tudor period. Around 1500, an Italian visitor declared that in "no country in the world are there more robbers and thieves than in England; insomuch, that few venture to go alone in the country, excepting in the middle of the day, and fewer still in the towns at night."[10] In the first decade of the seventeenth century, the much-traveled Sir Thomas Chaloner asserted that economic depressions brought "more to the gallows in England in one year than a great part of Europe consumeth in many."

The city, with its heterogeneous population and abundance of movable goods, provided ample opportunities for stealing. Crimes against property were much more common in the bigger cities than in the countryside; but with regard to violent crimes against people, such rural-urban differences were largely erased or even reversed. During Elizabeth's reign the murder and manslaughter rate of rural Sussex (1.4 per 10,000) was actually double that of Essex (0.7 per 10,000), a county that had already come under the commercial influence of London.[11]

England was an outpost of Europe. How did the mainland fare at this time? For a picture of the Mediterranean world we can depend on Fernand Braudel's magisterial survey. In countries bordering the Mediterranean Sea, poverty and strife rose sharply toward the end of the sixteenth century, and became even more pronounced in the next. Throughout this period, as Braudel puts it, "disturbances broke out regularly, annually, daily even, like mere traffic accidents which no one any longer thought worthy of attention." Historians now find it difficult to classify and explain these disturbances. Were they revolts, rebellions, feuds, vendettas, unorganized plunder and murder by desperate people, the primordial struggle of man against man? However classified, their widespread occurrence and frequency indicate an extremely insecure social landscape, one in which violence, injury, and sudden death were permanent features. And whatever the other explanations, an underlying cause was poverty—desperate indigence existing side by side with opulence and power.

Poverty produced vagrants and vagabonds, beggars, thieves, cutthroats, and bandits. One sixteenth-century writer believed that there were 150,000 of them in Spain alone.[12] Such undesirables flocked into towns, from which they were periodically driven out again to plague the countryside. Around Saragossa, a Venetian reported in July 1586,

> one has to travel in blazing heat and in great peril from cutthroats who are in the countryside in great numbers, all because at Valencia they have issued an order expelling from the kingdom all vagrants after a certain time limit, with the threat of greater penalties; some have gone to Aragon and some to Catalonia. Another reason for travelling by day and with a strong bodyguard!

No region in the Mediterranean world was free from the scourge of banditry. It cropped up everywhere: at the gates of

Alexandria and Damascus; in the countryside around Naples, where watchtowers were built to warn of brigands; in the Roman Campagna, where authorities sometimes used brush fires to smoke out robbers in hiding; and along the principal highway in the Turkish Empire, sections of which might be fringed with scores of hanged outlaws. In Spain, the road between Saragossa and Barcelona—a major artery of the empire—was extremely dangerous. Noblemen traveled in armed caravans; official couriers were frequently robbed or even failed to get through. In Catalonia, as in the lower Rhône valley, all farms were fortified houses.

Mountains and frontier zones, where state authority was weak, were the strongholds of outlaws: for example, the Dalmatian highlands between Venice and Turkey; the vast frontier region of Hungary; the Pyrenees near the French border; and the rugged terrain of Calabria. Highwaymen ruled almost openly large tracts of Calabria and Apulia. When travelers there sought to avoid the perilous roads, they risked falling into the hands of pirates who infested the coastal waters. In general, Italy, being a mosaic of petty sovereignties, was a brigands' paradise. They could seek refuge in an adjoining state when their home base of operations was no longer secure.

Noblemen on the mainland, like those in England, often abetted or actively directed the activities of outlaws. There were undoubted ties between the Catalan nobility and brigands in the Pyrenees, between the Sicilian nobility and robbers in southern Italy, between the magnates of the Papal States and the outlaws around Rome. These noblemen were often impoverished younger sons or adventurers who had lost their fortunes.

Bandits perpetrated atrocities of all kinds. They plundered the land, maimed or killed travelers, destroyed the crops and livestock of those who resisted them, burned houses and raped and killed the residents, kidnapped for ransom, and desecrated churches. Mountain outlaws held the rich farms on the plains in bondage. Every rumor of an impending attack incited panic. Once caught, bandits were brutally punished. An official notice dated the end of September 1585 impassively reports: "This year in Rome, we have seen more heads of bandits on the Ponte Sant-'Angelo than melons on the market place."[13]

In the seventeenth century, banditry and rural violence instigated and led by the local nobility continued to afflict the poorer parts of Europe—southwestern France, for example, in that broad belt of impoverished soils surrounding the productive Aquitaine basin. This region, during the reign of Louis XIII, was notorious for its lawlessness. Between 1628 and 1644, riots and even peasant wars flared up periodically throughout the area. The ferocity of the rural nobility, gentleman brigands as well as the most illustrious families, cast an oppressive pall over the entire land. No one and no property was safe. "The nobility for the most part recognizes neither reason nor justice, only force and violence," reported the Marquis de Sourdis to Richelieu in July 1640.[14]

When we turn to the eighteenth century, the countryside in the prosperous parts of England and France seems to offer smiling landscapes unshadowed by the bloody conflicts and fears of earlier times. To the gentry even wild nature was beginning to appear sublime, a source of inspiration rather than a minacious presence to be avoided; talented landscape gardeners were converting country estates into works of pastoral art. By contrast, the cities seemed overcrowded, crime-ridden, chaotic, and dirty. This antithesis between country and city, to judge from the literary evidence, was and remains to this day a common view.

Yet, another view is possible. We might ask, How did the eighteenth-century countryside look from the city? To a London gentleman it probably looked appealing but also difficult of access. No suburbia sprawled interminably beyond the London of that time. However, what did surround the city was even less attractive. The land adjoining the roads out of London was watered from drains and thickly sprinkled with refuse and manure heaps. Numerous hogs found a home there. A chain of smoking brick-kilns encircled the greater part of London, and in the brickfields vagrants, thieves, and footpads lived and slept, cooking their food at the kilns.[15]

Highways out of London all suffered in varying degree from the predations of bandits. The Great North Road and Epping Forest were the playing fields of Dick Turpin, Jerry Abershaw, and Captain Mcheath. Elsewhere scores of desperadoes, known and unknown, frequented on horseback the undrained and uncultivated heaths and commons—Hounslow, Bagshot, Wimbledon, Hampton, Hatton, Harlington, Wandsworth, and Finchley —all of which had thick growths of furze bushes and bulrushes.[16] A journey without incident through such country was a matter for surprise and congratulation. "I was robbed last night as I expected," wrote Prime Minister Lord North to a friend in the autumn of 1774. Horace Walpole was moved to complain that one was "forced to travel even at noon as if one was going into battle. . . . What a shambles this country is grown."[17] While country houses, with their iron gates and guarded grounds, were no doubt havens of peace and beauty, the roads that linked them to each other and to the capital, especially where they passed through heath and forest, could only have been viewed with alarm by travelers. Would the coach be mired in mud? Could the wheel axle withstand another shock? Who might be hiding in the next thicket?

Turning to Paris, we find that travelers had similar trepidations. A ring of forests and woodlands partially enclosed Paris in the late eighteenth century. On the beautiful pen-and-wash maps drawn up mostly in the 1760s and 1770s the forests appear as pleasing patches of dark green. "But," writes Richard Cobb,

> nothing could in fact have been less reassuring once these conventional colours had been translated into the reality of stark winter forest, the branches cracking like alarming reports in the deep forest, or of thick summer coverage . . . as the prudent traveller walked or rode, preferably in company, well to the middle of the road, with the almost felt presence of those who watched through the thickets and branches. The highroads were but uncertain, fragile frontiers between huge areas of primeval jungle; and the pretty colours of the cartographer's palette tell us nothing . . . of the wild pigs and wolves . . . of the mutilated, half devoured bodies lying in thickets, sometimes a few paces from the King's military roads.

The forests also harbored human predators. One of the worst areas was the Bois de Boulogne. "Many poor female pedlars, on their return from a fair or a market in Versailles, would find themselves robbed, and more occasionally, raped and then murdered, on this last lap of their walk through the late afternoon and the dusk."[18]

Robbers and highwaymen could make the countryside look sinister. Although the most notorious among them (Dick Turpin and Louis-Dominique Cartouche, for instance) were city bred, most bandits had rural backgrounds, their prior occupations being farm hand, day laborer, or herdsman.[19] Landed peasants rarely became outlaws, except perhaps under extreme duress. However, violence was certainly not alien to their way of life. In eighteenth-century France, few urban dwellers were inclined to see peasants as peace-loving rustics in a bucolic setting. There was little sentimentality in that regard. Parisians indeed tended to look upon the inhabitants of the countryside surrounding Paris as more or less naked savages and cannibals, people who were innately nasty, brutal, and bloody. A variety of incidents lent support to this perception. Rural folk showed little tolerance for customs other than their own; they were quick to take offense and resorted easily to physical force.

> A soldier had been beaten to death in a village because quite unwittingly, he had sinned against rural tribal *mores,* by initially refusing to drink out of a glass offered him by a countryman who had already drunk out of it. . . . A 15-year-old boy was stabbed to death apparently because he could not make out what the villagers were trying to say to him.[20]

In the eighteenth century, certain parts of rural France—the Lyons region, for instance—suffered from outbreaks of collective violence. Some of these riots flared spontaneously between families, and some were directed without much forethought against tax collectors or seignorial rights; others, however, showed an almost ritualized periodicity.[21]

One circumstance which permitted and perhaps encouraged these sorts of violent incidents, particularly those at set intervals, was the extended free time of farm workers. Young English laborers, who had much less leisure than their French counterparts, channeled their energies into vicious sports; but a young French farm hand had a right to as many as sixty or seventy days of holiday a year. How did he fill them? He sought release in semiritualized forms of conflict. On *fête* days a group of agricultural workers might walk five or ten miles to the next village for no better reason than to start a brawl with its workers. They fought with fists and tore each other's clothes. Contests of this kind between parishes and villages were commonplace. Society accepted them as the means by which farm youths settled their vendettas. In general, the rural poor hurled insults and used physical force with unconscionable ease. The wrongful pasturing of a cow, the straying of a voracious goat, or the misuse of ponds and streams led not to litigation but to beatings and threats. One family was set against another. Olwen Hufton, in a recent study, notes:

> Housewives came to public blows in streets or markets or at washing-places. Stocking knitters relieved the monotony of their employ as they sat at the door of their shacks by pouring obscenities upon women of dubious repute or upon those they personally disliked, as they passed by. Shepherds on lonely mountainsides would while away the hours in violent quarrels with their handful of companions, would beat up a lonely traveller, not with theft in mind, but because they had a genuine taste for violence.[22]

Such pictures of country life shake our deeply held belief in the peaceful rustic. Yet if we reflect, life on the land—stripped of civilization's cushioning artifice and sophistries—must oftentimes be hard and cruel. Countryfolk live close to violence. The farm is often a place for killing. Although it is an excess of sentiment to lament the fate of plants, there remains the slaughtering of animals, a common experience of the farmer from which city people can turn their eyes in distaste. One wonders whether over the years physical hardship, combined with this necessity to kill, dulls the farm worker's awareness of suffering in himself, in other human beings, and in animals. Richard Jefferies, writing in 1874, commented on the "brutal manner" with which agricultural laborers treated boys under their control, and the same "unfeeling brutality" toward the cattle under their care.[23] Ronald Blythe, in the 1960s, reported equally emphatically on the insensitivity of Suffolk farm youths to killing. Capital punishment was all right with them, an attitude in striking contrast to that of their age peers living in the city. "They all have a streak of cruelty. They kill animals in a way which would disturb the ordinary town boy. . . . Death is as familiar as birth. To take a murderer's life is just sensible to them."[24]

In the United States, proneness to violence and readiness to kill have been a part of the frontier tradition. On the plains and in the forests, farmers in isolated homesteads and communities felt from time to time that they had to take the law into their own hands. They put their trust in guns and in vigilante groups formed to protect not only property but their strongly held beliefs and customs where these seemed threatened by outsiders. In the South, lynching was more likely to occur in small rural towns than in the few large cities.

Despite an awareness of crime and bloodshed in the countryside, Americans tend to romanticize their rural past. "Crime" immediately suggests the city. It is a common belief that as cities grew rapidly in the nineteenth century, so did the national crime rate. The evidence for this trend is at best ambiguous. Roger Lane suggests that in Massachusetts the rate for serious crimes actually fell when the urban population surged upward between 1835 and 1900. In 1835, Massachusetts had a population that was 81 percent rural and still overwhelmingly preindustrial and native born. No town had a police force; and although Massachusetts rural areas scarcely constituted frontier society, the people living there were more free than law-abiding. By 1900, population in the commonwealth had increased more than fourfold and was 76 percent urban. "The move to the cities had produced,

for better or worse, a more tractable, more 'civilized,' more so-
cialized generation than its predecessors. What had been tolerable in a casual, independent society was no longer acceptable in
one whose members were living close together. . . . All cities and
many towns had acquired police forces."[25]

Rural people are exposed to the rough as well as the gentle
sides of nature. The harshness of nature is seldom depicted in
geographical sketches of the country scene, except where the
topic is frontier settlement. Too often we are presented with the
warm palettes of spring and summer, or the poetic hues of autumn, rather than the bleak, discomforting grays of winter.
Summer and winter are two different worlds, as peasants in
middle and high latitudes have always known. Richard Jefferies
wrote in 1874:

> In the summer the warm sunshine casts a glamour over the rude
> walls, the decaying thatch, and the ivy-covered window [of the
> farm laborer's cottage in England]; but with the cold blasts and
> ceaseless rain of winter all this is changed. The hedge, once the
> leaves are off, is the thinnest, most miserable of shelters. The
> rain comes through the hole in the thatch, the mud floor is damp,
> and perhaps sticky. The cold wind comes through the ill-fitting
> sash, and drives with terrible force under the door.[26]

To isolated communities in the mountains of Appalachia, winter is a state of siege. A child said to Robert Coles in the 1960s:
"In the winter it's the worst time—the weather, and the food
starts running out—so we'd stay away from school then. Come to
think of it, we'd hibernate, just like the animals do. We'd go into
the cabin and stay there." The mountaineer mother explains to
her child why they are hiding: "Son, we're hiding because if we
don't we'll die. We'll freeze to death, or we'll starve to death,
because we only have enough food to fuel a quiet body, and no
more, and maybe not even that much."[27]

To the well-to-do American farmer who lives in a substantial
house, winter presents no great hardship. Drought or excessive
rain may cut down his income but does not endanger his life or
that of his family. Threat to life and limb comes from another
source. Working on the modern, mechanized farm is lonely and
it can be dangerous. Vehicles are the leading cause of death in
farm accidents, and the aloneness contributes to this danger, for
out in the field an accident—when flesh tangles with steel—
cannot receive immediate medical care. As James Dickey
dramatically put it in his novel *Deliverance:* "The work with the
hands must be fantastically dangerous, in all that fresh air and

sunshine. . . . the catching of an arm in a tractor part somewhere off in the middle of a field where nothing happened but that the sun blazed back more fiercely down the open mouth of one's screams."[28] Through the 1950s, statistics collected by the National Safety Council show that farming is a hazardous occupation in the United States, its rate of injury being exceeded only by construction, mining, and the manufacturing industries. In California for the same period, agriculture ranked third, not fourth, in injury rate.[29]

We have seen how the countryside is exposed to different kinds of violence. Perhaps the most burdensome of them all, from the standpoint of the tillers of the soil, have been those committed by landlords and field bosses. Peasants in ages past lived in anxious fear that they might lose their land and certain vestigial rights, such as pasturage on the commons. Landless farm workers had no certainty of employment: they could be let go, following repeated summer rains and diminished harvests that required fewer hands to bring them in. And they could be dismissed upon the whim of the farmer. With the loss of work went also the low-rent cottage that was tied to the job.

Oppression in the countryside, however, is not egregiously visible and seldom leaves any lasting imprint. Consider the enclosure movements in England, which resulted in greater agricultural productivity and in the neat, hedged fields that we have all come to admire. This was the success story embossed proudly on the land. Behind it lay numerous tales of deprivation and fear which, but for the literary record, would have faded from our consciousness because they left their mark largely on the perishable bodies and minds of the people.

In the Tudor period, as arable fields were fenced in and turned into pastures, a common lament was that "the land raised sheep rather than men."[30] Revolts broke out in 1536 and 1549, and again in 1554 and 1569. There were enclosure uproars in Oxfordshire in 1596. Agrarian grievances in the Midlands in 1609 led to armed rebellion. Enclosure movements in the eighteenth century affected arable fields less; hence their impact on the rural population—driving people off the land—was also less severe. Nonetheless, the number of small farmers declined and farm hands found that, as village communities with merging social and economic classes began to disintegrate, so did their hope of bettering themselves through thrift, hard work, and wise marriage.[31]

Even in the early part of the twentieth century, oppression and anxious fear could be the daily burden of a farm laborer. This is the most shocking revelation from Ronald Blythe's report on a Suffolk village. One elderly worker recalled what it was like in the 1920s:

> Today you can be a man with men, but not then. . . . I lived when other men could do what they like with me. We feared so much. We even feared the weather! Today a farmer must pay for the week, whatever the weather. But we were always being sent home. We dreaded the rain; it washed our few shillings away.[32]

The United States boasts great agricultural wealth. Americans are aware of this plenitude not so much from production figures as from the evidence of the senses: wealth and abundance can be seen in the cornfields and substantial farmsteads of the Middle West, in the bounteous herds of cattle on the plains, in the machines of agribusiness in Texas and California, but above all in the cornucopia of supermarkets—the stands overflowing with the handsome produce of orchards and market gardens.

Who pick these vegetables and fruits? The work is done by some two million migrant workers from the poorer parts of the South, from Mexico and Puerto Rico. Annually, they move northward in branching streams, following the ripening of the crops. Without their sweated labor, that grapefruit or Caesar salad would not appear on our table. Yet we may drive from New York to California, from Dallas to Minneapolis, and not notice any migrant camps; nor are we likely to detect their existence by poring over the most detailed topographic maps. Migrant workers and their flimsy shacks are invisible. Middle-class America wants it that way. One has to drive on side roads and search before one can discern a line of cabins too modest to make a statement on the landscape. The curiosity of an outsider is, in any case, strongly discouraged by "no trespass" signs and armed guards.[33]

Migrant workers are recruited and supervised by crew leaders who control their charges through a mixture of glowing promises and dire threats. Behind the crew leaders, reported Robert Coles, "stands a virtual army of assorted private guards, 'hired men,' supervisors, foremen, 'patrol men,' who in turn can usually depend upon sheriffs and deputies." To the growers and their hired guards, migrant workers are animals, or at best children, who require constant attention and discipline. As one guard said to Coles:

> In the cabins they live like pigs. They throw things all over. When they're not being pigs they're being wild like a wild animal is—tearing up whatever we've built for them. In the fields they

turn lazy on you.... [At night, they will want] to drink and if you
don't keep them here on the property, they'll get lost and never
show up again. A lot of them get killed. They fight when they
drink.[34]

To the migrant worker, life is dominated by a pervasive sense
of powerlessness from which arise recurrent feelings of anxiety
and fear. Men and women are promised "good pickin' " down the
road, but will the crop be ripe when they get there? Often it is
not. The workers may have to wait a week or two, during which
time they will be so indebted to the crew leader for basic suste-
nance that their first meager earnings will simply melt away.
What are they doing in a crowded, accident-prone bus or truck
that takes them farther and farther from home? Why are they
in this strange field, cursed at by armed men? Will they in fact
receive the full pay promised them, and, if not, what can they
do? What if they fall sick?[35]

A migrant child, Tom, drew a picture for Coles. It showed dark,
jumbled fields, guarded by a black fence and the outlines of some
dark faceless men. Fields and roads, for families like Tom's, are
both fearful and promissory. Tom explained:

If it's real bad on the farm, you can sneak away in the middle of
the night. The guards will fall asleep, and before they wake up,
you can be on your way, and then you've got a chance to find a
better place to work. That's why you have to keep your eye on the
road, and when you leave it to stay in a cabin near a field, you
should point the car so it's ready to go.[36]

The road may lead to work. It spells another chance, but to
migrant laborers it is more often a band of constraint than a
symbol of freedom. Migrants have to keep moving. The police
see to that. "If they catch you sitting by the road, they'll take you
to jail," said Tom. "They won't let you out so easy, either. They'll
make you promise to go away and never come back."

Children see the countryside with mixed emotions. The field
is a workplace for them and for their parents: it means some
money, but also back-breaking labor. Potentially, a field by the
highway is an area of rest and play after the long confinement
within a crowded vehicle. In reality, it may turn out to be an
alluring trap.

Once I was really scared, and so was everyone else. We went way
down a road that we thought was safe, and there was a little pond
there, and we went and played in it.... Then the man came. He
said we would all be arrested and we were no good, and we
should be in jail and stay there forever.[37]

The countryside nearly always exudes an air of innocence. Even abandoned cottages can look picturesque. If, from the window of our speeding car, we happen to see the bent backs of men, women, and children picking tomatoes in the field, our immediate response is more likely to be "the wholesome life of outdoor labor" rather than "oppression, pain, and fear." As Raymond Williams reminded us in his study of the English scene, suffering leaves no mark in the country. The processes of rural exploitation have been "dissolved into a landscape." It is in the city that they emerge conspicuously as law courts, money markets, political power, and the arrogant display of wealth.[38] The city, in many ways the supreme achievement of humankind, also stands as a monument to human greed and guilt.

12.

Fear in the City

The city manifests humanity's greatest aspiration toward perfect order and harmony in both its architectural setting and its social ties. Wherever urbanism emerged independently, we find that its root lay in a prestigious ceremonial center rather than in a village.[1] An early and essential function of the city was to be a vivid symbol of cosmic order: hence its simple geometric design with walls and streets often oriented to the cardinal points, and its imposing monuments. Corresponding to this desire for physical perfection was the longing for a stable and harmonious society.

In ancient times, people discerned a stability and predictability in the heavens that they could not find on earth. The Greeks, for example, distinguished explicitly between an orderly nature above the orbit of the moon and a disorderly nature below it, a distinction that was maintained by European thinkers in the Middle Ages. Elsewhere, the difference between these two realms of nature was at least implicitly recognized. In the heavens, a Babylonian or Chinese astronomer could observe the fixity of the North Star and the regularity of astral motions, particularly the daily and seasonal trajectories of the sun. Close to earth, however, nature seemed far more erratic and complex. Who could predict the weather, or discern a rational pattern to the hills, valleys, and streams? Who could master the ways of humans and animals? People have always feared chaos. To counter its lurking presence, the ancient civilizations of Mesoamerica, the Near East, India, and China built ceremonial centers and geometric cities that mirrored the regularity of the heavens.

In the eyes of kings and rulers, the social order that best conformed to the cosmic city was a hierarchical one. At the top were the paternal ruler and his court of priests and officials; at the base was a loyal and hard-working populace engaged primarily in what the Chinese called the "root" activity of agriculture. Working on the land fitted in well with a cosmic world-view, for farmers submitted to the swing of the seasons and were conscious that they lived under the aegis of the sun, the moon, and the stars. For their part, court astronomers, claiming special competence in reading the charts of the heavens, issued calendars which were intended to benefit the farmers.[2] Ceremonies conducted within the capital were meant to embrace the whole world, and not only those who lived behind the city walls. The great ruler himself, as mediator between heaven and earth, might participate in the seasonal rites.

This ideal of a perfect physical and social order rarely lasted anywhere more than a few decades. Its existence depended on force—the stringent application of rules to regulate human behavior. The use of force, however, was ineffective. Too much of it killed the life of the city and reduced it to a mere ceremonial center of splendid monuments. Too little, and a capital would continue to attract swarms of people engaged in economic and commercial activities, whose presence inevitably disrupted the idealized order.

Powerful rulers sometimes tried to control nonagricultural occupations by confining them to certain quarters within the geometric city, or by limiting them to markets beyond the city gates. Despite such efforts, in a few years profane outskirts tended to overwhelm the ceremonial core. These outskirts, bursting with an extremely heterogeneous population free from day-to-day governmental control, often proved a particular threat to the ideology of a hierarchical, imperial order. As craftsmen, small traders and merchants, they seemed rootless—without ties either to the land or the seasonal cycles of nature. The environment in which they lived and did business was a wild confusion of ramshackle houses, shops, and tortuous alleys—a vivid contrast to the harmonious form, calm, and magnificence of the ceremonial center. However much the city has changed in the course of time, the conflict persists between the desire for an imposed socio-aesthetic order and the reality of masses of human beings living in a dynamic but confused world.

It is deeply ironic that the city can often seem a frightening place. Built to rectify the apparent confusion and chaos of nature, the city itself becomes a disorienting physical environment in which tenement houses collapse on their inhabitants, fires break out, and heavy traffic threatens life and limb. Although every street and building—and indeed all the bricks and stone blocks in them—are clearly the products of planning and thought, the final result may be a vast, disorderly labyrinth.

Consider some of the manifestations of disorder in the city as a physical environment, beginning with noise. Unless one lives close to a thunderous waterfall, noise is not a problem in the countryside. Human beings, in any case, are inclined to accept most sounds in nature—from surf pounding on the beach to the chirping of crickets—as peaceful. Noise in the city is another matter. To newcomers, urban cacophony may initially be their most disorienting and frightening experience. Noise is auditory chaos, and most people are better able to tolerate visual than auditory disorder because sound tends to affect emotions more elementally than does sight.[3] In time, one learns to tolerate noise and it is no longer frightening. But it continues to create tension and anxiety—to be a reminder of chaos.

Noise is not the egregious defect of modern cities, despite heavy motor traffic and airplanes. The commercial quarters of traditional cities were sometimes much more raucous. In fact, complaints about urban noise have been recorded since ancient times. In Imperial Rome, citizens could find areas of beauty and calm in more than forty parks and gardens. But on the streets there reigned an intense animation, a breathless jostle, an infernal din. The numerous traders at work were largely responsible both for the zest and the cacophony. Roman satirists pointed to the cadence of their tools, the rush and hustle in their toil, and their swearing. The approach of night brought no peace because it was then that wheeled carts could legally enter the city. Juvenal might not have exaggerated much when he said that night traffic condemned Romans to everlasting insomnia.[4]

The prosperous medieval town was full of the sound of bells and of bustling people. Bells tolled the beginning and the end of the day; church bells rang almost incessantly. Human cries filled the air. At dawn a crier proclaimed that the baths were open and the water hot; then followed others bawling out their wares—fish, meat, honey, onions, cheese, old clothes, flowers, pepper, charcoal, and other goods. Mendicants and begging friars were everywhere, seeking alms. Public criers announced deaths and other news.[5]

By the eighteenth century, bells chimed less often, but the number of aggressive street criers had increased and made more noise. In 1711, Joseph Addison complained:

Milk is generally sold in a note above E-la, and in sounds so exceedingly shrill, that it often sets our teeth on edge. The chimney sweeper is confined to no certain pitch, he sometimes utters himself in the deepest bass, and sometimes in the sharpest treble. . . . The same observation might be made on the retailers of small coal, not to mention broken glasses or brick dust.[6]

London shopkeepers still maintained the ancient custom of having an apprentice stand at the door and bawl out invitations to buy. Even streets of private houses did not escape from such sales tactics. They were invaded by a never-ending procession of hawkers who shouted their services and goods.

In the medieval town as in the eighteenth-century city, people of different social classes and occupations lived close together; and although they showed far greater tolerance for noise and confusion than we do now, there were limits. One reads about a student in medieval Germany who was permitted to remove from his house a smith whose incessant hammering disturbed his studies, and about another student who unsuccessfully tried to compel a noisy weaver to change his lodging. At Jena, "a certain cooper used to get up at midnight and made so much din putting hoops on his casks that the health of his neighbors was imperilled through constant loss of sleep."[7] In eighteenth-century Paris, noise from carriages and vendors made repose all but impossible except in the dead of night.

The rapid increase of wheeled traffic during the eighteenth century was a major new source of deafening noise. In colonial America travelers were impressed by the sharp contrast between the quiet countryside and the hubbub of the crowded towns. Philadelphia, for example, was noted for its many carriages, its din, and the particularly terrifying turmoil of traffic north of Market Street. When the botanist James Young entered the city one July day in 1763, he gave the traffic no thought until he found himself "tangled amongst Waggons, Drays, Market Folks and Dust." A medical student living on Second Street wrote home and decried "the thundering of Coaches, Chariots, Chaises, Waggons, Drays, and the whole Fraternity of Noise [which] almost continuously assail our Ears."[8]

In 1771, London had a thousand hackney coaches. These were at first very heavy vehicles with perforated iron shutters; their wheels grinding on cobbled streets created an excruciating din.[9] Shopkeepers complained bitterly but to no avail. A century later, traffic noise was, if possible, even worse; not only had the number of vehicles increased, but their heavy wheels as yet unshod by rubber still bore down on streets paved with stone blocks. "In the middle of Regent's Park or Hyde Park," Stephen Coleridge recalled, "one heard the roar of traffic all round in a ring of tremendous sound; and in any shop in Oxford Street, if the door was opened no one could make himself heard till it was shut again."[10]

Traditionally, the poor, far more than members of the middle or upper classes, have been assaulted by noise. But a danger confronts the poor compared to which noise must seem a relatively minor affliction. The fact is that, in the city, the structures built to shelter people can themselves be a threat to life and limb. Tenement houses are hastily put up to accommodate the poor, or the poor move into old houses in varying stages of ruin. Though we see this happening today, we seldom hear of an apartment building collapsing on its inhabitants—at least not in Western society. This was not true in the past. Jérôme Carcopino, writing about Imperial Rome, noted that "the city was constantly filled with the noise of buildings collapsing or being torn down to prevent it."[11] Juvenal put the blame on unscrupulous landlords.

> Who, on Tivoli's heights [a summer resort of Rome], or in a small town like Gabii, say, fears the collapse of his house? But Rome is supported on pipestems, matchsticks; it's cheaper, so, for the landlord to shore up his ruins, patch up the old cracked walls, and notify all the tenants they can sleep secure, though the beams are in ruins above them.[12]

In late medieval and Renaissance times, tall houses tended to be top-heavy and unstable. The upper stories protruded and shop fronts, weighted by heavy metal signs, leaned dangerously toward the street. As the supporting timbers began to rot, walls crumbled. In eighteenth-century London old, decrepit houses collapsed with a regularity that made such disasters seem almost normal. Dorothy George wrote:

> To Samuel Johnson in 1738 London was a place where "falling houses thunder on your head." When a messenger ran into a City tavern with an urgent piece of news, the instant supposition (in 1718) was that he had come to warn the inmates that the house was falling. . . . The collapse of new or half-built houses is frequently commented on in eighteenth-century newspapers.[13]

Charles Dickens, in *Bleak House,* described one of the worst of London's slums, called Tom-all-Alone's:

> Twice, lately, there has been a crash and a cloud of dust, like the springing of a mine, in Tom-all-Alone's; and each time, a house

has fallen. These accidents have made a paragraph in the newspapers, and have filled a bed or two in the nearest hospital. The gaps remain, and there are not unpopular lodgings among the rubbish. As several more houses are nearly ready to go, the next crash in Tom-all-Alone's may be expected to be a good one.[14]

A city may boast handsome buildings and orderly squares, and yet its overall effect is one of disarray. Rome in the time of Augustus and Trajan had its dignified, measured spaces, but juxtaposed against them were a wild confusion of fragile dwellings and gloomy, narrow alleys that zigzagged, rose and fell steeply on the Seven Hills. On moonless nights the streets were plunged in impenetrable darkness. Cautious citizens kept indoors. Party-goers returning late and somewhat tipsy risked getting lost even if they escaped thieves and robbers. Petronius described what it was like:

> For nearly an hour we stumbled about, dragging our bleeding feet over the shards and splinters of broken crockery scattered along the streets, and it was only Giton's remarkable act of foresight which saved us in the end. Terrified of getting lost even in daylight, the boy had shrewdly blazed every column and pilaster along our route with chalk, and now, even through the pitch blackness, the blazings shone brightly enough to keep us on our path.[15]

The jumble of houses and lanes in late medieval towns has often been commented on. In Leeds, the open spaces and gardens that once stretched behind frontage houses and shops were, by the second half of the fourteenth century, already being built over and transformed into "dark and airless yards." In contemporary Florence, a much larger and more important town, houses were packed close together. Streets twisted and meandered without any sign of rational order. Building heights fluctuated crazily. Wedged between two massive towers eighty feet high might be a tiny one-story cottage, which at least allowed some light and air to penetrate into a district habitually dark, damp, and fetid.[16]

While medieval towns differed much in urban form and character, it is still possible to make some general comments on their streets: these were mostly unpaved and so badly maintained that they turned into rivulets of mud after each passing shower. The "throughways" of late medieval Southampton, for example, were described in a document of the time as "full of peril and a jeopardy to ride or go therein."[17] The narrowness and gloominess of alleys and lanes probably created contradictory feelings of constraint and chaos. Even the main arteries of Paris were less than twenty feet across, barely wide enough for two carts to pass side by side. A market street might begin with an ample width of fifty feet or more, but temporary stalls soon encroached upon it, and these in time became fixtures of a bustling commercial scene. The idea of an efficient throughway had not yet taken hold in the West: streets were as much places—centers of turbulent activity—as passages.

In Europe, even in much later times, the circulation of people and goods remained primitive. In the eighteenth century, the River Thames was still London's greatest highway. People in boats moved freely on it. The streets themselves hardly encouraged smooth locomotion. Pedestrians had to walk slowly and with great care. As Sir Walter Besant explained,

> The doorsteps projected—one had either to step into the muddy gutter or to walk over them. The cobbled stones of the pavement were broken up here and there, leaving small puddles of mud and filth. . . . Then, every house had its opening for the cellar, and its wooden cellar-doors constantly thrown up for the reception of coals or merchandise; and the shopkeepers vied with each other in pushing forward their bow-windows."[18]

In the early part of the nineteenth century, Parisian streets were such a labyrinth that to take even a short trip was a complex journey. Baron Haussmann, who as prefect of the Seine transformed Paris by creating airy boulevards, recalled the tortuous route that he in his student days had to follow in order to go from his home on the Right Bank to the School of Law in the Latin Quarter.

> Setting out at seven o'clock in the morning from the quarter of the Chaussée d'Antin, I reached first, after many detours, the Rue Montmartre and the Pointe Sainte-Eustache; I crossed the square of the Halles, then the rues des Lavandières, Saint-Honoré and Saint-Denis; I crossed the old Pont au Change, which I was later to rebuild, lower, widen; I next walked along the ancient Palais de Justice, having on my left the filthy mass of pot-houses that not long ago disfigured the Cité. Continuing my route by the Pont Saint-Michel, I had to cross the poor little square [Place Saint-Michel]. . . . Finally I entered into the meanders of the Rue de la Harpe to ascend the Montagne Sainte-Geneviève and to arrive by the passage de l'Hôtel d'Harcourt, the Rue des Maçons-Sorbonne, the Place Richelieu, the Rue de Cluny and the Rue des Grès, on the Place du Panthéon at the corner of the School of Law.[19]

Haussmann's long daily trek from home to school was atypical of his time. Normally, people stayed in their own mazes and ventured beyond them only on rare occasions. To local residents, their own neighborhood of winding streets, dead-end alleys, and courtyards might seem familiarly complex and intimate. To strangers, however, it was a bewildering and frightening place to stray into as the sun began to set and the shadows lengthened.

Especially for small children, streets in medieval towns were full of hazards, not so much from wheeled traffic as from the large number of animals more or less on the loose. Urban and rural functions were not spatially segregated: just as orchards and fields penetrated the heart of a town, so did livestock. Pedestrians suffered from peregrinating hogs, horses, cows, and sheep. The swine, though they made good scavengers, were a dangerous nuisance. In late medieval times, city councilors issued ordinances to control the movement of swine, but with little success. Galloping horsemen trod children underfoot. All kinds of accidents could and did occur from a traffic that was almost totally unregulated.

Wheeled carriages made their entry into European cities in the sixteenth century. A few lanes were broadened and straightened to accommodate them, and this had the beneficial effect of improving circulation and allowing more light and air to penetrate. However, the carriages soon added their own kind of chaos and danger to the street scene. For the first time, the wealthy were separated from the poor in the streets. Patrons of carriages enjoyed privacy and safety, while their vehicles endangered those who walked.[20] To protect the life and limb of pedestrians as well as storefront property, posts were driven into the roadsides, limiting the area carriages could use. This was the beginning of the pavement or sidewalk. The better commercial streets in Europe and colonial America had such posts in the early years of the eighteenth century. Without doubt fatal accidents declined, but pedestrians still suffered the indignity of being spattered with malodorous filth as carriages sped by. A sense of the turmoil and risk of living in a colonial American town was sketched by Carl Bridenbaugh:

> Back and forth through [the] streets coursed horsemen, gentlemen's chaises and chariots, a variety of tumbrils, carts, trucks, and great wagons drawn by from one to eight horses or oxen and large numbers of packhorses, plus numerous laborers pushing wheelbarrows and countless porters carrying parcels large and

small. Everywhere children died under hoofs and wheels; nor were their elders spared by galloping horsemen, reckless carters, or racing gentlemen whose equipages smashed into other vehicles on the streets.[21]

Bridenbaugh attributed most of the accidents to speeding. A more basic cause was the absence of rules governing street traffic. In 1765, for the benefit of both town and country readers in the Boston area, four newspapers printed regulations for riding and driving in the city, drawing attention in particular to one rule "which is strictly adhered to by all well regulated Cities in Europe . . . namely, always keep on the Right-Hand side of the Way."[22] In fact, European cities were badly managed and had few traffic rules that could be enforced. Arrogant aristocrats and rich merchants, on their horses and in their carriages, were among the worst offenders. Toward the end of the eighteenth century, Parisian authorities ordered that all horses be provided with sleigh bells so that pedestrians might be warned and be given a sporting chance to save their lives.[23]

The aspect of the physical environment that aroused the greatest fear in the city was, however, not traffic but fire—raging, uncontrollable fire that gave the people of medieval times their vivid imagery of hell. Fire had not been a major hazard in the great ceremonial capitals of the past. Many buildings were made of nonflammable materials such as stone and earth. Moreover, they normally occupied spacious grounds, which served as firebreaks. For instance, in Ch'ang-an, capital of China during the T'ang dynasty (A.D. 608–917), the avenues that divided the city into walled rectangular blocks were exceptionally wide, ranging from 220 to 480 feet.[24] Fire that blazed up in one crowded quarter would be prevented by these walls and broad avenues from spreading. During the Sung dynasty (960–1279), as cities became much more densely packed and the streets narrower, fire emerged as a constant hazard and a particular cause of uneasiness among the urban populace. Kai-feng, capital of the Northern Sung, had only one broad street, the Imperial Way; all the others were much narrower than those of Ch'ang-an. It was in this constricted city that a fire-fighting organization was first established. Hang-chou, capital of the Southern Sung, was even more crowded than Kai-feng. Hardly a year passed in Hangchou without a major outbreak of fire, and several might occur in the same year. Officials did what they could to combat the menace. Watchtowers, manned day and night, were erected in the crowded quarters, and 3,200 soldiers were formed into squads for the purpose of putting out flames both within and outside the city walls.

Fire haunted dwellers in these towns who knew that their houses of wood and bamboo, jammed together along narrow alleyways, were highly flammable. Panicking was frequent. An imperial edict forbade rumors of fire and alarming reports of incidents that had occurred. Terror of fire sought relief in superstition. Thus when fire broke out not long after a whale was found stranded near Hang-chou in 1282, people attempted to link the two events. Temples were dedicated to gods of the river and to dragon kings in the hope that these water divinities would protect the capital from conflagration.[25] Fire was emblematic of anger and ferocity. In temples that catered to folk belief, fierce Buddhist deities were depicted with halos bordered by flames.

A similar story can be told of Rome in the first century A.D. Houses easily caught fire, because they were made of flimsy material supported by wooden beams. The movable stoves that heated the houses as well as the lamps and torches that lighted them at night provided additional risks of ignition. Finally, water was scarce and often did not reach the upper floors of tenements in any case.

Augustus in A.D. 6 created a fire brigade consisting of seven cohorts, each numbering 1,000 to 1,200 men, organized under the command of a prefect. The post became one of great importance and its holder a high police officer second in rank only to the prefect of the city.[26] During Trajan's reign (98–117), despite the emperor's concern for the safety of the city, outbreaks of fire were a daily event. Rich men who worried about their mansions and other worldly possessions might keep troops of slaves to guard them against the devouring flame. Dread of fire was an obsession among rich and poor alike. Juvenal was prepared to quit Rome to escape it: "No, no, I must live where there is no fire and the night is free from alarms!"[27]

In 1183, William Fitz Stephen observed: "The only plagues of London are the immoderate drinking of fools and the frequency of fires."[28] Medieval houses and shops were extremely vulnerable to incendiarism and accidental burning. Throughout most of European history, in fact, town dwellers lived in anxiety about fire, which, once started, spread rapidly across the densely packed quarters, consuming wooden buildings thatched with straw with the utmost ease. Few houses had stone walls. In the twelfth century, the few stone houses built by rich men were considered so remarkable that their building material might be proudly registered in a property deed. Even churches were thatched with reeds or straw.[29] In the reign of Richard I (1189–1199), the mayor of London published an ordinance which required houses to have their common walls made of stone. Needless to say, the ordinance was not strictly enforced, least of all in the poorer quarters.

Thatched roofs were a tinder to fire. In the thirteenth century, tile roofs began to replace them. The law governing the use of tiles was strictly enforced in London during 1302, but relaxed again later.[30] Officials encouraged citizens to build with stone and bricks, but few could or were willing to do so. One reason for this reluctance was the vertical growth of houses in the fifteenth century, not only in London but also in Genoa, Paris, and Edinburgh. Under the pressure to accommodate more and more people, houses rose in height from the characteristic two stories of an earlier time to four and even six stories. Bricks were shunned as construction material because it was easier to make high and light walls with wood.

London did finally turn to brick during Elizabeth's reign, though this transformation was not completed until the fire of 1666 had destroyed three-quarters of the town. Paris began to change into a stone town in the same period. The process was slow, however, and many Paris houses even in the eighteenth century had only a stone foundation, the upper floors still being made of wood. In the Petit-Pont fire on April 27, 1727, the wooden houses blazed fiercely like a "great limekiln into which one saw whole beams fall."[31]

In colonial America, Boston seemed especially prone to what were called "great" fires, the first of which occurred on March 14, 1653, and led to the passing of the town's first fire code. Another disaster overwhelmed Boston on November 27, 1676, and prompted the purchase of a fire engine from England. As early as 1649, Boston selectmen adopted the English curfew. A man was hired to ring a bell at nine o'clock in the evening and at half past four in the morning. Between these hours all fires were to be covered (curfew=*couvrir feu*) to diminish the risk of combustion. New Amsterdam and other villages had similar rules.[32] The threat of fire, however, increased rather than diminished in the early decades of the eighteenth century as towns became more crowded. Though houses showed improvement in construction, many suffered from defective chimneys, which were the most common cause of fires in colonial settlements. New York and Philadelphia enjoyed relative immunity from burning because most of their houses were built of brick or stone.

Of course, fear of fire is not just a nightmare from the past. Almost every day the front pages of our newspapers report fires that have consumed homes and shops overnight. Occasionally, a major disaster strikes; we learn in the morning news that smoke and flame have engulfed a well-attended theater or club, searing and killing its panic-stricken patrons. A film like *The Towering Inferno* plays on the anxiety of people who work or live in high-rise buildings and who can easily imagine how it feels to be trapped on the fiftieth floor without any hope of escape. The sound of rushing fire trucks, their sirens shrieking, is a familiar enough aspect of a modern city's audio-environment. Although today we seldom hear of fire destroying an entire city, it is by no means rare for flames to gouge several city blocks before they are checked. In 1972, fires in the United States resulted in 12,000 deaths, inflicted serious injuries on over 300,000 people, and caused some $2.3 billion in property losses.[33]

Fear of the city as a physical environment cannot be neatly isolated from fear of the city's human denizens. It is suggestive that many Occidental children want to be firemen or policemen when they grow up, thus expressing a need to assume authority and overcome their sense of impotence and anxiety before both the physical environment and strange adults. Also suggestive is the fact that the first curfews were instituted to control not only fire but strangers. Fire and the unruly crowd have much in common. Fire, according to Elias Canetti, is a crowd or mob symbol. Sudden and violent, fire can begin anywhere and once started its course of destruction is hard to predict. Its movement, surging in one direction and then turning suddenly in another, is like that of a maddened human mob. Both the fire and the mob are ruthless destroyers of boundaries: the city's carefully erected containers, physical and social, are shattered.[34] In sixteenth-century Nuremberg, the steps taken to combat fire were like those taken against a human enemy: "This is worthy the noting that when any house chanceth to be on fyre . . . they which kepe watch smyte the Laram belles. The Towne gates are shutt, and all the Citie up in armour, with their Captains . . . placed in Battail array as if the Enemie were already entred."[35]

Again, consider the common image of the city as a "jungle." This metaphor may refer to the city's physical environment of tangled streets, or it may refer to the streets' deviant and dangerous population. The two components can rarely be separated. We see them merge naturally into each other in Henry Fielding's description of the cities of London and Westminster in the middle of the eighteenth century:

> Whoever considers . . . the great irregularity of their Build-
> ings, the immense Number of Lanes, Alleys, Courts and Bye-
> places must think that, had they been intended for the very
> purpose of Concealment, they could scarce have been better
> contrived. Upon such a View, the whole appears as a vast
> Wood or Forest, in which a Thief may harbour with as great
> Security as wild Beasts do in the Desarts of Africa or Arabia.[36]

From an Aristotelian and sociological perspective, the city is
not "sticks and stones," but rather a complex society of heterogeneous people living close together. Ideally, people of different
backgrounds dwell in harmony and use their diverse gifts to
create a common world. Whenever this happens the city is, in
that duration of time, a superb human achievement. But
heterogeneity is also a condition that encourages conflict.
Throughout its history the city has been burdened by violence
and the recurrent threat of chaos. Among the many intricate
themes of this story, the following merit special attention: violent conflicts among urban magnates and the creation of a fortified landscape of fear; danger from and anxiety about strangers in an urban milieu; fear of anarchy and revolution, that is,
of the overthrow of an established order by unassimilable and
uncontrollable masses; distaste for and fear of the poor as a
potential source of moral corruption and of disease; and urban
fears in the lives of poor immigrants.

As already noted, magnates and their retainers might engage
rivals in bloody battle and terrorize the countryside. This type of
feuding had its parallel in the Italian cities of the late medieval
and Renaissance periods. Indeed, violence in the towns of
Romagna between 1450 and 1500 was often of rural origin, feuds
between landowners in the countryside being continued in
towns which, though *città* in a technical sense, were in size and
importance merely *cittadine,* not true urban centers but large
villages. In such Romagna communities as Imola and Forli,
rival families seem to have fought in a spirit of pure vendetta
rather than for political power.[37]

Violence and crime transcended class in Renaissance Italy.
In Florence, every social class was well represented in the
criminal courts; however, the incidence was greatest at the extremes of the social scale. Magnates and the desperately poor
had the most volatile tempers and were liable to fight under
the slightest provocation. Small shopkeepers and merchants,
with some hard-earned wealth to defend, tended to be less im-
petuous. The two extreme social groups were violent for different reasons. Patricians cultivated an ethos of individual pride

and assertiveness which was at odds with the demands of orderly social exchange essential to the growing commercial world in which most of them lived. Often their fits of combativeness were attempts to satisfy their carnal desires or their self-esteem. Acts of violence by the populace, in contrast, were more likely to be the result of chance encounters. In Venice, an incident such as two boats ramming into each other might lead to a fight to the death. A casual jostle on the street could have the same result. "Even such banal matters as an argument over whether fish or meat should be served at the seamen's mess, the obstinacy of two claimants to a chair in a public place, or a groom's offense at a passerby's use of his stable as a privy could culminate in killings."[38]

A characteristic of the Italian Renaissance city was the social and economic heterogeneity of its districts and neighborhoods. No quarter was reserved solely for the rich, nor were there ghettos inhabited exclusively by the poor. Each district was a mélange of palace and cottage, factory and retail shop, parish church and monastic foundation. Nobles, rich bankers, and industrialists lived in the same streets as indigent workers and prostitutes. This pattern arose, in part, out of a social need which in time became a consciously maintained tradition. Prominent families had established themselves in various precincts during the twelfth and thirteenth centuries, depending for their political and physical strength on the help of family members and relatives, but also on quick support from friends, servants, and retainers who lived in the same precinct. Noble families and their dependents thus banded together for protection against attack from a rival house. Cities such as Genoa, Florence, and Rome consisted of hundreds of such family nuclei, each of which was a center of economic and military power. A chance altercation between clan members, or even between the servants of rival houses, could end in bloody battle.

Anarchy constantly threatened city government. Urban architecture attested to the insecurity of the times. Barricades enclosed Genoese neighborhoods during periods of prolonged factional strife. Defensive towers, usually placed between the interior square and its most vulnerable entrance, rose far above the eighty-foot maximum that the city government tried to impose. In the thirteenth century, aristocratic Florentine families continued to live in tall and narrow fortified houses that looked like medieval towers. These had few windows, and those so small that they provided the barest minimum of light and air to the lower stories.[39] The German historian Ferdinand Gregorovius described thirteenth-century Rome as though it were a battlefield—a landscape of fear:

> Everywhere that the eye rested might be seen gloomy, defiant, battlemented towers, built out of the monuments of the ancients, with crenelated enceintes of most original form, constructed of pieces of marble, bricks and fragments of peperino. These were the castles and palaces of Guelf and Ghibelline nobles, who sat thirsting for battle in ruins on the classic hills, as though Rome were not a city but an open territory, the possession of which was to be disputed in daily warfare. There was not a single nobleman in Rome at the time who was not the owner of a tower. . . . Families dwelt amongst ruins, in uncomfortable quarters, barred by heavy iron chains, with their relatives and retainers, and only now and then burst forth with the wild din of arms, to make war on their hereditary enemies.[40]

Such strife between rival families was a characteristic of Mediterranean cities; it did not appear in anything like the same degree in medieval towns north of the Alps. A more common source of disturbance in all urban centers was the stranger or vagabond. Unlike feuding households, unorganized strangers attacked most often after dark. One form of precaution against them and against the possibility of rowdiness among the local inhabitants themselves was the imposition of curfew. With the ringing of the curfew bell, people were supposed to stay indoors, or as a Leicester ordinance of 1467 put it: "That no man walke after IX of the belle be streken in the nyght withoute cause resonable in payne of impresonment." Authorities did their best to minimize the temptations to roam. Shopkeepers and taverners were ordered to close their premises after the bell had tolled, though it was easy enough for them to pretend deafness. In English towns curfew sounded at eight o'clock in the evening in winter and about an hour later in summer. Londoners were sometimes allowed to walk abroad until ten o'clock, but this was the latest hour ever permitted.

All rules were applied more stringently to strangers. At Beverley, England, they were to retire indoors an hour earlier than did natives, and their hosts had to vouch for their good behavior. In London as early as 1282, each alderman was to take two of the best men of the ward and visit every hostel to check on its inmates. Nighttime walkers who could not give a satisfactory account of their activity were taken either to prison or to an inn and kept there until the next morning when they could be examined by a bailiff.[41] At Cambridge in 1445, burgesses were especially warned against sheltering any suspicious-looking person. In medieval Germany, the law barely extended its protection to outsiders. Well-to-do residents of Augsburg, when they infringed the law, were treated courteously at the time of arrest or conviction. Strangers received no such courtesy, but were rudely apprehended and punished. Moreover, a citizen might abuse and even kill an officious stranger with impunity. A stranger wounded by a citizen outside the city could not obtain satisfaction in the city's courts. Strong group morality went side by side with the fear of all things alien, including people.[42]

Colonial towns in North America were deeply suspicious of strangers. Boston set the pattern for excluding poor and undesirable outsiders in 1636, when its selectmen forbade any inhabitant to entertain a nonresident for more than two weeks without official permission. Similar steps were taken in Charles Town and Philadelphia in 1685. A year earlier New York had codified and published laws against "forriners." Constables were instructed to search out all strangers and present a list of them to the mayor.[43]

Medieval European and early colonial American towns were small places with populations of less than 10,000. They could use the curfew because relatively few suspicious-looking strangers roamed the streets and their movements could be supervised. In a large metropolis, such as Rome in the second century A.D. or eighteenth-century London, curfew without the support of a well-manned police force would have been totally ineffective. Instead, as night approached, the citizens themselves recognized the need to withdraw into the security of their homes, abandoning the dark alleys to thieves and foolhardy revelers. On moonless nights the warrens of Rome no doubt looked extremely sinister. Respectable people barricaded the entrances to their houses; the shops fell silent, and traders drew safety chains across the leaves of the doors. If rich party-goers stepped into the streets, they did so protected by slaves who carried torches to light them on their way. Carcopino wrote:

> No ordinary person ventured abroad without vague apprehension. Juvenal sighs that to go out to supper without having made your will was to expose yourself to the reproach of carelessness. He contended that the Rome of his day was more dangerous than the forest of Gallinaria or the Pontine marshes.[44]

Crime in eighteenth-century London was rampant. After dark townspeople were reluctant to go out into the ill-lit streets. London's city marshal noted in 1718:

It is the general complaint of the taverns, the coffee-houses, the shopkeepers and others, that their customers are afraid when it is dark to come to their houses and shops for fear that their hats and wigs should be snitched from their heads . . . or that they may be blinded, knocked down, cut or stabbed; nay, the coaches cannot secure them, but they are likewise cut and robbed in the public streets.[45]

In 1751, Fielding, as magistrate of Bow Street, reported: "The innocent are put in terror, affronted and alarmed with threats and execrations, endangered with loaded pistols, beat with bludgeons and hacked with cutlasses, of which the loss of health, of limbs, and often of life, is the consequence; and all this without any respect to age, dignity, or sex." Fielding observed that street robberies commonly took place at night, and that people who traveled in chairs and coaches were attacked no less than those who walked.[46] Samuel Johnson, who loved the stir of the metropolis and equated Fleet Street with life, knew how dangerous the streets could be: he himself always walked with a stout cudgel.[47] Many citizens went about armed. Friends, when they were to return from a coffeehouse or tavern, made up parties for mutual protection. Many families refused to go to the theater on account of the dangers of the homeward journey. Jonas Hanway complained in 1775: "I sup with my friend; I cannot return to my home, not even to my chariot, without danger of a pistol being clapt to my breast. I build an elegant villa, ten or twenty miles distant from the capital: I am obliged to provide an armed force to convey me thither."[48]

Criminals operated boldly in the heart of London. Moreover, large sectors of the metropolis were wholly given over to them. Not only ordinary citizens but officers of the law hesitated to venture into these blighted areas, known as "Alsatias" in the eighteenth century and as "rookeries" a hundred years later. The origin of the Alsatia lay in the medieval sanctuary, which was a place where debtors might seek protection against imprisonment and where malefactors could hide before they faced the bailiff or abjured the realm.[49] An act of 1623 abolished the sanctuary, but in practice it continued to exist, perhaps in a different part of town, as a criminal area. Thieves and robbers found haven in the maze of dilapidated courts and alleys that sprang up largely during the period between the rules of Elizabeth and Cromwell. By the end of the seventeenth century, London was blighted by several notorious criminal districts. Alsatia (or Whitefriars) provided the generic name, but the Southwark Mint was reputed to be even worse. The Minories, Baldwin's

Gardens, and Gray's Inn Lane were other convenient refuges for hard-pressed thieves.[50] The Improvement Acts of the eighteenth century cleaned up some of these crime-infested warrens but not all of them, and new ones appeared elsewhere.

In the nineteenth century, rookeries were an important part of the sordid environments to be found in Liverpool, Manchester, and London. St. Giles's in Holborn was one of London's worst rookeries. Charles Dickens described it as

> a black, dilapidated street, avoided by all decent people; where the crazy houses were seized upon, when their decay was far advanced, by some bold vagrants, who, after establishing their own possession, took to letting them out in lodgings. Now, these tumbling tenements contain, by night, a swarm of misery. As, on the ruined human wretch, vermin parasites appear, so these ruined shelters have bred a crowd of foul existence that crawls in and out of gaps in walls and boards.[51]

A recurrent fear exhibited by rulers, officials, and propertied citizens was of public disorder and violence on a scale that could lead to revolution and anarchy. The sight of masses of people all in one place, mostly poor and without obvious ties to family and possessions, aroused unease. All governments assumed the necessity to maintain public order, but in their methods of control they differed enormously. The traditional Chinese city represents an extreme example of rigid control. Indeed, in the eyes of some scholars, the capital city of Ch'ang-an during the Han and T'ang dynasties was run almost on the model of a ritualized military camp, or even of an enlightened prison. The multiple walls with their few guarded openings might well suggest a prison. While the ostensible purpose of the ramparts was to protect the inhabitants against evildoers and alien armies, they also served as an effective device for internal surveillance.

The Han Empire was able to attempt a census of its vast population in A.D. 2 because it had the necessary bureaucratic machinery to keep track of the comings and goings of its subjects, most of whom lived in walled settlements. Consider the rigidly boxed-in character of Ch'ang-an. The city had an irregular outer rampart. Within it land was subdivided into 160 wards, each of which had its own enclosure pierced by only one gate. Within each settled ward the individual households had enceintes of their own: residential gates opened outward to narrow alleys rather than directly to a street. People wanting to go from their homes to the countryside had therefore to pass through three sets of gates—those of house, ward, and city—all of which were closed at night and guarded.

During the T'ang dynasty, the rules were relaxed to the extent that an official of high rank could have the gate of his residence open directly onto the street. A further sign of relaxation was that most of the wards had four gates rather than the single aperture normal in Han times.[52] Nevertheless, life in T'ang Ch'ang-an was highly regimented. The curfew imposed a daily rhythm on the entire populace. Until 636, the ward gates opened at dawn to the shouts of a military patrol, and thereafter to the beating of drums in the streets. The *New History of T'ang* described the policing of the capital thus:

> At sunset, the drums were beaten eight hundred times and the gates were closed. From the second night watch, mounted soldiers employed by the officers in charge of policing the streets made the rounds and shouted out the watches, while the military patrols made their rounds in silence. At the fifth watch, the drums within the Palace were beaten, and then the drums in all the streets were beaten so as to let the noise be heard everywhere; then all the gates of the wards and markets were opened.[53]

The ward system of urban government and control could not, however, endure under the pressure of an expanding market economy. Even in the eighth century, this pressure was already felt in the western market of T'ang Ch'ang-an. The Sinologist E. H. Schafer describes it as "a busy, raucous, and multi-lingual cluster of bazaars and warehouses, whose visitors were also entertained by prestidigitators and illusionists of every nationality, not to mention story-tellers, actors and acrobats." In the latter part of the ninth century, as the money economy continued to expand, public houses of prostitution sprouted near busy places everywhere, including city gates, markets, and temples. Several alleys were devoted to prostitution.[54]

Rules governing the ward system progressively weakened. Markets first gained the right to open at night; they then spilled, without fear of penalty, beyond their designated areas into residential quarters; finally, the walls enclosing markets came down.[55] By the eleventh century, the ward system of population surveillance no longer functioned. Throughout the Sung period (960–1279), boisterous commerce took over larger and larger portions of capital cities, destroying their calm, hierarchical order. In the Northern Sung capital of Kai-feng, it was not unusual for the homes of dignitaries and commoners, government buildings, and markets to be juxtaposed.[56] In the Southern Sung capital of

Hang-chou, pigs could be heard squealing as they were slaughtered not far from the Imperial Way.

In Europe, control of population was never attempted on the scale and with the rigor that Chinese rulers undertook, though fear of rebellion certainly existed. Curfew, widely imposed in medieval times, served to check both local violence and the possibility of large-scale revolt. Governments regulated the carrying of arms by day or night, especially for foreigners. Townsmen were warned against wearing armor unless they had at least the rank of knight or squire. In the fourteenth century, London authorities legislated against the donning of masks or any other type of facial covering in public places during Christmas and other times considered volatile.

These signs of nervousness were periodically justified by events. Rebellions did occur; constituted power could totter and fall. Renaissance Florence was well protected by walls from external enemies. Strict curfew created a semblance of calm during normal times, but these times could not be counted on to last. In a particularly turbulent period between June 1342 and August 1343, the communal regime was thrice overthrown by force. And greater chaos threatened. In the summer of 1378, the specter of anarchy haunted many of the wealthier Florentines as they saw about them the numerous hungry poor, the crowds of unemployed workers many of whom carried arms, and a weak regime that could barely maintain control. With the first signs of disturbance in June, prominent citizens fled to the countryside, shops and factories closed, and nearly all business activities ceased. Rumors spread that the workers were going to sack the city. Leonardo Bruni, in his official history written in 1415, articulated the fear common to the ruling class of his time with these words: "There was no end or measure to the unbridled desire of the lawless rabble, who lusted after the property of rich and honoured men, and thought of nothing but robbery, slaughter and oppression."[57]

City officials, in times past even more than today, grew nervous when they saw the poor flocking into their jurisdiction. In the sixteenth century, the expansion of London beyond its ancient limits excited official alarm. For about a hundred years, starting with Elizabeth I, attempts were made to restrain building on new foundations. This policy failed utterly to check growth: indeed, it succeeded mainly in creating slums tenanted by criminals, the very condition the authorities feared. Paris expanded slowly in the four centuries preceding the Grand Siècle. At the start of the seventeenth century the wall of Philip

Augustus (of late-twelfth-century vintage) stood intact on the Left Bank. Paris was still a contained city of modest size. During Louis XIII's reign (1610–1643), a rapid population increase created the uneasy feeling among officials that the capital might become too large and complicated for effective government. The king alleged that the city's recent growth made it difficult to dispose of filth and ensure food supplies. He also claimed that it was a cause of uncontrollable larceny, robbery, and murder.

Under Louis XIV, Paris began to organize itself in earnest against crime. The office of lieutenant of police was established. In 1667, its first occupant personally led two hundred armed men and a squadron of sappers to storm and capture Paris's most infamous retreat for criminals, the Cour des Miracles. In the same year, a municipal street-lighting system was inaugurated, and Paris for the first time emerged from its nocturnal gloom. Businessmen in the short winter days no longer needed to rush home before nightfall. During the day hours as well, Paris looked brighter with the construction of the first public squares worthy of the name, which allowed sunlight to penetrate the constricted quarters.[58] Despite improvements in law enforcement and in lighting, fear of public disorder retained its grip as country folk continued to pour into Paris. A series of royal edicts in 1724 and 1726, renewed in 1728 and 1765, attempted to curtail the growth of the city by forbidding construction beyond a fixed point; most worrisome to the government was the problem of food supply and the threat of bread riots.[59]

In the nineteenth century, Louis Napoleon's transformation of Paris served several purposes, one of which was to facilitate the enforcement of public security. Critics of Louis Napoleon said that he ordered the building of straight boulevards so as to provide more effective sight lines for his artillery, that he made the boulevards broad to forestall the erection of barricades, and that he cut them through the crowded working-class quarters in order to break up and, if necessary, encircle these potential areas of rebellion and of resistance. Modern historians consider these criticisms unfair. Napoleon III wanted to attach the populace of Paris securely to his regime, but he hoped to accomplish this by creating an orderly and beautiful city rather than through the threat of force. On the other hand, some of these strategic considerations must have entered Napoleon's plans as they had the plans of preceding governments. After all, between 1827 and 1848, barricades were thrown across Parisian streets eight times in the densely settled eastern half of the city, and on three occasions they had been the prelude to revolution.[60]

In America, fear of the stranger and of public disorder was commonplace in the rapidly expanding towns of the eighteenth century. Indians and blacks, slave and free, were perceived to be the greatest threat to law and order. By 1740, the black inhabitants of New York made up one-fifth of the city's total population. Out of fear white citizens treated them harshly, with the predictable result that they became increasingly restless. Constant dread of black uprisings culminated in hysterical rumors of a "Negro conspiracy" during 1741. The militia was called out. Hundreds of people fled the town. Blacks were rounded up, and before the frenzy attenuated thirteen of them were burned alive, eight hanged, and seventy-one transported from the colony. Although there were instances of Negro crime and disorder, the "conspiracy" itself probably existed only in the imagination of the anxiety-ridden townspeople.[61]

Philadelphia, the City of Brotherly Love, was the "City of Brotherly Fear," according to the historian John Alexander. In the late eighteenth century, fear was of strangers and of the poor. Philadelphia was a cosmopolitan city: strangers speaking in alien tongues were everywhere. German residents were numerous enough to warrant the printing of signposts in both German and English. Irish immigrants and the descendants of Irish stock formed another large segment of the population. Toward the end of the period, French was introduced by refugees from the French Revolution and from the revolt of the blacks in Haiti. Established residents had reason to be afraid of the poor and of new immigrants who could not find jobs and became desperate. "Records from the city court indicate that for the period 1794–1800, at least 68.3 percent of the criminals convicted were either born in Ireland or black. Less than 12 percent of the criminals were born in Pennsylvania, and less than 6 percent were born in Philadelphia."

The city was spatially segregated: at the center lived the well-to-do and at the outskirts the poor in run-down housing. Respectable citizens complained constantly of disorder in the streets, especially near the fringes of the city where the indigent congregated. Proper Philadelphians lamented the growing visibility of "evildoers" of all kinds—including "rude, unsupervised children." In the minds of some merchants and householders, dread of the poor and fear of fire were confounded: the poor were suspected of resorting to arson in order to plunder the burnt-out ruins.[62]

The urban fears of upper-class Americans and intellectuals were complex. At a time when city government still lay largely in the hands of an elite class, there was deep suspicion of the propertyless, volatile mob and of agitators who could incite it to violence. Fear of unruly masses was intensified by the example of the violent Parisian mobs of 1789, 1820, 1848, and later. In the second half of the nineteenth century, as immigrants poured into American cities and in time organized powerful political machines, the patricians lost control of urban governments. Their political fears then became tinged with ethnic animus, a visceral feeling of disgust for the clannish ways and uncouth speech of the new Americans. Furthermore, patricians who took pride in their capacity for calm and rational thought felt an aesthetic distaste for what they perceived to be the urban populace's predisposition to panics and transports.

In Europe, governments and well-to-do citizens also viewed with growing alarm the swelling populations of their metropolises. What did this massive influx portend? Passing through Manchester in 1842, Cooke Taylor observed that no one could "contemplate these 'crowded hives' without feelings of anxiety and apprehension almost amounting to dismay. The population is hourly increasing in breadth and strength. . . . We speak of them as of the slow rising and gradual swelling of an ocean which must, at some future and no distant time, bear all the elements of society aloft upon its bosom, and float them—Heaven knows whither."[63] Businessmen and other members of the rising middle class were repelled by what they did not understand. To them the lower orders were dangerous, their alleys and tenements "rife with all kinds of enormity." A sprawling metropolis or industrialized town was often described as grotesque and lurid, labyrinthine and obscure. Its people—dark and stunted in comparison with the well-fed members of the upper middle class—seemed invincibly alien, pagan, and hostile; they spoke a slang that sounded like some primitive, foreign tongue. From the 1860s onward, literate Englishmen began to talk of "darkest London" and "darkest England" as they did of "darkest Africa." They saw London's East End as an "unknown" region to be explored.[64] They felt as never before that a threatening primitivity lay, not just in a distant corner of their empire, but in their midst. Social reform in Victorian England was prompted to some extent by Christian zeal, but also by fear of a new human "subrace" that could contaminate or do violence to middle-class society.

This sense of unease among the urban middle class was not, of course, restricted to Britain. It notably affected the French, the Germans, and the Americans: Eugène Sue, influenced by English examples, wrote the novel *Les Mystères de Paris* in 1843, and Charles Loring Brace published his sociological tract *The Dangerous Classes of New York* in 1877. The French, in the early part of the nineteenth century, barely distinguished laborers from criminals. Newspaper reports and illustrations in novels tended to show both groups as made up of brutal and vain types, unpleasant to rub shoulders with and repulsive when seen up close.[65] Brace described his dangerous classes as consisting mainly of American-born children of Irish and German immigrants, who he felt were far more brutal than the peasantry from whom they descended. Almost boastfully, Brace noted that the "intensity of the American temperament" made the American children of vice more unrestrained than their European counterparts.[66]

Besides fear of their violence and a sort of aesthetic distaste for them, middle-class Europeans shunned the poor because they were believed to be carriers of disease. We have seen how medical opinion overwhelmingly attributed the spread of epidemic disease to corrupted physical environment—particularly the air—rather than to infected people. This was the miasmatist theory. By the nineteenth century, however, the rival contagionist theory was gaining increasing acceptance. To the miasmatists, slums had to be removed or at least contained lest their pestilential vapors poison middle-class districts. To the contagionists, the poor themselves were suspect. Ladies and gentlemen avoided the odorous poor who were thought to bear deadly *contagia* in their blood, breath, and clothes. Describing the horrors of a slum in the shadow of Southwark Cathedral, Charles Dickens drew attention to a denizen's corrupted blood, which "propagates infection and contagion" everywhere. "It shall pollute, this very night, the choice stream (in which a chemist on analysis would find the genuine nobility) of a Norman House, and his Grace shall not be able to say Nay to the infamous alliance." Everything about the slum dweller was threatening: "There is not an atom of [his] slime, not a cubic inch of any pestilential gas in which he lives, not one obscenity or degradation about him, not an ignorance, not a wickedness, not a brutality of his committing but shall work its retribution."[67]

Mob, rabble, mass, the "great unwashed"—these are some of the terms that established residents and officials use to express their disgust and horror as they see strange people crowding into their city. An orderly world is threatened by chaos, and every effort is made to contain it. We have seen such fears of dissolution in the past, and we see it today. They are primarily the fears of the propertied and articulate members of the upper and middle classes. How does the city look to impoverished newcomers from the countryside or a foreign land? What are their fears when confronted by an alien and hostile environment? Answers are difficult to obtain for earlier historical periods. We know the urban fears of the Tudor monarchs of England and of Louis XIII of France through the decrees they promulgated and other documents. In the nineteenth century, middle-class distress over the swelling mass of people in the metropolises is amply recorded in the literary works of social reformers and novelists. The poor and the oppressed, on the other hand, often suffered in silence; or if they cried out in pain, their cries went largely unheeded and unrecorded unless accompanied by desperate action.

Although direct evidence from the mouths of the underprivileged is rare, we can infer their fears from the ways they were forced to live. This indirect evidence is sufficiently abundant and varied to give us, for example, a picture of how an urban immigrant might have felt in the last decades of the nineteenth century. The record is particularly rich for New York City, the main port of entry into the United States. To most immigrants, coming to the United States and establishing a foothold there was a harrowing experience in which brief phases of hope alternated with long periods of depression and deep shock. Even in the 1860s, a journey across the Atlantic Ocean might take a month. Crowding, sickness, lack of food and fresh water, and other deprivations made the sojourn in the ship seem more a diabolic form of punishment than a method of transportation. The first sight of New York's harbor and skyline brought a moment of euphoria, followed soon by a period of intense anxiety as the newcomers ran the gauntlet of immigration and health officials. Would they be rejected at the last moment? Some were, though the majority surmounted the last hurdle to enter the Promised Land. An immigrant family might be met by a fellow countryman, known as a "runner," who offered to cart their luggage to a boardinghouse. The optimism raised by that gesture of welcome was dashed as soon as the newcomers saw the boardinghouse, a crumbling structure in which flies, bedbugs, and wharf rats were permanent guests. The keepers charged exorbitant rates not only for the rooms but for the cartage and storage of baggage. If the boarders could not pay they were thrown penniless into the street, while their belongings were kept as security.

The establishment of efficient immigrant-aid societies and

central receiving stations (Castle Garden and Ellis Island) made the gross exploitation of newly landed immigrants by "runners" less common from 1855 onward. However, the newcomers still had to find a cheap place to live, and this was often an old private residence converted into a tenement house to receive people like them. These tenement houses, jammed together, were airless, dank, and dark warrens in which a single small room might accommodate a family with four or five children. To the peasant from rural Ireland or southern Germany, the lack of ventilation and sunlight was a shock. The noisy and dirty industries that stood among the tenement buildings delivered another shock. These factories, slaughterhouses, stables, lumber and coal yards, shipyards, and docks in the lower wards of Manhattan physically threatened the immigrant families who lived in their midst. Exposed machinery caused accidental death and maiming, as did the heavy traffic of bulk materials and merchandise. Timber and bricks fell from rickety structures; walls collapsed, and entire buildings might crumble on their foundations. Fire, often caused by the coal stoves in crowded tenement rooms, was frequent. The mere rumor of fire incited panic, because residents knew that their buildings burned easily, that the front door and windows were the only fire escapes, and that many rooms had no windows at all.[68]

The social environment seemed equally threatening. Income from hard manual labor barely supported an immigrant household. Many jobs were temporary. "When construction workers finished a project, they found themselves back where they started—looking for a job, with few savings. This time, though, they were a little older and weaker; with every project they risked injuries that might make them unfit for any work." Russian and Polish Jews who poured into New York's Lower East Side at the turn of the century offered urban skills which found employment in the "needle trades," making clothes of all sorts. The pay, already miserable, could be further reduced by the employer for the most trivial of offenses, such as giggling or staring out of the window.[69] Tenants feared eviction. For those who had acquired a little personal property, eviction spelled disaster. Failure to pay rent might result in the seizure of the tenant's property. Landlords projected such power that tenants put rent before clothing and fuel, seldom failing to pay.[70]

To immigrants struggling for survival in their squalid ghetto, the outside world was at once alluring and terrifying, filled with riches but also with hostility. The ghetto itself, despite the filth and the crowding, at least offered the companionship of one's own kind, people who spoke the same language and practiced the same religion. On the other hand, the immigrant ghetto was far from being a community. The relentless pressure to survive strained all social bonds, including those of the family. Some husbands simply vanished, unable to face the recurring quarrels, the distress of seeing their dependants go hungry, or the shame of living with wives who earned more than they could. Many marriages were formally broken. By 1903, the Lower East Side had the highest divorce rate of any district in New York. Gambling, alcoholism, crime, and mental illness were other routes of escape from misery.[71]

Nevertheless, immigrants of European stock could at least dream that their children would in time be accepted by the larger society and become prosperous citizens. Even when prejudice was most virulent, Americans never maintained that every European endangered the American way of life. Attacks focused on the "scum" and "dregs" of Europe, thereby implying that there were exceptions. Those antagonistic to Orientals, however, tended to reject them all as members of a despised race. Even in 1900, when Chinese immigration had ceased and the Chinese no longer competed with Americans for desirable jobs, a labor union could refer to that people as "more slavish and brutish than the beasts that roamed the fields."[72] The Chinese lived in humiliation and fear. Casual brutality was "John Chinaman's" daily lot. Cutting his queue was a favorite sport of bullies, and a shower of rocks might greet him whenever he ventured beyond his neighborhood. "No one will ever know how many Chinese were murdered in California; in the best-known outrage, about twenty Chinese were shot and hanged in the sleepy village of Los Angeles during one night in 1871." Justice could not be obtained through the courts, for Western juries acted on the belief that the Chinese were "born liars."[73]

From 1880 onward, the Chinese began to move out of California and settle in metropolitan areas in different parts of the country. Thus was established a scattering of Chinatowns, of which the largest are now those in San Francisco and New York. Chinese immigrants were denied entry into so many trades and professions that they could expect to make a living only in the larger cities where humble services and modest businesses such as hand laundries, cafés serving Chinese food, and curio shops attracted American customers.

The Chinese gathered in one area of the city because they were not allowed to, or were afraid to, live elsewhere. They sought security in the midst of their own kind. Their social institutions were more creatures of adversity than of pride. China-town was and is a ghetto. This fact tends to be lost amid a welter of contradictory public perceptions. In the late nineteenth century, Americans were prone to view the Chinese quarter as a place of temptation, corruption, and fear. Concentrated in it, they believed, were gambling and opium dens, houses of prostitution, gangsters, and white-slave traffickers. An opposite image has emerged in the twentieth century, particularly since the Second World War. Chinatowners as well as American society at large successfully promoted the idea that the ghetto was a thriving community in which traditional Confucian virtues of family love and filial piety were upheld and crime, especially among juveniles, rarely occurred.

If Chinatown as a den of iniquity was a distortion, so also was the later, rosy myth. No doubt happy families and good community services existed in Chinatown, but so did an intense factionalism that periodically erupted in violence. Wars between secret societies, many of which took root at a time when the Chinese population was predominantly male, did not cease in the 1920s, as commonly believed. Twenty and even thirty years later, mutual-aid and clan associations—penetrated by secret-society members—continued to fight each other over employment and power. Hiring thugs for purposes of blackmail and harassment persisted in contests for dominance.[74] Yet, when confronted by threats from the outside world, rival groups would unite to defend themselves against a common enemy, so that for a time at least, Chinatown resembled a true community.

Bonds of desperation can emerge in the ghetto. Consider, as another case, the seamstresses who, in the early 1970s, compose the largest labor force employed by any single industry in Chinatown. There is no doubt that they are grossly underpaid and in other ways exploited by their Chinese employers. Workers complain about their bosses in the privacy of their homes. Antagonism and conflict certainly exist, but so does a strong sense of solidarity, for seamstresses and shop owners are well aware of the powerful and hostile world outside, before which both groups—despite their unequal status within the ghetto—see themselves as victims.[75]

Ghetto dwellers seldom ventured beyond the confines of their small world. At the start of the twentieth century, Chinatowners in San Francisco were restricted within a seven-block area. To cross the boundaries defined by such streets as Kearny and Broadway was to risk almost certain physical abuse. When Chinatowners occasionally left the ghetto to shop in Union

Square, they were obliged to carry a police whistle, though when they were attacked by thugs, blowing the whistle rarely elicited the help of a policeman. In the far more enlightened age of the 1940s, a Chinese working-class family could actually move out of the ghetto and live among white Americans; but it lived in fear. Even when white neighbors appeared tolerant and friendly, there was always the feeling that at any time they could turn hostile. To guard against such possibility, a Chinese family might try to placate the local businessmen with offerings of food on national holidays, as though the barber and the bartender next door were minor gods of uncertain benevolence.[76]

To the poor and oppressed, the ghetto is home, but also a most dangerous place. In fact, immediate threats to life and property come from people of the same ethnicity who live or "hang out" in the same area rather than from white society which, however powerful and oppressive, is distant. When gang wars flare in Chinatown, safety lies in one's immediate neighborhood where one's own clan members and allies are concentrated. In a black ghetto, safety may be confined to a short block or a street corner, or reduced ultimately to the haven of home. A black person may feel so ineffectual and vulnerable that he or she withdraws into the only space—the home—over which control can still be exercised. Before the flickering TV screen in a darkened room, with a beer in hand, a person is safe; beyond the four walls are demands and threats, continual reminders of an individual's isolation and inadequacy.

An ethnic ghetto can often give a deceptive impression of unity. The houses, streets, people, and activities have a distinctive stamp, from which an outsider may infer a community of interests, a wide social bond that is not there. Characteristics of the ghetto in the United States are social fragmentation and a pervasive sense of wariness that can be transformed into overt hostility among the fragmented groups. Gang war is the most dramatic manifestation of this phenomenon. Rival gangs divide the ghetto into turfs and fight each other for the right to rule over patches of run-down streets, littered parking lots, crumbling playgrounds, schools, and homes. They terrorize the local populace, the old as well as the young. In a study of a black district in Philadelphia, the geographer David Ley notes: "Fear of gangs is a major deterrent upon adolescent movement, including the journey to school." Boys might be afraid to attend the local cinema for fear of "harassment from the youth of other neighborhoods, either on the journey or inside the theatre."[77]

Crime, so long as it is confined within the ghetto, is often overlooked by authorities in the larger society. The myth of the peaceful Chinatown, for example, was made possible partly because the victims of violence were mainly Chinese rather than whites, and partly because the leaders of Chinatown preferred to settle the conflicts themselves and thus gain greater power rather than cooperate with the outside judicial system. Ghetto fears and frustrations, however, might not be containable. In the 1960s, Chinese youth gangs in San Francisco fought not only among themselves but also with black and white gangs. The Watts (Los Angeles) riot in August 1965 quickened America's awareness of the possibility of widespread and violent disaffection among the nation's urban blacks. Even though black fury on that occasion was confined within Watts and caused the destruction of white property rather than persons, middle-class white America felt threatened.[78]

When the leaders of established society sensed such impending chaos coming from elements of the population that they did not want to or could not assimilate, what did they do? Historically, they resorted to creating landscapes of fear: an earlier one of public torture and execution, followed by the subtler arts— diabolical or redemptive, depending on one's point of view—of confinement.

13.

Public Humiliation
and Execution

A tribal community has no permanent enclave of strangers living in its midst who might disturb the peace. As for deviants within the social net, ostracism is normally sufficient to bring them to heel. Witches, it is true, are enemies from within, and they must sometimes be killed, but the killing is not justified as a deterrent. The machinery of justice and punishment need not be put on display, because tribe members respond to more subtle cues. However, where rootless "strangers" form a large component of society, social sanctions lose effectiveness. Rulers, from fear that their world might shatter, use force to impose order. For force to be an effective deterrent, people in authority once believed that it must be both severe and visible. The result was the creation of a landscape of punishment which, in Europe, became especially prominent and ghoulish between the late Middle Ages and the end of the eighteenth century.

When human beings had faith in the after life and, moreover, believed that their ruler had power over both this life and the next, the use of grisly forms of physical punishment was not essential. In Egypt at the time of the Old Kingdom, a man who infringed upon temple immunities suffered the loss of civil status and with it the right to a ritual burial. This meant that the offender lost not only his freedom in this life but also the possibility of enjoying blessedness in the next. By New Kingdom times, however, metaphysical fears had so diminished that they needed to be augmented by the fear of corporeal punishment, which included beating, mutilation, and death by impalement.[1]

Ancient Rome provides another illustration of this process. In the Republican period, the punishment for treason was a form of civic excommunication which had the effect of reducing the culprit to a state of nonbeing. Exile (imposed under the decree known as "interdiction of fire and water") could seem worse than death. By the Imperial period, however, such a loss of civic rights and a sentence of exile, especially in its milder form of *relegatio*, no longer induced overriding fear or even great inconvenience; the offender might withdraw to the provinces and lead a tolerable life supported by friends and relatives. To command terror, punishment had to be made more physical. Under the Empire, citizens convicted of crimes against the state could be banished to a desert island, where their chances for survival were slim, or could be given the death penalty. By A.D. 222, death had become the punishment for all but the mildest forms of treason.[2]

Various factors account for the introduction of harsher laws in the Imperial period. One was the infiltration of Roman society by what might be called the military analogy. As a citizen at home the Roman enjoyed extensive protection against the arbitrary judgment of a magistrate, but as a soldier in the field he was subject to the commander's discretion in matters of discipline. This was exercised with a minimum of legal restraint.[3] The emperors, who step by step arrogated to themselves the arbitrary powers of the commander at war, came to see Romans not as citizens but as subjects and soldiers under discipline. The severest penalties, including mutilation and death, could then be laid on free men.

Another factor in the increasing tolerance of harsh sentences was the daily spectacle of cruelty inflicted on slaves. Civic sanctions did not apply to slaves, who were taught obedience through fear of pain and death. Romans, free and unfree, were exposed to the common sight of slaves being publicly flogged or executed by crucifixion, for which there was a special place—the Campus Esquilinus. Similar places of execution, complete with crosses and other instruments of torture, probably decorated every large city in the Roman Empire, as a warning to slaves and all lawbreakers, and as a sign of a strict and merciless regime.[4] Under these circumstances, any sensibility toward the rights of citizens naturally deteriorated. To those in authority, it seemed necessary to use cruel methods at first to control slaves, then persons of low rank (the *humiliores*, or rabble), and finally the citizens themselves, especially since the class of citizens had vastly expanded under the Empire. A landscape of fear was deliberately created because it came to be believed that the infliction of pain and death had to be public if it was to serve as a deterrent to potential rebels and criminals. As Quintilian put it, "Wherever we crucify the guilty, the most crowded roads are chosen, where the most people can see and be moved by this fear. For penalties relate not so much to retribution as to their exemplary effect."[5]

Compared with the Romans, the Germans at the fringes of the Empire treated their offenders more humanely. From Tacitus we learn that capital punishment was imposed only for crimes against the community such as going over to the enemy and disgraceful retreat in battle, while the worst offense against the individual, namely, homicide, merely incurred the payment of a certain number of cattle and sheep.[6] In a society where every fighting man was a valuable asset, execution and mutilation were not considered suitable punishments for mere murder and theft. A similar system had developed in England. King Ethelbert of Kent, in the seventh century, promulgated laws that provided a list of fines for a wide assortment of offenses ranging from fornication to murder. The amount of compensation to be paid in each case was carefully adjusted to the status of the victim and of the perpetrator.

By the middle of the tenth century, punishments had become more severe. This occurred at least in part because people in authority were more aware of the problem of thievery and of other signs of social disorder. When Athelstan introduced harsh laws into his kingdom, both his own administrators and the bishops praised him. Death and mutilation replaced material compensation for a growing number of offenses. Witchcraft and sorcery, if they brought on death, incurred the penalty of death under the laws of Athelstan. By a law of Canute's, a woman forfeited "both nose and ears" for adultery.[7]

Although William the Conqueror abolished capital punishment, he substituted for it the equally terrible—often worse—punishment of maiming. If a person was found guilty of certain crimes, his eyes were torn out, or his limbs chopped off, or he was reduced to his head and trunk, which were to act as a witness to his crimes. William's law, according to a modern writer, "populated the country with ghastly objects whose head and trunk only remained. Blind, armless and legless, they could only move by directionless rolling. Their usually short lives were sustained by the charity of their relations and friends if they were fortunate enough to have any."[8]

By the sixteenth century, maiming had become a grotesque public ritual. Half a dozen or more officials might be needed to cut off a man's hand. First, the Sergeant of the Woodyard brought in a block and cords. The Master Cook then handed the Dressing Knife to the Sergeant of the Larder, who used it to perform the deed. The Sergeant of the Poultry stood by with a rooster, whose body was to be wrapped around the stump of the wrist. Other attendants who had roles were the Yeoman of the Scullery, the Sergeant Farrier, the Chief Surgeon, the Groom of Salcery, the Yeoman of the Chandry, and the Sergeant of the Pantry.[9] Such elaborate procedure served to emphasize the majesty of the law and the heinousness of crime.

This ancient practice of mutilation probably offends modern sensibilities more than any other form of punishment. It has had a long life. In Europe it continued to be used for certain non-homicidal crimes until well into the eighteenth century. From the viewpoint of the authorities mutilation enjoyed at least two advantages: it was relatively cheap, and it produced victims who dramatically advertised the power of court, king, and state.

In the Middle Ages, every town and village of any size and every feudal castle had its instruments of retention and of punishment. Unlike those of modern times, medieval instruments were on display: they stood prominently by the roadside, next to public buildings, and in market squares. They were a normal component of the landscape. To judge from early medieval prints, the English relied on stocks for the punishment of many offenses. These they put at the entrance of a town, or fastened to a courthouse. Stocks served as an open-air jail for runaway servants and laborers; immobilized, they waited for their masters to claim them. Persons suspected of criminal offenses were also placed in stocks prior to trial; some did not survive to be tried, whereas others might lose a foot as a result of interference with blood circulation. Under a statute for laborers in 1351, every village that did not have stocks was required to set them up.[10] In 1405, a statute was passed which would have demoted every town or village to the status of a hamlet if it did not possess this apparatus. As late as 1890, stocks might still be seen in isolated villages, though their last recorded use was in 1872 at Newbury, Berkshire, when a man suffered this ancient indignity for drunkenness and disorderly conduct in a parish church.[11]

The pillory was also a conspicuous and familiar sight in the towns of Europe. Excepting perhaps stocks, no engine of punishment was more generally employed. Almost every market had a pillory, because local authorities who neglected to keep one on hand for immediate use ran the risk of forfeiting their right to hold a market. In London, men were put in the pillory for scores of different offenses, including the use of magic, begging under false pretenses, and the forgery of letters, bonds, and deeds. But men suffered in the pillory most often for deceitful trading practices. Hence the appropriateness of putting this instrument of torture and humiliation in the marketplace, where buyers and sellers could be forewarned. In the great market of Cheap in London, the nature of the offense was clearly indicated. A butcher who sold putrid meat, for example, might have his smelly commodity piled before him and burned under his nose.[12] The pillory inflicted greater pain on its victim than did the stocks. Both hands as well as the head were pressed between two boards, and sometimes the ears were pinned back and nailed to the frame. Prolonged exposure before spectators who jeered and threw things could easily end in the culprit's death. France also used the pillory to expose dishonest tradesmen, but especially to punish blasphemers. An edict of 1347 required that a blasphemer be pilloried; the same edict specifically allowed people to throw filth in his face.[13] Given such mistreatment, death was a common occurrence.

The pillory, unlike the stocks, sometimes attained monumental size. In the sixteenth century, Paris's apparatus, located at the center of the market, was an imposing tower sixty feet tall. Like the stocks, the pillory enjoyed a long life; it was one of the more stable elements in Europe's shifting landscape. As recently as 1830, English officials were still using the pillory to punish perjurers. An act of Parliament finally abolished it in 1837.

From the late medieval period to around 1600, the methods of punishment were both diabolically cruel and varied. The death penalty was given for the most inconsequential of crimes when these threatened the interests of landowners or detracted from the respect due to a city. In late medieval Germany (ca. 1400), a man caught girdling trees could have his intestines torn out and wrapped around a tree. The punishment for a destroyer of boundary stones was a painful death inflicted with a plow. Customs varied from town to town. In south Germany the modes of execution included breaking on the wheel, quartering, pinching with red-hot tongs, live burial, and burning. Some techniques were so cruel that even the executioners considered them excessive. In 1513, the official punishers at Nuremberg complained about the unpleasantness of their job, particularly when it called for live burial. They no doubt had in mind the difficult death of Elizabeth Schellen-Claus, a hardened thief, who was buried alive beneath the gallows in 1497. "This poor creature struggled until the skin on her hands and feet was so lacerated that the people greatly pitied her." Compared with such barbarity, death by hanging seemed merciful. However, unlike quarterings and live burials, the traces of which quickly disappeared, gallows with dangling corpses were an enduring and conspicuous feature of the European landscape; in south Germany they plainly marked the neighborhood of an important court, especially a city court.[14]

In England during the same period, the methods of punishment were equally cruel and varied. There were regional differences which seemed to reflect both the nature of the crime and deeply rooted local traditions. Thus the historian John Bellamy writes:

> The customs of Sandwich decreed that all who were condemned for homicide should be buried alive in a place allotted for this purpose at Sandown, called the "thiefdowns." At Pevensey any man "of the franchise" found guilty on a plea of the crown was to be taken to the town bridge at high tide and thrown over into the harbour. At Portsmouth any man who slew another was burned. At Halifax execution of thieves was by means of the original guillotine.[15]

Such individuality in methods of physical punishment did not please the English kings, who sought to centralize power in their own hands. They were reluctant to allow any special device of execution if no ancient local custom sanctioned it. They favored hanging which, from the standpoint of deterrence value, enjoyed the advantage of enduring visibility.

Tacitus noted that the Germans hanged their traitors. From at least the first century A.D., the stringing up of an offender on a tree or post was the most common method of public execution. With gallows and gibbets as omnipresent as church towers and castles, it is not surprising that they also became motifs in European decoration and artwork. In England, a gallows or tree with a man hanging on it was so frequent an object outside of towns and in the countryside that it seems to have been considered almost a natural ornament of the landscape, and was thus introduced into certain medieval manuscripts.[16] Poets and artists depicted gallows and swinging bodies in their works, purposefully as in François Villon's "Ballade des pendus," or matter-of-factly as in Hieronymus Bosch's *Wandering Fool.*[17]

Machines of execution were a feudal right. Charles V of France (1337–1380) granted leave to certain districts to have gallows with two posts, the number of posts in a machine being a symbol of prestige. The lord who had the right to an eight-post gallows could look down on a cousin entitled to only two posts on his engine of death.[18] From the Middle Ages to the eighteenth century, condemned criminals in France were executed by hanging more frequently than by any other method. As a result, in every town and in almost every village there stood a permanent gibbet, which, owing to the custom of leaving the bodies on the post until they crumbled into dust, was very rarely without some corpses or skeletons attached to it.

Paris, from the twelfth century onward, became the central place for hangings as for so many other functions. A monumental gibbet was built on the eminence of Montfaucon, between the faubourgs of Saint-Martin and the Temple in Paris. This notorious structure was made of heavy masonry. Ten or twelve layers of rough stone formed an enclosure of forty feet by thirty feet. Sixteen pillars rose above the fundament, each about thirty feet high. The pillars were joined to one another by double bars of wood and bore iron chains on which the criminals were suspended. Montfaucon was used not only to carry out the death penalty but also to expose corpses transported from execution grounds in every part of the country. In 1466, it was equipped to display the bodies of fifty-two malefactors. Fresh corpses hung there as well as the mutilated remains of criminals who had been boiled, quartered, or beheaded; these were shown in sacks of leather and wickerwork. It does not take much imagination to envisage the hideous scene: the massive scaffold on its eminence, at twilight against a backdrop of towering storm clouds, the thousands of crows feasting on the bodies that swung on the iron chains.[19]

In England, the gibbeting of executed offenders was an accepted practice by the fourteenth century. Its widespread use in later times may be inferred from old road books and guides that mention gallows and gibbets as landmarks. For example, the following directions appear in John Ogilby's *Itinerarium Angliae,* a work which was first published in 1675 and reprinted in various editions during the first two decades of the eighteenth century:

> By the Gallows and Three Windmills, enter the suburb of York. . . . Beyond the suburbs (Durham), a small ascent, between the Gallows and Crokehal. . . . Pass thro' Hare Street, and at 13'4 part of Epping-Forest, a Gallows to the left. . . . Pass by Pen-menis-Hall, and at 250'4 Hildravaght Mill both on the Left, and Ascend a small Hill, a Gibbet on the Right. . . . Leave Frampton, Wilberton, and Sherbeck, on the Right, and by a Gibbet on the Left, over a Stone Bridge cross. . . . From Nottingham ascend a Hill, and pass by a Gallows.[20]

To combat the "Horrid Crimes of Murder," an act was passed in 1752 that made it legal to preserve a felon's body in tar for prolonged and prominent display. As a consequence, more and more tarred bodies in varying stages of disintegration appeared in the English countryside, frightening the local inhabitants to the extent that, at night at any rate, people might go several miles out of their way to avoid such a spectacle. However, avoidance was not always easy. English officers of the law had an eye for the significance of place; they attempted to erect the gibbet close to the scene of the crime, or in sight of the malefactor's own home. Visibility itself was an important consideration. William Levin, executed in 1788, was hung in chains on the most elevated part of Helsby Tor, about eight miles from Chester. At that exposed location the corpse could be seen from several counties. Gibbets were also made as high as possible. A pillar twenty-one feet tall was used to exhibit the body of a William Jobling, executed in Durham in 1832 for murdering a magistrate.[21]

London was the center of capital punishment in England, and Tyburn the center of hanging in London and Middlesex. The earliest execution at Tyburn of which a record exists was in 1177. Expanding business required the addition of two more gallows in 1220. By then Tyburn was probably the chief hanging place in the country. During Queen Mary's reign, Tyburn had so much work to do that extra gallows were set up beyond the city, at Hay Hill, Mayfair, Charing Cross, Fleet Street, Cheapside, and Bermondsey. During the reign of Elizabeth I, the continued pressure on Tyburn's facilities called for an unusual extension to the old gallows. A triangular frame was built capable of accommodating at least twenty-four felons at a time.[22] Tyburn's machine achieved thereby a measure of monumentality, though not quite on the scale of Paris's Montfaucon. By 1783, when execution was abolished at Tyburn, the gallows there had, in their 650 years of service, strangled to death at least 50,000 human beings.

Much has been written on the charm of English gardens and landscapes in the eighteenth century; what we tend to forget is this odious landscape of punishment. Much has also been written on the architectural elegance of certain parts of London in the eighteenth century; what we may not remember is that London had by then earned a ghoulish title—"City of the Gallows." W. C. Sydney believed that this title was justified:

No matter by what approach the stranger then entered London, he had the fact of the stringent severity of English criminal law most painfully impressed upon him by a sight of the gallows. If he entered the metropolis by its northern suburbs he would have passed Finchley Common, and have beheld not one, but perhaps five or six gibbets standing at a short distance from each other. If he traveled outside or inside a stage-coach that ran through the western quarter of the metropolis to Holborn or Picadilly he passed within sight of the notorious gallows at Tyburn. If, hailing from some foreign shore, he sailed up the River Thames to the port of London, his gaze would have been certain to have fallen on some of the skeletons of those who had paid with their lives the penalty of mutiny or piracy on the high seas, suspended in chains from numerous gibbets erected in the marshes below Purfleet on the Essex side and Woolwich on the other. If he traversed on foot any of the numerous heaths or commons in the vicinity of the metropolis, he would, unless possessed of unusually strong nerves, never fail to be terrified by the sudden creaking and clanking of the chains in which the corpse of some gibbeted highwayman or foot-pad was slowly rotting away.[23]

At night and alone, a passerby could be excused for shuddering at the sight of a gibbet. What he feared was not the dire consequence of running afoul of the law, but rather the corpse itself. He experienced primordial dread. Public execution and gibbeting were not, however, designed to produce a sense of the uncanny; rather they were intended to overawe the populace, to inspire in them a healthy respect and fear of duly constituted power.

Hanging was to be a public event. Quintilian called for "the greatest number of spectators," and Dr. Johnson voiced the same sentiment. To him, "executions are intended to draw spectators. If they do not draw spectators, they don't answer their purpose."[24] In the eighteenth century and the early part of the nineteenth, hangings attracted enormous crowds. The lower classes considered an execution day at Tyburn a holiday. The occasion generated a festive mood and much rowdiness; hence it was called a "fair" (Tyburn Fair) and a "hanging match." Craftsmen in different parts of the metropolis might abandon their work to attend a major execution. As the day approached, people from all directions converged on the three-mile stretch between Newgate prison and Tyburn. They came on foot, on horseback, and in coaches. They packed the nearby houses, filled the adjoining roads, climbed ladders, platforms, and walls for a view, and at Tyburn itself stood shoulder-to-shoulder in the contiguous pastures.[25] Crowds became so large and unruly, the disruption of normal traffic and commerce so severe, that the authorities finally decided to forgo the procession and hang criminals at

Newgate, where they were jailed. The crowds, however, did not diminish. Some 45,000 spectators attended the execution of John Holloway and Owen Haggerty on February 23, 1807. They jammed the spaces in front of Newgate prison and all adjacent streets. In the crush of excited bodies, twenty-seven persons died. At the execution of Fauntleroy in 1824, a multitude estimated at 100,000 assembled. Hangings were as popular in the provinces as in London. The size of the crowd attending an event in an assize town rivaled that of the capital, with people from rural areas flocking there when news of an execution reached them.[26]

Across the Atlantic in the United States, the same kind of morbid drama was enacted in the antebellum South. No spectacle in South Carolina was better attended or more vividly remembered than the strangulation of a felon. Hangings were advertised well in advance, even weeks ahead, and on the appointed day citizens gathered from all parts of the district as if for a great social occasion. The authorities in charge were solicitous. They erected the gallows on a "low, flat place" bordered by high ground that served as an amphitheater. And where the natural slope was insufficient, they built wooden platforms so that the rearmost spectators might not be deprived of a good view.[27]

Public executions succeeded in attracting crowds, but failed to impart their intended lesson. The majesty of the law made little impression on the people, many of whom used the occasion for drunken rowdiness, violence, and thievery. The spectators did not look contemptuously down on the felons about to be hanged; they rarely jeered at them as they did at petty offenders suffering in the stocks or pillory. Indeed, crowds often cheered the felons as though they were heroes. Proximity to death lent them glamour. Spectators credited them with their own pleasurable feelings of excitement, their intoxication. Awe for the condemned went even beyond death. In various parts of England, magical powers were attributed to the corpse of the hanged. Simple folk thought that touching it could cure skin disease, goiter, or a bleeding tumor.[28]

None of the effects had been anticipated by officers of the law, who saw in the public execution a secular morality play and believed as well that it acted as a powerful deterrent. In England, an early and eloquent critic of public execution was the novelist Henry Fielding. His appointment as a police magistrate in 1748 gave him an insider's knowledge of London's criminal class. He was convinced that hanging did not deter crime; on the contrary, he thought it a cause of the increase in robbery at mid-century. If the populace was to be taught fear, the lesson might be better imparted away from the carnival of public hanging. "A murder behind the scenes, if the poet knows how to manage it, will affect the audience with greater terror than if it was acted before the eyes."[29] How can one create a more effective landscape of fear? Jeremy Bentham, a reformer who sought to ease the harshness of criminal law, nonetheless advocated, not private hanging, but a better-staged ritual that could strike terror into the hearts of criminal and onlookers alike. A black scaffold, officers of justice bedecked in black crepe, a masked executioner, and somber religious music would perhaps prepare "the hearts of the spectators for the important lesson they were about to receive."[30]

Public execution was abolished in England in 1868. Through the early part of the nineteenth century, evidence accumulated to show that the grisly carnival promoted rather than discouraged social disorder and violence. If it frightened people, it frightened the wrong people—sensitive and law-abiding citizens —not hardened criminals and the rabble.

Charles Dickens was a strong advocate of reform. He powerfully articulated the sentiment of a rising number of lawmakers who deplored the macabre and frenzied atmosphere of a public hanging. Dickens witnessed the execution of Mr. and Mrs. George Manning at Horsemonger Lane Gaol in 1849. He saw the dawn break on droves of thieves, prostitutes, thugs, and drifters. The thousands and thousands of upturned faces, gilded by the bright gold sun, seemed to him brutal and inexpressibly odious. The people looked so obscene in their mirth that he thought "a man had cause to feel ashamed of the shape he wore." Three years later, Dickens recalled the scene again. He could not forget the two forms dangling on the top of the entrance gateway. "I never could, by my uttermost efforts, for some weeks, present the outside of that prison to myself (which the terrible impression I had received continually obliged me to do) without presenting it with the two figures still hanging in the morning air."[31]

Of the ideas and sentiments that converged to end public execution in England as well as (somewhat earlier) in the United States, one was the growing sensibility of a large and expanding middle class. Its members were less and less able to tolerate what they considered crude and vulgar. As their tastes became more genteel, they wanted to remove themselves from, or to have removed, all the outward signs of raw and violent life. It would be best if the poor, the mentally sick, and the lawbreakers did not exist. Next best was to segregate them: the poor in slums and ghettos, the mad and the criminal in asylums and prisons—as far away as possible from the suburbs.

14.

Exile and Confinement

Complex societies are intricate codes of exchange. Some of these codes are formulated into laws and regulations; most are internalized patterns of behavior that the dominant institutions of society have more or less succeeded in inculcating. Yet a complex society is never immune from the threat of anarchy (or rebellion). Its diversified and stratified population inevitably contains elements which, for different reasons, deviate from the generally accepted norms, or which seek deliberately to subvert them. Madmen do not obey rules of polite behavior. Neither do vagrants and loiterers and, in general, the dispossessed and rootless poor. To members of established society, such people are unstable drifters; they have no ties to place, family, and worldly goods. They are seen as violent, ready to commit crimes against property and persons.

What does society do with such fringe members? In the past, if they were not violent and had some legitimate means of support, their presence was tolerated. Mental defectives, beggars, vagabonds, and the helpless poor lived in the midst of the respectable and the rich. If people at the fringes of society committed a crime, they might be swiftly and harshly punished. We have seen how brutal the exercise of force could be before modern times. However, most societies had two other methods for imposing order or forestalling the dangers of internal chaos: exile and confinement. With exile, danger is expelled from the communal body; with confinement, it is isolated in space, thereby rendering it innocuous.

In ancient Rome and China, high-class offenders were banished to desert islands and remote provinces where, with the connivance of family and friends, they could live in reasonable comfort. Low-class felons were also banished, but they had to wear chains and perform hard labor.[1] In the modern period, transportation was an important type of punishment. From the seventeenth century to the early part of the nineteenth, both England and France dispatched their debtors and felons to the colonies. The general outline of this story is familiar and need not be repeated here. Less familiar is exile at the local level—banishment from the community.

What could a community do with inhabitants who were disreputable, jobless, and potentially a source of crime? The answer was that unless such people could demonstrate their membership in the community by virtue of birth or long residence, they were expelled. Small towns feared strangers who might become an economic burden and disrupt the tightly knit social order. Cities could afford to be more tolerant, but even a large community would be under pressure to remove its parasitic members if too many of them congregated. Toward the end of the sixteenth century, Paris had a population of 100,000, of whom some 30,000 were beggars. Obviously, no city thus burdened could hope to survive for long. In 1606, a decree of Parlement ordered that the beggars of Paris be whipped in the public square, branded on the shoulder, and driven out. To protect the capital against their return, an ordinance of 1607 established companies of archers at all the city gates.[2]

How is society to cope with its insane? Mad people are those whose minds wander. Without the control of rational minds, their behavior is erratic, either harmlessly adrift or violent. From ancient Greek times to the late medieval period, madmen received—other than medicine of a magical or sacral nature—two basic kinds of treatment: the violent were chained in private houses and religious institutions; the harmless were lightly supervised and allowed to mingle with the populace. When the insane became too numerous and troublesome, they were ejected from the city and encouraged to drift through the countryside. The step of transporting lunatics farther afield was undertaken between the late Middle Ages and the sixteenth century. City authorities hired sailors and merchants to conduct the mentally confused to distant towns where they might in the most literal sense be lost.

Naturally, societies would like to be rid of their mad people. When it could be shown that they had come from other places, they were often returned there. Towns in Germany engaged in this practice, as did those in other countries. How far were local officials willing to go? The councilors of Nuremberg, between

1377 and 1397, dispatched thirteen madmen at public expense to Bamberg, Passau, and Regensburg, and to places as distant as Vienna and Hungary.[3] A more kindly act was to put them on boats and send them on pilgrimages to shrines such as the popular shrine of Saint Dympha in Gheel near Antwerp. Along the Rhine River and among the Flemish canals could be seen these "ships of fools" carrying their deranged cargoes to distant places. This treatment, recorded in Sebastian Brant's well-known satire *Das Narrenschiff,* attained a peak of popularity in Western Europe during the fifteenth century.[4] In the "ship of fools," the images of madness and water were aptly conjoined: water, a fluid medium signifying a state that lacks definition, is an appropriate symbol for madness. By contrast, sanity is the firm land the drifting mind hopes to reach and anchor itself in.

To our way of thinking, the simplest answer to the threat of unruly people is to confine them in space, that is, in prisons and asylums. This idea was not, however, put into practice on any scale before the sixteenth century. Of course prisons existed in ancient times, but they were not seen as a device for controlling disorderly people, nor were they intended to be a method of punishment. The Greeks made little use of prisons: Greek law forbade the arrest of anyone accused of a serious crime if he could find three persons to vouch for him. The Romans recognized the possibility of imprisonment but rejected it. According to Ulpian, a jurist who worked in the early part of the third century A.D., a prison *(carcer)* might be used to hold persons but not to punish them. It was a place for detaining suspects before trial and convicted criminals until the time came to execute the death penalty.[5]

This view of the prison's function remained little changed throughout the medieval period of European history. Confinement was a means, not an end. Debtors, for example, were thrown into jail until they paid their debts, and important captives were kept in a dungeon until their ransom was received. A prisoner might languish in a dark and musty cell for a year or more. He could not doubt that he was being cruelly punished, but society pretended to interpret his condition otherwise. This difference is important, because the moment society saw the prison as a place of punishment it also saw it as the place for redemption. Thus brutality and idealism, despair and hope intertwined and produced the contradictory images of prisons and asylums that continue to baffle us. To see how this ambivalence has come about, we should turn to Europe's first systematic attempt to create places of confinement: the leper houses.

Leprosy was pandemic in Europe between A.D. 1000 and 1400. Lazar colonies, as many as 19,000 of them, once pockmarked the face of Europe. In 1226, more than 2,000 appeared on the official registers of France. In the fifteenth century, Great Britain had 362 leper houses, of which 285 were in England.[6] Nearly always, they were located outside of settlements; a leprosarium would be moved as the edge of the town expanded toward it. The defiled nature of the institution is suggested by the fact that at Rostock, Cologne, and other places, it was located at the site where criminals had once been executed. Also, wherever possible, the lazar house was built downwind from the town so that its foul air might not contaminate healthy inhabitants. Lepers were isolated. The religious ceremonies used to set them apart from the world differed little from the office for the dead.[7]

Why was there such fear of lepers? Fear in our time is based on the suspicion that the disease is communicable. Were people in the Middle Ages well aware of this fact? In 1346, Edward III issued an edict expelling all the lepers residing in London: he thought they might seek consolation in numbers by deliberately infecting the wholesome.[8] By the end of the fifteenth century, there can be little doubt that infection was the compelling reason for isolating lepers. Less clear is what motivated the construction of lazar houses and colonies in the early Middle Ages. Danger from infection did not then seem to preoccupy people's minds. Nothing in the foundation charters of the hospitals reveals any urgent concern to stem a floodtide of disease. The afflicted were known to seek admission to a hospital: acceptance into one was considered a privilege, expulsion from it a punishment. If people dreaded the disease, the dread did not suffice to prevent the old and the infirm from seeking food and shelter in a leper house. Moreover, although the afflicted lived apart, they were not under house arrest. A sufferer could without great difficulty obtain permission to visit a neighboring town and even stay there overnight.[9]

Some fear of contagion probably always existed, especially when ugly sores were visible; nonetheless, a major reason for segregating lepers in the eleventh and twelfth centuries was that they were believed to carry the stigma of defilement. Leprosy was seen as a moral disease, its victims threatening society by their evil behavior as much as through infection. Leprosy and lechery were linked in the medieval mind. Lepers were obscene and lecherous people, sinners. Yet although they were sinners, they were somehow, unlike other sinners, exculpated from the full burden of responsibility for their sins. The Church pronounced them dead to the world, but their souls could still be saved.

Leper hospitals were essentially religious institutions; even those administered by the burgesses of a town functioned under the auspices of the Church. Regulations in leper hospitals stressed the saving of souls. In some establishments the religious personnel far outnumbered the patients. Under the influence of the Church, attitudes toward leprosy became highly contradictory: the disease was the outward mark both of the damned sinner and of someone under God's special grace—that is, a person worthy to participate in Christ's own agony and humiliation for the salvation of the world. Saint Hugh of Lincoln (1140–1200) rhapsodized over lepers as the flowers of Paradise, pearls in the coronet of the Eternal King.[10] The bishop of Tournai urged in 1239 that the disease be considered a gift from God. Leper colonies were indeed places of horror, "cities of the damned"; on the other hand, through the lens of mystical vision they were perceived to be endowed with heavenly grace.

Around 1400 the virulence of leprosy began to decline. The affliction ceased to terrorize society. Leper houses fell into decay, and thus one form of sequestration came to an end. But not sequestration itself. In fact, we may think of the fifteenth century as the beginning of an "age of confinement" to which we still belong. What forces and events directed this change? The more salient among them may be summarized as follows. Western Europe suffered severe social and economic dislocations during the fifteenth and sixteenth centuries. Some of these dislocations signified progress in the sense that Europe was moving from a feudal to a capitalist economy. Population rose rapidly, wages declined, and unemployment was widespread. The towns gained new industries and prospered, but at the same time they swarmed with poor and unemployed people. In the English countryside fields once tilled were enclosed and turned into sheepfolds by well-to-do farmers. Jobless and landless peasants drifted about the country roads and into towns. Wars contributed to social chaos and the propensity for violence. Deserters, demobilized soldiers, and men from disbanded private armies joined the swelling streams of beggars and vagrants. While the demand for charitable institutions increased, the religious bodies that once ran the almshouses and hospitals were in a state of decay, and could not even minimally meet the needs of the poor and the sick.[11]

Rulers and governments viewed this mounting tide of vagrancy with alarm. Individual beggars were unsightly and a nuisance; and, even worse, many vagrants terrorized the country in organized bands. They stole, plundered, raped, and killed; they made pests of themselves at weddings and funerals; and the more politically conscious among them preached sedition.[12]

The Tudor monarchs of England recognized vagrancy as a threat to public order and a challenge to their rules. Periodically, tough laws were passed to restrain aimless movement. The whole weight of Tudor legislation and policy was directed toward confining the poor people within their home parishes. The parish was the basic unit of responsibility. Those who left it were to be returned there. A statute of 1495 required all local officers from the sheriff down to petty constables to put vagabonds in stocks on only bread and water for three days and two nights, and then compel them to return within a six-week period to the parishes of their birth or long residence. In 1531, a statute laid heavy penalties against begging by unlicensed persons; vagrants and unruly loiterers were whipped and then sent back to their home parish.[13]

The poor, in short, were to stay put. What was the local community to do with them? Ideally, worthy paupers unable to look after themselves found charity in an almshouse. Able-bodied beggars and loiterers, on the other hand, were placed in a house of correction where through work, prayer, and the acquisition of regular habits they could become productive members of society. The first English house of correction opened in London in 1556. It was converted from an old palace named Bridewell that had belonged to Edward VI. The refurbished palace received sturdy vagabonds and prostitutes, who were all forced to work: the women did carding and spinning; the men labored in a bakery, ground corn on a treadmill, or made nails in a smithy. In 1576, Parliament attempted to reduce pauperism by ordering every county to set up at least one "bridewell," or house of correction, within its borders. Perhaps as many as two hundred bridewells were thus established. A bridewell was not intended originally to be a place of punishment. Its ostensible purpose was to employ the poor, teach juveniles a trade, and reform vagrants. A few of these institutions, especially in the early phase of their founding, enjoyed a measure of success in restoring their inmates to an orderly life, but by the end of the seventeenth century they had become indistinguishable from common jails.[14]

Inspired by the English prototypes, hundreds of houses of correction sprang up in Europe during the seventeenth and eighteenth centuries. The earliest of these was the *tuchthuis,* or house of discipline, in Amsterdam. Founded in 1598 and occupying an abandoned nunnery, it catered to a very mixed population which ranged from serious offenders and lifers, through moderate misdemeanants such as beggars and runaway apprentices, to the incorrigible sons of wealthy burghers. The *tuchthuis* was planned by its first founder as a reformatory in which inmates, receiving vocational training in a variety of skills, would learn to be industrious and God-fearing. In fact, these Dutch houses soon turned into municipal factories with a captive labor force that was cruelly exploited for the profit of merchants and manufacturers. The Dutch institutions provided models for the establishment of similar workhouses in other parts of Europe. The first German workhouse, doubling as a house of correction, was built in Hamburg in 1620. Its spacious quarters could accommodate 500 inmates. Although the institution provided work for willing paupers, its primary purpose was to take beggars, drunkards, and idlers from the streets and force them to earn their livelihood by hard labor. At the end of the eighteenth century, Germany had sixty such institutions.[15]

The largest of the European houses of confinement was the Hôpital général in Paris. Soon after its founding in 1656, its occupants increased to the astonishing number of 6,000, which meant that one out of every hundred persons in Paris had spent time there. Despite the claim that the Hôpital général was to be a shelter for the poor and the sick, its operation showed a total disregard for the concept of medical care. The institution's primary concern was order—order as the absolute monarchy and the rising bourgeoisie understood it. Idleness was the source of all evil, and evil itself could be defined simply as the force for dissolution and chaos. In work—hard, persistent work—lay personal and societal salvation; all means could be used to enforce it, including irons, chains, the whip, and the dungeon. The Paris model was deemed a success. A royal edict, dated June 16, 1676, called for the establishment of an *hôpital général* in every city of the kingdom.[16]

Who were thought to benefit from sojourns in such places of confinement? An extraordinary variety of human types, it would seem, from the inhabitants of Paris who found their way into the Hôpital général: felons, debauchers, libertines, blasphemers, lunatics, spendthrift fathers, prodigal sons, childbearing women, cripples and incurables, beggars, discarded infants, homeless juveniles, and homeless old people. Although the Paris institution attempted to segregate its inmates by some rough rule of sex and age, this was often a haphazard affair: thus the unit known as the Salpétrière, intended for women and girls, included old men and young boys as well, and among the females a gallimaufry of types from raving lunatics to sick mothers.[17]

In the seventeenth and eighteenth centuries, respectable society in Western Europe tended to show less and less tolerance for the visibility of people it considered deviant and unruly. Outcasts and marginal persons were, if not a physical threat, then at least a source of shame; it hardly mattered whether they were felons or debtors, drunkards or lunatics, provided they were removed from respectable society and incarcerated. A great evil of European houses of confinement, as the English reformer John Howard pointed out in the last quarter of the eighteenth century, was this indiscriminate mixing of inmates.[18]

The theory and practice of confinement were rich in contradictions, paradoxes, and ironies. We have already noted the irony of converting a palace or a convent into a house of correction. In fact, most jails in mid-eighteenth-century Europe were forbidding places, viewed from both outside and inside. None in England had been built especially for the purpose of housing miscreants unless one includes the castle dungeon. The types of structure put to use included the cellar of a house and the gatehouse in a city wall—Newgate, for example. On the other hand, there were a few places of confinement, almost palatial in grandeur, which had been built with a sense of communal pride. Paris's Hôpital général was the supreme example. Its scale and prestige inspired the construction of London's new Bethlehem Hospital for the insane, which opened in 1676. This asylum—New Bedlam—was much admired in its time. The diarist John Evelyn considered it "very magnificent." Foreign visitors were lavish with praise. Soon after its opening, a ballad writer produced a broadsheet of a hundred lines entitled "Bethlehem's Beauty, London's Charity, and the City's Glory."[19] The institution, however, embodied glaring contradictions. One was between the splendid architectural exterior and the putrid cells, the chains, irons, and whips, to be found within. Another, equally painful now that we are aware of it, yawned between the degraded state of the mad people and their popularity as a tourist attraction. In the seventeenth century and early part of the eighteenth, the lunatic was viewed as the lowliest human creature, someone reduced almost to a state of pure animality though still possessing a soul that could be saved. Where the criminal and the madman were confined together, pity went to the crimi-

nal for the company he had to keep. Yet not only the rabble but
the most refined members of society flocked into Bedlam for
entertainment. Just as people in our day might cruelly tease
animals caged in the zoo, so in this earlier era visitors to Bedlam
deliberately tried to enrage the inmates chained to their cells, or
intoxicate them with gin so as to obtain more grotesque perfor-
mances. Before its doors were finally closed to the public in 1770,
Bethlehem Hospital came to admit 96,000 visitors annually. Re-
ceipts from the gates supported the institution.[20]

Of the different classes of disreputable people confined behind
bars, only lunatics attracted regular troops of curious viewers.
Felons, beggars, and vagabonds in their cells had no special
appeal. Prisons were shunned; they aroused uneasiness if not
fear. In England, since at least the fifteenth century, the term
"gaol fever" was in use and spoken in dread: it was applied
loosely to the sicknesses that almost invariably overcame prison
inmates. Parliament made halfhearted attempts to curtail the
virulence of jail fever in the seventeenth century, to little effect.
It remained a common affliction more than a century later. Why
did it persist, seemingly ineradicable? For answer, Dr. William
Smith, writing in 1776, pointed an accusing finger at the prison's
layout and its deplorable state of maintenance. The cells of some
prisons were underground; into them "prisoners were lowered,
to fight with rats for the meagre pittance of food thrown to them
through a trap-door." Often the cells were damp or even had
their floors covered by several inches of water. Prisons had no
chimneys, no fireplaces, no beds but bundles of straw, and these
were left unchanged so long that they reeked with "foul exhala-
tions."[21] From John Howard's survey of continental Europe, it is
clear that the prisons there were no better.

People, of course, had good reason to fear imprisonment:
dreadful things happened behind prison walls. In the middle of
the eighteenth century, however, both the English and the
French suddenly saw the places of confinement as sources of an
evil that could not be contained; it would spread and threaten the
city even if the felons remained behind bars. The fear was of an
undifferentiated rottenness both physical and moral. It was felt
that the violence and degradation of the prisons and asylums
generated a poisonous air that could be smelled hundreds of
yards away. The idea of fermentation, then new to science,
added to the suspicion. All kinds of noxious vapors and corrosive
liquids might be brewing in the confined spaces of the wards,
from which they would surely escape to attack neighboring residential areas.

More than localized jail fever was feared. A specific event intensified England's apprehension of what could be an uncontrollable evil. In April 1750, two diseased prisoners from Newgate infected the Old Bailey where they were standing trial. Fifty people died as a result, including the judge, the jury, the lawyers, and many spectators. "This disaster convinced the Corporation of London to set about negotiating with Whitehall for financial assistance in rebuilding what Sheriff Janssen had called 'that abominable sink of Beastliness and Corruption.' "[22] When an epidemic spread through Paris in 1780, citizens were so convinced that the infection had come from the Hôpital général that they talked of burning down the buildings of Bicêtre.[23]

Old Europe was a mixture of splendor and decay; across the Atlantic lay a fresh New World. How did the expediency of confinement evolve in North America during the colonial period and in the early decades of American independence? The story, well told by David Rothman, differs from and yet resembles the European experience.[24] In the early colonial period, institutions of confinement could hardly be said to exist. The houses of correction that began to proliferate in Europe by the second half of the seventeenth century found no echo in the New World. The main reason was that poverty did not overwhelm local communities; families took care of their own dependents. Only a handful of towns maintained an almshouse, and they used it as a last resort. New York opened a multipurpose asylum in 1736. It was a "Poor-House, Work-House, and House of Correction." The mildly insane were also admitted and worked along with the other inmates. Discipline differed little from that of a normal household, and indeed the architecture of the institution simulated that of an ordinary residence. The same could be said of the Boston almshouse and of similar asylums elsewhere. They usually stood well within the town boundary, and lacked anything distinctive in either appearance or governing procedures. Jails of the colonial period also resembled the household in structure and routine. They were not designed to intimidate criminals. Escapes were easy and frequent.

On the other hand, it is evident that colonial America retained many of the attitudes of the Old World toward criminals, vagabonds, and lunatics. Physical punishment was harsh and included the stocks, the pillory, and the gallows, which were all standard furniture in settlements of some size. Rigorous codes were passed to confine beggars and vagabonds. In the New York colony, the code of 1683 empowered town constables to return drifters to "the county from whence they came." Regulations against vagrancy were reinforced in 1721.

Treatment of the severely insane resembled that of Europe. The first general hospital in colonial America, the Pennsylvania Hospital, opened its doors to patients in 1756. The mentally ill were confined to the cellar. They were often chained to iron rings fixed on the floor or wall of their cells. The keeper carried a whip and used it freely. Lunatics were regarded as wild animals. Local people entertained their out-of-town guests by bringing them to observe and tease the mad people. A cruel fantasy of the time was that the insane, like wild beasts, were insensitive to weather and therefore could be kept in their cells naked. The enlightened Dr. Benjamin Rush fought against this sadistic practice, but he was hardly free of the notion that mad people were subhuman. He believed, for example, that the insane could be "tamed" by the total deprivation of food, citing in support of his idea the fact that in India wild elephants were subdued by denying them victuals until they became thin shadows of their former selves. He also suggested that the methods used in breaking wild horses be applied to violent patients.[25]

According to Rothman, two major changes in penal thought occurred in the period between Independence and the Civil War. From Independence to the first decade of the nineteenth century, Americans under the influence of Enlightenment ideas sought to curtail physical punishment, especially the use of the gallows, in favor of a graduated system of incarceration that matched the severity of the offense. Fear of certain imprisonment rather than of the uncertain application of the gallows was to deter crime. During this period, emphasis was placed on the need to reform the legal system and to introduce prisons as its material arm. But how confinement might affect inmates and the free society outside the prisons received little attention.

In the second decade of the nineteenth century, the focus of American penal thought shifted from the legal system to deviants and the penitentiary. Between the 1820s and the Civil War the philosophy and construction of places of confinement underwent changes that were revolutionary, idealistic, and rich in irony. A key idea of the time was that society, not sin, bred crime. And how did Americans of the Jacksonian era view their society? They were proud and yet also deeply disturbed: proud because they had abandoned the cruelties of the recent past, and disturbed because they could see virtue in the earlier social order, in the stable communities and fixed ranks that their predecessors enjoyed but which were challenged in their own day.

Society seemed on the verge of chaos. It was felt that youngsters without the support and discipline of their beleaguered families could easily succumb to the numerous temptations of the town: taverns, theaters filled with dissolute customers, houses of prostitution, and streets whose habitués included many thieves and drunkards.[26]

What could be done? One might try to shut down taverns and houses of ill repute. An alternative solution was to create a special setting for deviants: remove them from the society that had corrupted them and put them in a corruption-free environment, namely, a prison. Such an ideal setting called for almost total isolation and the strictest discipline. It would obviously be foolish to remove criminals from their depraved surroundings only to expose them to the evil influence of other convicts. They must be set apart from fellow prisoners as well as from the outside world; not even their own families should visit them. Obedience was to be absolute, and the whip freely applied.

A striking tenet of the reformist faith at this time was the belief in the power of architecture to change human personality. Reformers exerted themselves, and spared no expense, in creating physical settings that they felt would re-educate the fallen creatures by regulating their time and space down to the most minute details. Architecture was exalted as an important moral science. The intricate interior of the penitentiary reflected the need for isolation and control. The massive exterior conveyed a sense of power. Prisons in the Jacksonian era, usually built in a pastoral setting, looked like medieval castles surrounded by their demesnes.

There can be little doubt that citizens were proud of their penal institutions, which attracted not only local tourists but distinguished reformers and writers from abroad, including Alexis de Tocqueville. By the 1830s, American penitentiaries had become world-famous.[27] It is strange, to say the least, that a country that boasted of its freedom also offered its ruthlessly controlled prisons for the world's admiration. Indeed, some proponents of the penitentiary were so taken with their creation that they suggested it as a worthy model for the wider society. Almshouses and workhouses, they thought, would clearly benefit from the arrangements of the idealized prison; furthermore, in the opinion of the Boston Prison Discipline Society, such arrangements could also "greatly promote order, seriousness, and purity in large families, male and female boarding schools, and colleges."[28]

Before 1800, the mildly insane were taken care of by their families in their homes, or at public expense in almshouses along with sick paupers. The severely afflicted were treated as criminals if they committed acts of violence, or as subhuman creatures to be tamed either in confinement at home or in the cellar of a hospital. Enlightenment ideas as well as the beliefs and practical charity of the Quakers eventually transformed attitudes toward the treatment of the mentally deranged. In 1792, the year in which the physician and reformer Philippe Pinel dramatically freed the insane from their chains at Bicêtre, was also the year in which the Quakers of York, England, established the Retreat, a hospital for mental defectives operated along humane lines. In 1817, the Quakers of Pennsylvania opened an asylum in Frankford which was inspired by the York Retreat.[29] Until around 1820, however, steps taken to improve asylums were mostly private and haphazard; thereafter, they became far more ambitious, systematic, and public. By 1850, almost every Northeastern and Midwestern legislature supported an asylum; in 1860, twenty-eight of the thirty-three states had public institutions for the insane.

What brought about the change? The change is less surprising if it is seen as part of the broad move toward confinement as a solution to society's problems in the Jacksonian era. Under Enlightenment and Quaker influence, insane people were being treated more humanely, but Americans began to see that gentle care did not necessarily lead to cure, and by the 1830s they came to believe that insanity was increasing. What was the cause? Influential opinion, medical and political, did not doubt that insanity had organic and biochemical roots, but they were even more convinced that the primary cause lay in the chaotic nature of society. Europeans had long suspected a link between civilization and madness, but Americans, with their strong antiurban bias, boosted the suspicion into a doctrine. Fast-paced and turbulent town life, social mobility, the intellectual challenge of political participation, and the agonies of choice in religious freedom —all these had put too great a strain on the mind. The mad, to be cured, must be removed from the startlingly fluid social order of the new republic and placed in an isolated and specially created environment of order and disciplined routine.

The cure, as with the reformation of criminals, was architectural and administrative. Insane asylums multiplied. They jutted above flat rural landscapes and the small houses of new suburbs. Their sturdy walls became familiar landmarks in pre-Civil War America. Improvements occurred within the asylums;

prison architects no longer thought it necessary to have dark cells in the basement.[30] Treatment of patients in the 1830s and 1840s was often benign. Medical superintendents abolished whips and chains, substituting a highly regimented life based on the studious performance of manual tasks. No doubt the mental hospital was repressive in the extreme. Its ponderous appearance, so different from that of ordinary houses, symbolized the power of a totalitarian system. Yet the power was intended to restore order to the mentally deranged; and the hospital, in both its physical design and its administration, had some of the characteristics of a rigidly organized "utopian community" that sought to distance itself from the incessant and conflicting demands of the world.

A new nation in the New World might have its quota of felons and mad people but, surely, not of dissolute paupers. During the seventeenth and eighteenth centuries American settlers did not in fact show much concern with the problems of destitution. By English standards, the number of indigents dependent on public charity was small. As late as 1814 the influential journalist Hezekiah Niles pointed out that the Philadelphia Almshouse, which sheltered some 700 paupers, would have had to care for 18,000 if poverty had been as prevalent in that city as it was in England.[31]

Early in the nineteenth century, however, a change in perception occurred. Americans acquired a new sensitivity to pauperism as a social problem and as a potential source of unrest. The poor must somehow be regulated and made productive. Respectable people manifested little sympathy for able-bodied paupers, whom they regarded as lazy, weak-willed, and intemperate. Society did not hold itself to blame for them as it did—to a degree —for felons and lunatics. Society in the larger sense was, of course, guilty of providing temptations in the form of taverns, grog shops, and gambling halls, but respectable people believed that no matter how few the taverns or how well hidden the gambling halls, the poor would locate them with a diligence they had never demonstrated in finding a job. What would a solution be? Not surprisingly, in this area as in so many others the American answer in the Jacksonian period was confinement. In the first three decades of the nineteenth century the number of poorhouses swelled rapidly, first in Massachusetts and New York, then in the New England, Middle Atlantic, and Midwestern states. In the Middle West the appeal of confining the poor was so great that almshouses were established in settlements that had scarcely any poor to occupy them.[32]

The American experiment with confinement enjoyed, at best, only temporary success. An idealized setting in which the criminal, the lunatic, or the pauper could be re-educated through disciplined labor had a chance to endure only if it were small and received dedicated support from the community. Such was rarely the case. As the number of deviants and paupers increased, institutions quickly became overcrowded and were forced to change character. The Hartford Retreat, which opened in 1824, could accommodate 40 patients, but an estimated total of 1,000 insane persons required care in Connecticut. The Boston House of Industry, erected in 1823, was intended to be a model institution for the employment of the able-bodied poor. Only ten years later, it became a catchall place for the sick, the insane, and destitute children.[33] During the 1850s, almost every type of asylum was losing its special qualities, and by the 1870s few traces remained of the original designs.[34] The orderly world that was to be created behind walls yielded, or threatened to give way, to near chaos. The idea of moral treatment or reform faded as custodians were increasingly preoccupied with the simple maintenance of security. By the end of the nineteenth century the hulking shapes of asylums, no longer draped in an idealistic mantle, stood naked in the landscape as objects of embarrassment and revulsion.

Incarcerating deviants did not solve society's problems. What better devices are available? The prevailing wisdom of the twentieth century is to return felons, and since the 1950s the mentally retarded and the insane, to the bosom of society at the earliest justifiable occasion.[35] The prison with its fortresslike walls and guard towers still stands as an awesome reminder of an earlier belief in reform through confinement. It is now being replaced by a new ideal, partly prompted by shame, of invisibility: thus a modern prison may, from a distance, look like a high school, or it is low-slung and tucked into the hill slopes so that it can barely be seen from the highway.[36]

15.

The Open Circle

We seek security and are curious: this describes not only human beings but all higher animals. "Security" and "curiosity" have a common root in the Latin *cura,* which means anxiety, care, medical care, and cure. In a secure place we are cared for and are without care. But never wholly without care, for the world is full of surprises. Moreover, we know, as all higher animals know by virtue of their brain and distant sensors, that there is always another world beyond whatever space we have encircled, conquered, and made safely our own. To be curious is to feel anxiety and the need to dissolve that anxiety with further inquisitiveness. If temporary, surprise and anxiety can be pleasant as long as we have ultimate control. The infant, from the safety of its crib, enjoys surprise and takes pleasure in games of peek-a-boo. The toddler seeks the thrill of exploration, using the mother as a point of departure. Children delight in disorientation—tumbling, swinging, or hanging upside down from the limbs of trees. Adults, well fed and secure in their work world, seek pleasurable stress—"eustress"—the happiness that comes from overcoming fear in risky sports such as mountain climbing.[1] Risk should be differentiated from danger. Experienced climbers abhor danger while welcoming risk, because risk presents difficulties that can be estimated and controlled.

> The north face of the Eiger [in the Bernese Alps] is often tried despite its formidable death toll, because the accidents have been due primarily to the climber's failure. By contrast, Marinelli Gully, whose avalanches have killed many, does not have the same attraction. The manageable risks that make a route difficult do attract climbers, while the uncontrollable dangers do not.[2]

Insofar as we survive, we have known security. The size and character of that secure world vary enormously from person to person. The healthier individuals are, the bigger and more complex is the stage on which they act with confidence. To schizophrenics and other sufferers from mental illness, on the other hand, life's supportive stage is narrow and fragile indeed. A survey of the landscapes of fear will seem incomplete without a brief tour of the confined circles of the mentally ill, for whom security is an insistent concern and the urge toward adventure seldom—if ever—arises.

At the Henry Ittleson Center, schizophrenic children (eight to twelve years old) find it difficult to experience both the self and the world as continuous in time and space. The children are confused and apprehensive. They make repeated attempts to stabilize a world that lacks unity, continuity, and permanence. Few things can be taken for granted; nothing is truly familiar. Clues for time are hard for them to interpret. When the sky is overcast and lights are turned on in the living room, is it day or night? Insecurity with "time" forces schizophrenic children to become excessively concerned with it. All their waking hours are secretly accounted for and any interference, delay, or alteration of their timetables may cause acute anxiety, which is frequently manifested in outbursts of anger.

Space and visual forms are often equally elusive to disturbed children. They cannot readily apprehend the most common visual cues. Though eyes, as our distant sensors, open up the world for us and effectively structure space, schizophrenic children seem to distrust this faculty. They make only reluctant use of sight and visual thinking, preferring the security of the proximate sensors—touch, smell, and taste. Because the perceptual world of these young patients is so lacking in natural stability and familiarity, they try to compensate with encyclopedic knowledge. They turn into compulsive geographers. They are preoccupied with maps and clocks, and ask endless questions about where things are and when. They become experts in factual information of the kind recorded on street maps and in bus schedules.

Large open spaces, which encourage aimless, vortical, anxiety-laden movements, have no place in any institution designed to help such mentally disturbed children. At the Ittleson Center, the open land surrounding the building is partitioned to advance purposive activities. Fences are erected to define small areas, each of which has a clearly assigned function: this is a bicycle area, that is a garden area. Interior space, too, is carefully delineated according to function and purpose. In all communication to the children, regarding space and time, the stress is on complete clarity. The children need to draw closed, safe circles around themselves; the open circle, the boundless area, and any space with ambiguous edges provoke anxiety rather than pleasurable excitement.[3]

Schizophrenic adults suffer in a like manner. A schizophrenic man sits in a simply furnished room, looks at the window or at the light fixture, and asks, "What's that for?" The boundary between self and environment is infirm, and that between fantasy and perception can, at times, dissolve altogether. A woman patient says, "The wall is moving . . . I don't know what's wrong with my hands, but I can't keep them still," as if her hands, like the walls, were uncontrollable inanimate objects. A male patient believes he is well and should return to the outside world, but once in a while he is alarmed by the sensation that the building he is in might fall. The fragility of his own ego is projected onto the external environment.[4]

Victims of agoraphobia are better off than sufferers from acute schizophrenia because with agoraphobics a more or less stable world does exist, and that is the home; so long as they stay within that charmed circle they feel competent—only beyond it is the frightening public space, the *agora*. One symptom of this affliction is the fear of crossing any large and open space. The sufferer feels dizzy, as though his body, like the space stretching before it, were about to lose its center and limits. If there is a wall and he can edge along it, the distress is somewhat eased; likewise if he can open his umbrella and walk under its small dome.[5] The agoraphobic's greatest fear is the loss of control. In public space, whether open and empty or closed and packed with people, he dreads the possibility of fainting, dying, or making a mess of himself. A long journey on a crowded train is a nightmare unless the train stops frequently and the sufferer knows he has ready access to the toilet.[6]

Decline into schizophrenia is often preceded by a growing sense of "queerness" in everything. Objects come to have a "deeper meaning"; they seem mysterious and sinister. Such is not the world of the normal child and adult, and yet it does have something in common with the world of exceptionally gifted people. They ask strange questions. What we take for granted they find queer; what we accept as stable and closed they perceive as changing and open. Unlike schizophrenic patients, however, geniuses welcome—or, at least, are highly tolerant of —uncertainty. The circle is breached, but they believe it can be healed at a higher level of generalization.

For geniuses, venturing beyond the familiar circle entails, of course, the risk of pushing to the edge of madness. Blaise Pascal, certainly a genius, is widely known for writing, "The eternal silence of these infinite spaces frightens me." To the schizophrenic at one extreme and to someone like Pascal at the other, the world is vast, unstable, and frightening. Pascal spoke for fearful people when he wrote:

> We sail within a vast sphere, ever drifting in uncertainty, driven from end to end. When we think to attach ourselves to any point and to fasten to it, it wavers and leaves us; and if we follow it, it eludes our grasp, slips past us, and vanishes for ever. Nothing stays for us. This is our natural condition, and yet most contrary to our inclination; we burn with desire to find solid ground and an ultimate sure foundation whereon to build a tower reaching to the Infinite. But our whole groundwork cracks, and the earth opens to abysses.[7]

Where is this solid ground we all yearn to find? Most people do not share Pascal's metaphysical anguish. Simply to survive, a faith in the trustworthiness of the space we occupy seems essential. Culture reinforces that faith. The degree to which culture is used for this reinforcement varies from group to group. Some peoples must establish a precisely articulated framework (mental and material) before they feel secure. The Balinese are an example. They display a seemingly inordinate need to be oriented. Their spatial frame, set to the cardinal points, is specific, is symbolically potent, and affects all aspects of their lives: it dictates, for example, the location of the village, of every houseyard and family shrine, and inside the house, of where people sleep. The Balinese dread disorientation. To be sick is to be *paling,* that is, disoriented. Although they appreciate a lively party and use spirits, they dislike drunkenness, for it means the loss of clues to the framework of life (the directions, the calendar, the caste system) that gives safety to adults in the same manner that the walking rail reassures young Balinese children. When a villager loses his bearings as he is taken for a motorcar ride, he quickly becomes anxious and may fall sick for several hours or enter deep sleep. The idea of deliberately seeking "eustress," of exploring the unknown, could not be farther from the thoughts of a Balinese villager.[8]

In Navaho dogma, good is control. Evil is the indefinite and that which is not ritually under control. Few things are wholly bad because nearly everything can be managed, and when it is, the evil effect disappears. Things predominantly evil such as snakes, lightning, and thunder may thus be transformed into good and even invoked as powers in the service of good. Such belief is widely shared—perhaps universal. The Navahos are distinctive in making it explicit. A ritual prescribes the control of space. Exorcists use evil chants to disperse evil, the farther away the better, the idea being that the more space encircles evil the less its power. It is not enough to simply drive out evil; good must be enticed with holy chants to fill the vacated space. Whatever is foreign and indefinite, being outside the Navaho's mastery, is bad. Closed circles are satisfyingly complete; and if they are small and therefore subject to control they are good. The healing hoop drawn on the ground is such a circle; in it is concentrated power which the patient can absorb. But the Navaho is also afraid of the closed circle. Evil may be trapped in it, and once trapped it cannot get out, nor can good enter. For this reason the Navaho favors the open circle.[9]

Cultures differ in the ways they define space, but define it they must. The minimum requirement for security is to establish a boundary, which may be material or conceptual and ritually enforced. Boundaries are everywhere, obviously so in landscapes of fences, fields, and buildings, but equally there in the worlds of primitive peoples. Boundaries exist on different scales. Minimally and perhaps universally, three are recognized: the boundaries of the domain, of the house, and of the body.

In the Western world the limits of a domain could be established by an ancient practice known, in Britain, as "beating the bounds." Legend has it that the founding of Rome required the drawing of a magical circle around the city to exclude all malevolent powers, including wolves and influences that caused barrenness. The ritual came to be called the Lupercalia, and was celebrated every year on February 15.[10] Under Christian auspices "beating the bounds," led by parish priests or village elders, continued to be a viable custom in isolated parts of Western Europe until the Second World War. Other cultures have similar procedures for defining a domain. In Bali, for example, the dragon dance encircles the village and thereby creates an area of safety.

The house is bounded space, but it has openings that must be protected. The Greeks put pitch on their doors as prophylactic against ghosts and demons; the Chinese use auspicious words and effigies of gate gods; the Temne of Sierra Leone employ the *kanta,* consisting of roots and barks of a plant and holy sentences from the Koran, to guard not only the farm and the house but also vulnerable openings—doors—within the house;[11] and the hillfolk of the Ozarks nail a horseshoe to the door, or drive three nails into it to form a triangle representing the Father, the Son, and the Holy Ghost.[12]

Finally, there is the human body itself with its apertures through which evil can enter. The mouth is notably exposed. The Athenian chewed buckthorn during the dangerous period known as the Anthesteria to prevent evil spirits from penetrating and possessing the body. The Balinese are exceptionally sensitive to the vulnerability of the mouth. Covering gestures with the palm or with a shawl show how almost constantly they feel the need to guard this opening. Betel-chewing is another way to diminish the aperture, as is putting a great wad of shredded tobacco into the mouth.[13] In Western society it is impolite to leave the mouth open while chewing. The food that enters the body nourishes but it can also cause indigestion and sickness; in the fifteenth century children were told to make the sign of the cross over the mouth before they ate.

We draw boundaries and protect their apertures. Nonetheless security is not absolute. Horror is the sudden awareness of betrayal and death in the inner sanctum of our refuge. In his story "The Masque of the Red Death," Edgar Allan Poe plays cleverly on this fear. No doubt something like what Poe describes has happened repeatedly in the past when bubonic plague besieged a city: the gates were closed, archers stood guard over them, and within the walls citizens danced in the illusion of security—until the disease suddenly appeared in their midst.

Fear of betrayal and of entrapped evil goes far deeper than historic experiences of this kind. It may well be that a desire for self-destruction lies buried in the core of our being, that the overpowering urge to live and grow is periodically vitiated by a longing for death. It is even more certain that the idea of betrayal is a lesson indelibly learned in early childhood. The mother is at the center of the small child's world, an ever dependable presence, a fount of love and nurture. Yet, unaccountably, she can turn into a threatening and punishing figure—a witch.

A basic fact of the human condition is the child's vulnerability, the long period of dependence on the parent; another fact, equally basic, is the need for adults to cooperate in order to survive and sustain a world. Nature's many challenges and threats could be met only when human beings banded together and exerted their power. Houses, granaries, and irrigation ditches are visible tokens of the human effort to control nature's vagaries, and the effort has been so successful that in a technological society nature seldom arouses fear. In the United States, natural disasters such as floods and tornadoes kill some 600 people a year, a small figure indeed when compared with the 55,000 annual deaths caused by traffic accidents.[14] This is a striking illustration of the predicament under which humans labor. Success over nature comes when people live together in large numbers and cooperate, but the greater the concentration of people in one place the greater is the likelihood of disorder and violence from within. The densely packed houses that keep out the weather may be incubators of contagious disease; the city wall that fends off external enemies encloses disaffected groups and individuals who periodically erupt in violence. Collective human power, once turned against nature, may be turned against the marginal and volatile elements of society, creating a landscape of punishment, or, more subtly, a vast system of bureaucratic control as powerful, arbitrary, and inaccessible as nature itself before it was subdued.

16.

Fears: Past and Present

Many people even in the modern and affluent Western world are haunted by fear. Almost daily we read about muggings and murders, and about elderly residents of the inner cities so afraid that they are virtually prisoners within their own homes. While well-educated young people do not usually live in dread of physical violence, more nebulous threats plague their lives. They often appear to be anxious about the future, their own as well as that of humanity. They have the uncomfortable feeling that "things are getting worse"; the future promises not only further deterioration of the inner cities but ecological crisis, racial tension, world famine, and nuclear disaster.

Such contemporary fears encourage the strong human bent to postulate a better—or at least much safer—world either sometime in the past or at a distant sheltered place. In extreme reaction we might deliberately slight the real achievements of the modern age, such as sanitation, and find something admirable in the horrors of the past, such as the ubiquity of pain and the capacity to bear it. John Wain, in his recent biography of Samuel Johnson, looked longingly to the comeliness of eighteenth-century landscapes, compared with which the modern English scene, ugly and begrimed, seems a desecration. However, Wain has to admit that there was an incongruous element in that vanished world of great beauty, namely, its large number of diseased and disfigured people and animals.[1] Many humanists today bemoan the banishment of all evidences of death from the modern town. Where are the picturesque graveyards that once lay among the houses of the living? Where are those realistic and healthy reminders of mortality? But these humanists conveniently forget that the graveyard was at the center of the old

European village because death occupied the center stage of life.[2]

We wish to know whether fear in the past differed in kind, intensity, and frequency from that of our time. The question bristles with difficulties. Fear is not only objective circumstance but also subjective response. A landscape of gallows and gibbets is, objectively, a landscape of fear. Certainly gibbets were put up for the purpose of inducing fear, and we do hear of people trying to avoid them when they traveled at night. On the other hand, in much of Europe, these ghastly instruments of execution had come to be accepted as a normal component of the urban and rural scene. They served as mere landmarks—like village ponds and windmills—in old road books. The historian Lynn White notes that in the fifteenth century, "Parisians liked to go on picnics to the Montfaucon gibbet outside the city where they could revel under the shredding remains of the dead."[3] We are shocked and uncomprehending. Yet instances of such barbarity can easily be multiplied. If we are doubtful that any moral progress has occurred in the history of the West, we should ask: What practices that we accept as normal today would deeply offend the moral sensibility of our ancestors? Would it be the cramped and seedy rest homes for the aged, the long prison sentences, the slums, the violence on television? Surely not, except perhaps in their magnitude.

Former fears may be closely bound up with values that we now consider good. This is a possible source of confusion when we try to compare fears of the past with those of the present. For instance, we sometimes lament the desacralization of nature. Woods, mountains, and streams were once the abodes of spirits and as such commanded respect and even fear. We have seen, for example, how the ancient Greek landscape was dotted with shrines to nature deities and to the spirits of dead heroes. Their departure from the landscape can seem to us a loss, a draining of power from the natural world so that its features are now merely pleasing rather than awesome. In fantasy, we long for the return of the guardian spirits of place, but could they re-enter nature and our lives alone, unaccompanied by demons and ghosts? Within the Christian tradition, a strong belief in angels has always been coupled with a strong belief in the dark forces of Satan. Those vivid landscapes of the past had bright patches of sunlight but also deep shadows.

In comparing fears of earlier times with those of our day, a further possible source of confusion lies in our failure to recognize the profoundly ambivalent nature of the communal ideal.

We often lament the looseness of human ties in the modern world, and yearn for that intimacy of human bonds that once existed (we feel) among members of a family, a neighborhood, a village or town. We forget that fear was and is a common reason for weaving close human ties. Remove the threats of environment, whether they be the forces of nature or human enemies, and the bonds of community tend to weaken. As an illustration, consider the nature of the family bond in the Mâcon country of France in the Middle Ages. The historian Georges Duby notes that the family in the ninth century was reduced to its simplest expression, the conjugal cell. Blood ties were very loose because they served no defensive or offensive purpose. "The peaceful organs of the old Frank state were still strong enough to allow a freeman to live an independent life and to prefer, if he so wished, the company of his friends and neighbours to that of his relatives." But after 1000, the dissolution of the state obliged people to form more closely knit and exclusive groups for protection. Nobles and knights sought refuge in family lineages and the bonds of blood, whereas peasants found security by strengthening the social webs within a village.[4] At the scale of the city, we have seen how certain Italian towns of the late medieval period consisted of fortified family nuclei. No doubt intense loyalty existed within each protected neighborhood of medieval Rome or Florence, but the bonds were clearly forged out of need and fear. At the scale of the nation-state, it is well known that citizens can develop a fervent sense of cohesiveness and national purpose under the threat of an external enemy. Thus, from the family to the nation-state, ties of community can be seen to wax and wane with fear. A cooling of passion and a loosening of communal bonds—though not necessarily of individual friendships—appear to be the price we have to pay for living in a world that has in some ways grown more secure.

Without doubt, fear of wild nature has greatly diminished throughout the world in modern times. "Wilderness" once signified a demonic power utterly beyond human control; now it is a fragile web of life needing human protection and care. We find it hard to think of vegetation as a menace. Yet it was such to primitive farmers who struggled to keep their plots from being overcome by weeds that seemed to move in with malignant intent. In the modern world, wild animals are protected. Very rarely, a bear mauls an unsuspecting visitor in an American national park and reminds us of dangers that we now encounter only in childhood tales. Storms and floods still cause vast damage to property, but in the developed Western countries so few lives are lost that people cannot easily be persuaded to take commonsensical precautions. Perhaps only a major earthquake, or the threat of one, is now capable of arousing the sort of terror that nearly all natural rampages could once provoke. When the earth itself trembles, we suddenly feel deprived of an ultimate source of security. Still, major earthquakes seldom occur. Californians, many of whom have houses built on active faults, are more likely to live in dread of economic than of geologic tremors. If the educated people of the Western world can still be said to fear nature, it is the paradoxical fear that plants and animals, even rivers and lakes, may die through human abuse. The fragility of nature, not its power, now makes us almost constantly anxious.

Every major human achievement appears to be attended by a feeling of unease, as though success might inflame the envy of the gods who alone have the right to create; or as though it had been forged at the expense of nature, which might then take revenge. The city is one such major human achievement. Building that artifactitious world, necessarily at the expense of the natural environment, aroused feelings of anxiety and guilt in ancient times. Consider the capital of Shang China (ca. 1500 B.C.). It was a city for the living as well as for the dead, the dead being the human sacrifices that were buried beneath every important edifice—indeed, beneath every pillar of an important edifice. As the buildings rose skyward, the spirits of the earth had to be propitiated.[5] The ancient Hebrews also appear to have doubted the propriety of great aspirations. In Genesis, we read that when Noah's descendants attempted to build a city in the land of Shinar and thus bring heaven to earth by their own strength, the jealous God intervened. He not only dispersed the builders, but made them speak in mutually incomprehensible tongues so that they could never congregate in sufficient numbers to form a great and proud society.

Success engenders pride, and pride is destined to meet, sooner or later, its nemesis. All the technological triumphs of the modern age have not been able to eradicate that ancient belief. Every step that seems to take us further from our rootedness in nature has caused unease among some elements of the population. When gaslight enabled human beings to "conquer night" for the first time, a Cologne newspaper in 1816 argued that it transgressed the laws of God and of nature: "Artificial illumination is an attempt to interfere with the divine plan of the world, which has preordained darkness during the night."[6] Such expressions of doubt and anxiety have been frequent since the beginning of the industrial revolution. However, rarely was the fear of hubris as intense and widespread as it is now. Of the technical developments that have contributed to the present malaise, the most important is the harnessing of nuclear energy. It is humankind's latest spectacular effort to bring heaven to earth—that is, to re-create the processes natural only to the sun in fragile manmade containers. After many premature alarms, have we at last unchained a force we cannot control that will wreck the earth and ourselves?

Another ancient fear, as we have seen, is of other people—strangers in particular. This fear, like the fear of nature, has diminished in modern times, at least when nations are not actually at war with each other. One reason for the abatement of anxiety about strangers is the emergence of a new and more flexible attitude toward the division of human beings into "we" and "they." In contrast to most nonliterate and traditional peoples, who tend to stress the differences between "we" and "they," modern society is inclined to minimize them: thus "we" is not a net of intimate and irrevocable bonds, nor "they" a permanent class of outsiders. To function at all, a modern man or woman must learn to deal with faceless institutions and the help of strangers. Furthermore, because relations among neighbors and kin are now less intense, the fear of betrayal has also diminished. Anxieties about witches and ghosts are much more likely to occur in a close-knit community than in a loosely structured group, in which human involvement even among relatives is far too cool to require enforcement by magical-conspiratorial means or continuation beyond the grave.

Strangers, even those of alien tongue, may be looked upon with tolerance and good will, especially in complex societies in peaceful times. However, the temptation to see the other as hostile and subhuman is always present, though it may be deeply buried. Under stressful conditions, strong feelings of envy, hatred, and fear can easily exaggerate and distort the slight cultural and biological differences between people into polarities of good and evil, angel and beast. Strangers then become the enemy, who may be killed and their homes demolished with a clear conscience. What we so readily entertain in our minds, many as readily put into action if the circumstances are right. Thus the human sojourn on earth is blighted by ruthless wars, conquests, and pogroms.

The will to annihilate has been repeatedly demonstrated. In ancient Mesopotamian wars, for example, cities were razed to the ground so that even the presiding deities had to flee. In the fourth century A.D., the nomadic conquest of northern China turned that long-established agricultural country into a barren steppe. Not only were historic cities like Ch'ang-an burned and depopulated, but the fields themselves lay fallow, abandoned by the peasants. Wolves and tigers prowled the once rich valley of the Wei River around Ch'ang-an. When the remaining Chinese populace, terrified of the wild animals, appealed to the nomadic chieftain Fu Sheng for help, he refused, saying sardonically that when the beasts had their fill of flesh the peasants would be left alone.[7] In our time, we face the possibility of total destruction in a nuclear conflict between the Great Powers. Our anxious fear is aggravated by an awareness of human culpability in the past. We know that our newly won power to annihilate is grafted on a still unregenerate will and on a lingering compulsion to polarize human beings into the irreconcilable camps of "self" and "other."

Since the beginning of civilization, brutal wars have periodically decimated cities and nations. We think of such events, however, as exceptional. Between them stretched—so we imagine—long periods of quietude in which peoples of earlier ages lived drowsily through their unvarying patterns of life. Compared with such an image of the past, our times seem to lack stability: both the physical environment and sociocultural values appear to be constantly shifting. We have no sense of permanence either in locality or in human relations. Yet what reason do we actually have to think that the world is now less stable—more full of unexpected and threatening events—than in the past? The Chinese peasantry of the nineteenth century lived in a traditional world, and "traditional" implies routine, the calm of predictable cycles. Yet few livelihoods were less secure than theirs. Could even five years lapse without a major disruption of their world by a natural disaster or civil strife? Some historians would have us believe that a contented people with well-adjusted personalities inhabited seventeenth-century England, free from the stressful uncertainties and conflicts of modern life. But, to judge from the diary of the clergyman-farmer Josselin, nothing could be further from the truth. Josselin was insecure and anxiety-ridden, and spoke almost constantly of accident, pain, and death. Though he earned an adequate living, he had good reason to be afraid for himself and for his family. His world, in fact, lacked stability: weather threatened his crops; a fire might not only kill his children but make him a pauper overnight, for of course there was no protection in the form of fire insurance; and, without modern remedies, even a small mishap such as pricking the thumb with a thistle might lead to gangrene and a painful death.[8]

In earlier ages, if physical circumstances were insecure, at least human relations enjoyed a degree of permanence unknown to modern times. That was the rock on which confidence and a sense of well-being could be built. So we fondly think. However, this too may be a myth. Death so often broke up human ties that people might have been inhibited from investing deep feelings and sympathies in them. We have noted how, before the eighteenth century, European parents often showed an apparent lack of devotion to their infants and young children. Infant mortality was extremely high. Why spend time and love on a child who might soon depart? Of youngsters who survived childhood accidents and diseases, few lived on to old age; those who did commanded the respect due to champions. We forget that two or three centuries ago it was rare for parents to live long enough to see the marriage of their offspring. Marriage itself was sacred and permanent, but what did permanence mean? In eighteenth-century France, a peasant couple who wed in their late twenties could reasonably look forward to a conjugal bond of only five to ten years before death would remove one partner. Widowers were then quick to remarry, widows a little less so. Divorce was hardly necessary when death so often performed the same service.[9]

The perception of rapid change in the present is subject to illusion. Two factors encourage us to discern greater changes in our own time than in earlier periods. One is that we are far more aware of the uncertainties in our own lives than in those of people who live either far away or long ago: spatial and temporal distance alone produce an illusion of stability. Another is "chronocentrism": that is, we boast of dynamism and progress in our time and relegate the past to a state of repetitive cycles in which nothing really new happened. It is a common belief that the number of technical inventions has soared without precedent in recent decades. For example, a person born in 1920 would have witnessed by now the appearance of television, computer technology, nuclear power, and space flights. This is true. On the other hand, a person born in 1860 and dying in 1920 would have seen the telephone, electric light, the automobile, the airplane, radio, and cinema. And a retiring and conservative person who lived between 1800 and 1860 would have been subjected to such unpleasant innovations as the coming of the railroad, the steamship, the telegraph, gas lighting, and the spread of factory-made clothing and household goods.[10] Even if it can be established that the pace of technical change was much slower in the earlier part of the nineteenth century, it is still possible that the people of that time experienced it as dizzyingly fast.

In the social sphere, we may rejoice in, or deplore, the striking changes that have transpired in the United States during the last two or three decades. On the other hand, are they really greater than those that occurred in the Jacksonian era—those turbulent years of population increase and social mobility which made even some idealists look back to the "fixed" social order of an earlier time with a trace of longing? To rectify our "chrono-myopia," we should read historical documents of bygone times, for we shall find in them abundant evidence of distress caused by social, economic, and even technological changes.[11]

The human mind is an ambivalent gift. It presents us with a large, orderly, and beautiful world, but also with images of chaos, evil, and death. Many contemporary fears are age-old: for instance, fear of being mugged in the city after dark. Some are new and reflect greater knowledge and growing awareness: for instance, the population "explosion," the world food crisis, the possibility of open conflict between the rich and poor nations, and grim scenarios of technological disaster.[12] People have always known food shortages and famines, but they usually confronted them as present realities in this or that place, not as a world-wide catastrophe yet to come. The global scale and the future tense are thus new. More and more educated citizens are anxious about the world and its future, even though they are not in serious doubt that they and their children will be comfortable and well fed. The established and the rich have always feared the poor. Again, the scale and the tense have changed. A Parisian in 1661 was afraid because he could see the beggars besieging the city gates. Today, a Parisian may well be anxious because he sees in his mind's eye the City (that is, the developed Western nations) besieged at some future time by the angry and hungry nations of the Third World.

At the personal and individual level, the critical mind un-weighted by tradition deprives modern man and woman of many beliefs that once gave comfort. Human beings are fragile, their sojourn on earth is subject to chance. Accidents, not suffering, are our most authentic *memento mori,* says Iris Murdoch. They remind us of our contingency. Anytime, our dear and familiar ways and life itself can be terminated by something totally unexpected and horrible—a fortuitous concurrence of events. I walk along the sidewalk whistling a tune; a flowerpot slips off the windowsill and falls on my head, killing me or reducing me to a vegetable. Human beings have always been aware of this element of fortuitousness, and have sought to guard against it with beliefs and devices that are as pathetic as they are ingenious, ranging from rabbit's foot to astrology. The critical person, who finds no haven in such beliefs, must learn to live in statistical uncertainty. As to death itself, it is well known that most people cannot face it except under the wraps of consoling fiction. We know the rewards of seeing clearly and well. The cost is the possibility of despair. Yet, such is the human paradox that even the refusal to be consoled by false images can become a source of comfort and strength.

Notes

1. Introduction

1. James J. Gibson, *The Senses Considered as Perceptual Systems* (Boston: Houghton Mifflin Co., 1966), p. 174.

2. T. Allison and D. V. Cicchetti, "Sleep in Mammals: Ecological and Constitutional Correlates," *Science* 194, no. 4266 (12 November 1976): 732.

3. Alex Comfort, *The Nature of Human Nature* (New York: Avon Books, 1968), pp. 70–71.

4. Konrad Lorenz, *King Solomon's Ring* (London: Methuen & Co., University Paperbacks, 1961), pp. 140, 185.

5. Bertrand Russell, *Power: A New Social Analysis* (London: George Allen & Unwin, 1963), p. 14.

6. Gustave Cohen, *Histoire de la mise en scène dans le théâtre religieux français du Moyen Age* (Paris: Honoré Champion, 1906), pp. 148–52.

2. Fear in the Growing Child

1. Vladimir Nabokov, *Speak Memory: An Autobiography Revisited* (New York: G. P. Putnam's Sons, 1966), p. 24.

2. John Bowlby, *Attachment and Loss,* vol. 1, *Attachment* (New York: Basic Books, 1969), p. 199.

3. D. G. Freedman, "The Infant's Fear of Strangers and the Flight Response," *Journal of Child Psychology and Psychiatry* 2 (1961): 242–48.

4. G. A. Morgan and H. N. Ricciuti, "Infants' Responses to Strangers During the First Year," in Brian M. Foss, ed., *Determinants of Infant Behaviour* (New York: Barnes & Noble, 1969), 4: 253–72.

5. S. Scarr and P. Salapatek, "Patterns of Fear Development During Infancy," *Merrill-Palmer Quarterly* 16 (1970): 59–90.

6. A. T. Jersild and F. B. Holmes, *Children's Fears* (New York: Bureau of Publications, Teachers College, Columbia University, 1935), p. 87.

7. H. E. Jones and M. C. Jones, "Fear," *Childhood Education* 5 (1928): 137–38.

8. J. van Lawick-Goodall, "The Behaviour of Free-Living Chimpanzees in the Gombe Stream Reserve," *Animal Behaviour Monographs* (London: Bailliere, Tindall & Cassell), vol. 1, 1968, pp. 173, 175–76.

9. R. Morris and D. Morris, *Men and Snakes* (New York: McGraw-Hill Book Co., 1965), p. 211.

10. Ibid., pp. 201–6.
11. Quoted in Malcolm A. Smith, *The British Amphibians and Reptiles* (London: William Collins Sons & Co., 1951), pp. 7–8.
12. Jersild and Holmes, *Children's Fears,* pp. 118, 124.
13. Ibid., p. 131.
14. Adapted from Carole Klein, *The Myth of the Happy Child* (New York: Harper & Row, 1975), p. xxi.
15. Alfred Kazin, *A Walker in the City* (New York: Harcourt, Brace & Co., 1951), p. 17.
16. Reported in *Los Angeles Times,* March 2, 1977, and *Time,* March 14, 1977.
17. Jean Piaget, *The Child's Conception of the World* (Totowa, N.J.: Littlefield, Adams & Co., 1969), pp. 91–112.
18. John E. Mack, *Nightmares and Human Conflict* (Boston: Little, Brown & Co., 1970), p. 60.
19. L. E. Ucko, "A Comparative Study of Asphyxiated and Non-asphyxiated Boys from Birth to Five Years," *Developmental Medicine and Child Neurology* 7 (1965): 643–57.
20. J. A. Hadfield, *Dreams and Nightmares* (Harmondsworth, Middlesex: Penguin Books, 1954), p. 184.
21. C. W. Kimmins, *Children's Dreams* (London: George Allen & Unwin, 1937), p. 22; Mack, *Nightmares and Human Conflict,* p. 67.
22. Iona and Peter Opie, *Children's Games in Street and Playground* (Oxford: Clarendon Press, 1969), pp. 106–8.
23. Klein, *Myth of the Happy Child,* p. 37.
24. Bruno Bettelheim, *The Uses of Enchantment: The Meaning and Importance of Fairy Tales* (New York: Alfred A. Knopf, 1976), p. 66.
25. *The Complete Grimm's Fairy Tales* (New York: Pantheon Books, 1972), p. 217.
26. Max Luthi, *Once Upon a Time: On the Nature of Fairy Tales* (Bloomington: Indiana University Press, Midland Books, 1976), p. 45.
27. Ibid., pp. 59–70; Bettelheim, *Uses of Enchantment,* pp. 44–45, 50–53.
28. Scarr and Salapatek, "Patterns of Fear Development," p. 85.
29. M. J. Konner, "Aspects of the Developmental Ethology of a Foraging People," in N. G. Blurton-Jones, ed., *Ethological Studies of Child Behaviour* (Cambridge: University Press, 1972), pp. 297–98.
30. Anna Apoko, "At Home in the Village: Growing Up in Acholi," in Lorene K. Fox, ed., *East African Childhood* (Nairobi: Oxford University Press, 1967), p. 56.
31. Marjorie Topley, "Cosmic Antagonism: A Mother-Child Syndrome," in Arthur P. Wolf, ed., *Religion and Ritual in Chinese Society* (Stanford, Calif.: Stanford University Press, 1974), pp. 234–38, 245.
32. Margaret Mead, *Growing Up in New Guinea* (New York: Blue Ribbon Books, 1930), pp. 7–8, 121, 126.
33. Beatrice Whiting, "Discussion" [Differences in Child Rearing Between Foragers and Nonforagers], in Richard B. Lee and Irven DeVore, eds., *Man the Hunter* (Chicago: Aldine Publishing Co., 1965), p. 337; see also H. Barry, I. Child, and M. K. Bacon, "The Relation of Child Training to Subsistence Economy," *American Anthropologist* 61 (1959): 51–63.

34. An example of individual training technique in Charles A. Eastman (Hakadah), *Indian Boyhood* (New York: Dover Publications, 1971), pp. 43–44.

35. George Devereux, "Institutionalized Homosexuality of the Mohave Indians," *Human Biology* 9 (1937): 498–527; Sue-Ellen Jacobs, "Berdache: A Brief Review of the Literature," *Colorado Anthropologist* 1 (1968): 25–40.

36. William Kessen, ed., *Childhood in China* (New Haven, Conn.: Yale University Press, 1976), pp. 69–70, 106.

37. Ibid., pp. 83–84; David C. McClelland, "Motivational Patterns in Southeast Asia with Special Reference to the Chinese Case," *Journal of Social Issues* 19 (1963): 6–19.

3. The Child as Unformed Nature

1. Seneca, *Moral Essays,* trans. J. W. Basore (Cambridge, Mass.: Harvard University Press, 1963), p. 145. References to Aristippus and Seneca in Lloyd deMause, "The Evolution of Childhood," in deMause, ed., *The History of Childhood* (New York: Harper Torchbooks, 1975), pp. 26, 27.

2. Marcus Aurelius, *Meditations,* bk. 10, sec. 35.

3. Philippe Ariès, *Centuries of Childhood: A Social History of Family Life* (New York: Vintage Books, 1965), pp. 38, 39.

4. M. Dorothy George, *London Life in the XVIIIth Century* (London: Kegan Paul, 1925), p. 43.

5. Thomas McKeown, *The Modern Rise of Population* (New York: Academic Press, 1976), p. 147.

6. William L. Langer, "Infanticide: A Historical Survey," *History of Childhood Quarterly* 1, no. 3 (1974): 359.

7. Ibid., p. 353.

8. Maria W. Piers, *Infanticide: Past and Present* (New York: W. W. Norton & Co., 1978), p. 49.

9. Ariès, *Centuries of Childhood,* pp. 365–66.

10. Claude Lévi-Strauss, *Tristes Tropiques* (New York: Atheneum Publishers, 1967), p. 170.

11. W. J. Bouwsma, "Christian Adulthood," *Daedalus* 105 (Spring 1976): 78.

12. Clifford Geertz, "Myth, Symbol, and Culture," *Daedalus* 101 (Winter 1972): 7.

13. DeMause, *History of Childhood,* p. 10.

14. Ariès, *Centuries of Childhood,* pp. 315–19.

15. DeMause, *History of Childhood,* pp. 37–39.

16. Morton Schatzman, "Paranoia or Persecution: The Case of Schreber," *History of Childhood Quarterly* 1, no. 1 (1973): 67–70.

17. Margaret Mead, "Children and Ritual in Bali," in Margaret Mead and Martha Wolfenstein, eds., *Childhood in Contemporary Cultures* (Chicago: University of Chicago Press, 1955), p. 42.

18. Joseph A. Lijembe, "The Valley Between: A Muluyia's Story," in Lorene K. Fox, ed., *East African Childhood* (Nairobi: Oxford University Press, 1967), p. 17.

19. Hamed Ammar, "The Aims and Methods of Socialization in Silwa," in John Middleton, ed., *From Child to Adult: Studies in the Anthropology of Education* (Austin: University of Texas Press, 1976), pp. 237, 240.

20. Dorothea Leighton and Clyde Kluckhohn, *Children of the People: The Navaho Individual and His Development* (Cambridge, Mass.: Harvard University Press, 1947), pp. 40, 51, 52.

21. Dio Chrysostom, *Discourses,* trans. J. W. Cohoon (London, 1932), p. 36; quoted in deMause, *History of Childhood,* p. 11.

22. Brigid Brophy, *Black Ship to Hell* (New York: Harcourt, Brace & World, 1962), p. 361.

23. DeMause, *History of Childhood,* p. 14.

24. Ibid., p. 12.

25. John Bowlby, *Attachment and Loss,* vol. 2, *Separation* (New York: Basic Books, 1973), pp. 226–27.

26. John Newson and Elizabeth Newson, *Four Years Old in an Urban Community* (Chicago: Aldine Publishing Co., 1968).

27. Ibid., p. 471

28. John Russell Taylor, *Hitch: The Life and Times of Alfred Hitchcock* (New York: Pantheon Books, 1978), p. 28.

29. M. J. Tyerman, *Truancy* (London: University of London Press, 1968), p. 39.

4. "Fearless" Societies

1. In "Notes on the Original Affluent Society" Marshall Sahlins has written: "The traditional dismal view of the hunter's fix is pre-anthropological. It goes back to the time Adam Smith was writing. But anthropology, especially evolutionary anthropology, found it congenial, even necessary theoretically, to adopt the same tone of reproach. Archeologists and ethnologists had become Neolithic revolutionaries, and in their enthusiasm for the revolution found serious shortcomings in the Old (Stone Age) Regime. Scholars extolled a Neolithic Great Leap Forward." In Richard B. Lee and Irven DeVore, eds., *Man the Hunter* (Chicago: Aldine Publishing Co., 1968), p. 85.

2. Colin M. Turnbull, *The Forest People* (London: Chatto & Windus, 1961); "The Lesson of the Pygmies," *Scientific American* 208, no. 1 (1963): pp. 28–37; "Mbuti Pygmies of the Congo," in James L. Gibbs, ed., *Peoples of Africa* (New York: Holt, Rinehart & Winston, 1965), pp. 281–310; *The Mbuti Pygmies: An Ethnographic Survey,* American Museum of Natural History, Anthropological Papers, vol. 50, pt. 3 (New York, 1965), pp. 149–212; "Legends of the BaMbuti," *Journal of the Royal Anthropological Institute* 89 (1959): 45–60. See also Paul

Schebesta, *Les Pygmées du Congo Belge,* Institut Royal Colonial Belge, Classe des Sciences Morales et Politiques, Mémoires, vol. 26, 1952. Schebesta puts greater stress on the division of labor among the Pygmies and less on the unique character of the spirit of the forest.

3. Turnbull, "Mbuti Pygmies of the Congo," pp. 308–9.

4. John Nance, *The Gentle Tasaday* (New York: Harcourt Brace Jovanovich, 1976); D. E. Yen and John Nance, eds., *Further Studies on the Tasaday,* Panamin Foundation Research Series, no. 2 (Makati, Rizal, Philippines, 1976); C. A. Fernandez II and F. Lynch, "The Tasaday: Cave-Dwelling Food Gatherers of South Cotabato, Mindanao," *Philippine Sociological Review* 20 (1972): 279–313.

5. D. E. Yen, "The Ethnobotany of the Tasaday: III. Notes on the Subsistence System," in Yen and Nance, eds., *Further Studies on the Tasaday,* p. 173.

6. D. E. Yen and Hermes G. Gutierrez, "The Ethnobotany of the Tasaday: I. The Useful Plants," in Yen and Nance, eds., *Further Studies on the Tasaday,* p. 98.

7. Nance, *The Gentle Tasaday,* pp. 60–61.

8. Paul Schebesta, *Among the Forest Dwarfs of Malaya* (Kuala Lumpur, Singapore: Oxford University Press, 1973).

9. Iskandar Carey, *Orang Asli: The Aboriginal Tribes of Peninsular Malaysia* (Kuala Lumpur, Singapore: Oxford University Press, 1976), p. 99.

10. See Ivor H. N. Evans, *The Negritos of Malaya* (Cambridge: University Press, 1937), pp. 256–65, for different versions of the idea of paradise.

11. Richard B. Lee, "What Hunters Do for a Living, or How to Make Out on Scarce Resources," in Lee and DeVore, eds., *Man the Hunter,* pp. 30–43.

12. Lorna Marshall, *The !Kung of Nyae Nyae* (Cambridge, Mass.: Harvard University Press, 1976), p. 308.

13. Lee, "What Hunters Do for a Living," p. 37.

14. Jiro Tanaka, "Subsistence Ecology of Central Kalahari San," in Richard B. Lee and Irven DeVore, eds., *Kalahari Hunter-Gatherers: Studies of the !Kung San and Their Neighbors* (Cambridge, Mass.: Harvard University Press, 1976), p. 115.

15. On neurological disease and suicide, see A. Stewart Truswell and John D. L. Hansen, "Medical Research Among the !Kung," in Lee and DeVore, eds., *Kalahari Hunter-Gatherers,* p. 171; on stealing, see Lorna Marshall, "Sharing, Talking, and Giving," in Lee and DeVore, eds., *Kalahari Hunter-Gatherers,* p. 370.

16. Elizabeth Marshall Thomas, *The Harmless People* (New York: Vintage Books, 1965), pp. 126–27.

17. Lack of strife in the sense of war, witchcraft, and sorcery, but not in the sense of "kidding" and fighting without malice. Colin Turnbull noted: "In some cases, a Pygmy camp may be characterized by innumerable disputes, many of which are almost deliberately created." In Lee and DeVore, *Man the Hunter,* p. 91.

18. Gina Bari Kolata, "!Kung Hunter-Gatherers: Feminism, Diet, and Birth Control," *Science* 185 (September 13, 1974): 932; Richard B. Lee, "Introduction," in Lee and DeVore, eds., *Kalahari Hunter-Gatherers,* p. 5.

5. Fear of Nature: Great Hunters and Pioneer Farmers

1. Glynn Isaac, "Stratigraphy and Cultural Patterns in East Africa During the Middle Ranges of Pleistocene Time," in Karl W. Butzer and Glynn Isaac, eds., *After the Australopithecines: Stratigraphy, Ecology, and Culture Change in the Middle Pleistocene* (The Hague: Mouton, 1975), pp. 495–529; "The Food-Sharing Behavior of Protohuman Hominids," *Scientific American* 238, no. 4 (1978): 90–108; Carl O. Sauer, "Seashore—Primitive Home of Man?" *Land and Life,* ed. John Leighly (Berkeley and Los Angeles: University of California Press, 1963), pp. 309–12.

2. Kwang-chih Chang, *The Archaeology of Ancient China,* 3rd ed. (New Haven, Conn.: Yale University Press, 1977), pp. 48–49.

3. Grahame Clark, *World Prehistory in New Perspective* (Cambridge: University Press, 1977), p. 36; Alexander Marshack, "The Art and Symbols of Ice Age Man," *Human Nature* 1, no. 9 (1978): 32.

4. Grahame Clarke and Stuart Piggott, *Prehistoric Societies* (London: Hutchinson & Co., 1965), pp. 64–97.

5. Peter Freuchen, *Book of the Eskimos* (Greenwich, Conn.: Fawcett Crest Books, 1965), p. 145.

6. Edward M. Weyer, *The Eskimos: Their Environment and Folkways* (New Haven, Conn.: Yale University Press, 1932), p. 132.

7. Freuchen, *Book of the Eskimos,* p. 153.

8. Kaj Birket-Smith, *The Eskimos* (London: Methuen & Co., 1936), pp. 160–74.

9. Knud Rasmussen, *Intellectual Culture of the Iglulik Eskimos,* Report of the 5th Thule Expedition, 1921–1924, The Danish Expedition, vol. 7, no. 1, 1929, pp. 56, 62.

10. Ibid., p. 74.

11. Knud Rasmussen, *The Netsilik Eskimos,* Report of the 5th Thule Expedition, 1921–1924, vol. 8, 1931, pp. 225–26.

12. Carl O. Sauer, *Agricultural Origins and Dispersals* (New York: American Geographical Society, 1952); J. E. Spencer, *Shifting Cultivation in Southeastern Asia,* University of California Publications in Geography, vol. 19 (Berkeley and Los Angeles, 1966), pp. 125, 160.

13. Pierre Gourou, *The Tropical World,* 4th ed. (London: Longmans, Green & Co., 1966), p. 34.

14. Colin M. Turnbull, *Wayward Servants: The Two Worlds of the African Pygmies* (London: Eyre & Spottiswode, 1965), p. 21.

15. W. T. Harris and Harry Sawyer, *The Springs of Mende Belief*

and Conduct (Freetown: Sierra Leone University Press, 1968), pp. 39, 47.

16. William F. Nydegger and Corinne Nydegger, *Tarong: An Ilocos Barrio in the Philippines,* Six Culture Series, vol. 6 (New York: John Wiley & Sons, 1966), p. 73.

6. Natural Calamities and Famines

1. James H. Breasted, *A History of Egypt* (New York: Bantam Books, 1964), p. 134; Karl W. Butzer, *Early Hydraulic Civilization in Egypt* (Chicago: University of Chicago Press, 1976), p. 41.

2. Thorkild Jacobsen, "The Cosmos as a State," in Henri Frankfort and others, *Before Philosophy* (Harmondsworth, Middlesex: Pelican Books, 1951), p. 139.

3. Samuel N. Kramer, *The Sumerians* (Chicago: University of Chicago Press, 1963), p. 262.

4. Georges Roux, *Ancient Iraq* (Harmondsworth, Middlesex: Pelican Books, 1966), pp. 360–61.

5. Wolfram Eberhard, *A History of China,* 2nd ed. (Berkeley: University of California Press, 1960), p. 23.

6. Marcel Granet, *Chinese Civilization* (New York: Meridian Books, 1958), pp. 191, 208.

7. Jacques Soustelle, *Daily Life of the Aztecs on the Eve of the Spanish Conquest* (Stanford, Calif.: Stanford University Press, 1970), pp. 95–102; Bernard R. Ortiz de Montellano, "Aztec Cannibalism: An Ecological Necessity?" *Science* 200 (May 12, 1978): 611–17.

8. Ch'ao-ting Chi, *Key Economic Areas in Chinese History,* 2nd ed. (New York: Paragon Books, 1963), p. 6.

9. S. Wells Williams, *The Middle Kingdom,* rev. ed. (New York: Charles Scribner's Sons, 1907), 1: 467–68.

10. W. R. Aykroyd, *The Conquest of Famine* (London: Chatto & Windus, 1974), pp. 52–54.

11. Ping-ti Ho, *Studies on the Population of China, 1368–1953* (Cambridge, Mass.: Harvard University Press, 1959), pp. 231–35.

12. Aykroyd, *Conquest of Famine,* p. 55.

13. Ho, *Population of China,* pp. 228–29.

14. Kalhana, *Rajatarangini,* trans. Ranjit Sitaram Pandit (New Delhi: Sahitya Akademi, 1968), p. 209.

15. Ho, *Population of China,* p. 231.

16. China Famine Relief Committee, *The Great Famine* (Shanghai, 1879), p. 5.

17. Jack Belden, *China Shakes the World* (New York: Monthly Review Press, 1970), pp. 61–62.

18. Jan Myrdal, *Report from a Chinese Village* (New York: Pantheon Books, 1965), p. 135.

19. O. H. K. Spate, *India and Pakistan* (New York: E. P. Dutton & Co., 1954), pp. 158–59.

20. Gregory of Nazianzen, *Patrologia Graeca,* ed. J. P. Migne, vol. 36, col. 541; quoted in Keith Hopkins, "Economic Growth and Towns in Classical Antiquity," in Philip Abrams and E. A. Wrigley, eds., *Towns in Societies: Essays in Economic History and Historical Sociology* (Cambridge: University Press, 1978), p. 46.

21. W. H. Mallory, *China: Land of Famine* (New York: American Geographical Society, 1926), p. 30.

22. Lynn White, Jr., "Death and the Devil," in Robert S. Kinsman, ed., *The Darker Vision of the Renaissance: Beyond the Fields of Reason* (Berkeley and Los Angeles: University of California Press, 1974), pp. 26–27.

23. Georges Duby, *Rural Economy and Country Life in the Medieval West* (Columbia: University of South Carolina Press, 1968), p. 295.

24. Pierre Goubert, *Louis XIV and Twenty Million Frenchmen* (New York: Pantheon Books, 1970), pp. 178–81; quotation on p. 216.

25. Peter Laslett, *The World We Have Lost* (New York: Charles Scribner's Sons, 1965), p. 119.

26. Andrew P. Appleby, *Famine in Tudor and Stuart England* (Stanford, Calif.: Stanford University Press, 1978), p. 113.

27. Alan Macfarlane, *The Family Life of Ralph Josselin: A Seventeenth-Century Clergyman* (Cambridge: University Press, 1970), pp. 71–76.

28. Olwen H. Hufton, *The Poor of Eighteenth-Century France, 1750–1789* (Oxford: Clarendon Press, 1974), pp. 355–56; Jan de Vries, *The Economy of Europe in an Age of Crisis, 1600–1750* (Cambridge: University Press, 1976), pp. 11–15.

29. *Tao Teh Ching,* trans. John C. H. Wu (New York: St. John's University Press, 1961), p. 7.

30. M. J. Merk, a resident in Punjab, quoted in W. G. Kendrew, *The Climates of the Continents* (London: Oxford University Press, 1937), p. 146.

31. Evon Z. Vogt, *Modern Homesteaders* (Cambridge, Mass.: Harvard University Press, 1955), pp. 90–91.

32. Kwai-shing Poon, "A Historical Geographical Study of Natural Disasters and Minor Agrarian Riots," unpublished M.A. thesis, University of Minnesota, 1976, pp. 57–65.

7. Fear in the Medieval World

1. Johan Huizinga, *The Waning of the Middle Ages* (Garden City, N.Y.: Doubleday Anchor Books, 1954).

2. Peter Brown, "Society and the Supernatural: A Medieval Change," *Daedalus* 104 (Spring 1975): 133–51.

3. Ernest Brehaut, *An Encyclopedist of the Dark Ages: Isidore of Se-*

ville, Columbia University Studies in History, Economics, and Public Law, vol. 48, no. 1 (New York, 1912), p. 71.

4. Norman Cohn, *Europe's Inner Demons: An Enquiry Inspired by the Great Witch-Hunt* (New York: Basic Books, 1975), p. 70.

5. Kenneth Clark, *Landscape into Art,* rev. ed. (New York: Harper & Row, 1976), p. 6; Lewis Mumford, *Technics and Civilization* (New York: Harcourt, Brace & Co. 1934), pp. 28–29.

6. Carolly Erickson, *The Medieval Vision: Essays in History and Perception* (New York: Oxford University Press, 1976), p. 19.

7. M. D. Chenu, *Nature, Man, and Society in the Twelfth Century: Essays on New Theological Perspectives in the Latin West* (Chicago: University of Chicago Press, 1968), pp. 102–3.

8. Marc Bloch, *Feudal Society* (Chicago: University of Chicago Press, 1961), p. 83.

9. Erickson, *The Medieval Vision,* p. 90.

10. Richard Cavendish, *The Powers of Evil* (New York: G. P. Putnam's Sons, 1975), p. 93.

11. Peter Hunter Blair, *Northumbria in the Days of Bede* (London: Victor Gollancz, 1976), pp. 67, 197–98.

12. G. G. Coulton, *From St. Francis to Dante,* 2nd ed. (London: David Nutt, 1907), p. 78.

13. Heinz von Foerster, Patricia M. Mora, and Lawrence W. Amiot, "Doomsday: Friday, 13 November, A.D. 2026," *Science* 132 (November 4, 1960): 1291–95.

14. Bloch, *Feudal Society,* pp. 84–85.

15. C. S. Lewis, *The Discarded Image* (Cambridge: University Press, 1964), p. 118.

16. *Malleus Maleficarum* (1489) trans. with an introduction, bibliography, and notes by Montague Summers (1928; reprint ed., New York: Benjamin Blom, 1970), p. 147.

17. Ibid., p. 190.

18. H. R. Trevor-Roper, *The European Witch-Craze of the Sixteenth and Seventeenth Centuries and Other Essays* (New York: Harper Torchbooks, 1969), pp. 103, 106–7.

19. Gavin Rylands de Beer, *Early Travellers in the Alps* (London: Sidwick & Jackson, 1930). Reference to Pilate's Lake, p. 16, and dragons, pp. 89–90.

20. Roderick Nash, *Wilderness and the American Mind* (New Haven, Conn.: Yale University Press, 1967), p. 2.

21. Quoted in ibid., p. 29.

22. Robert Steele, ed., *Medieval Lore . . . Being Classified Gleanings from the Encyclopedia of Bartholomaeus Anglicus on the Properties of Things* (London: Elliot Stock, 1893), p. 92.

23. G. G. Coulton, *Life in the Middle Ages* (Cambridge: University Press, 1930), 4: 45.

24. Coulton, *From St. Francis to Dante*, pp. 39, 60.

25. Fernand Braudel, *Capitalism and Material Life, 1400–1800* (New York: Harper Colophon Books, 1975), p. 34.

26. G. G. Coulton, *Medieval Village, Manor, and Monastery* (New York: Harper Torchbooks, 1960), pp. 115–16; A. Feillet, *La Misère au temps de Fronde et S. Vincent de Paul* (Paris, 1862), p. 72; see also Elias Canetti, *Crowds and Power* (Harmondsworth, Middlesex: Penguin Books, 1973), p. 67.

27. Edward A. Armstrong, *Saint Francis: Nature Mystic* (Berkeley and Los Angeles: University of California Press, 1976), p. 7.

28. G. G. Coulton, *Medieval Panorama: The English Scene from Conquest to Reformation* (New York: Macmillan Co., 1946), p. 112.

29. Armstrong, *Saint Francis*, p. 203.

30. G. Carson, "Bugs and Beasts Before the Law," *Natural History* 77, no. 4 (1968): 6–19; Walker W. Hyde, "The Prosecution and Punishment of Animals and Lifeless Things in the Middle Ages and Modern Times," *University of Pennsylvania Law Review* 64 (1915–1916): 708–9.

31. Coulton, *Medieval Panorama*, p. 108.

32. Ernest Jones, *On the Nightmares* (New York: Liveright, 1971).

33. E. J. Becker, *A Contribution to the Comparative Study of the Medieval Visions of Heaven and Hell* (Baltimore: John Murphy, 1899), pp. 2–3.

34. Ibid., p. 83.

35. William Fitz Stephen, *A Description of London (Descriptio Londonie)*, trans. H. E. Butler, in F. M. Stenton, *Norman London*, Historical Association Leaflets, nos. 93–94 (London, 1934), p. 31.

8. Fear of Disease

1. Forrest E. Clements, *Primitive Concepts of Disease*, University of California Publications in American Archaeology and Ethnology, vol. 32, no. 2 (Berkeley, 1932), pp. 185–252.

2. Clarence Maloney, ed., *The Evil Eye* (New York: Columbia University Press, 1976).

3. J. B. Loudon, ed., *Social Anthropology and Medicine*, Papers from a Conference, Canterbury, England, April 1972 A.S.A. [Association of Social Anthropologists] Monographs, no. 13 (New York: Academic Press, 1976).

4. Maurice Freedman, "On the Sociological Study of Chinese Religion," in Arthur P. Wolf, *Religion and Ritual in Chinese Society* (Stanford, Calif.: Stanford University Press, 1974), pp. 19–41.

5. Guido Majno, *The Healing Hand: Man and Wound in the Ancient World* (Cambridge, Mass.: Harvard University Press, 1975), pp. 238–44. See also I. Veith, *Huang Ti Nei Ching Su Wen* [The Yellow Emperor's Classic of Internal Medicine], rev. ed. (Berkeley: University of California Press, 1966); also Manfred Porkert, *The Theoretical Foundations of Chinese Medicine* (Cambridge, Mass.: MIT Press, 1974).

6. J. J. M. De Groot, *The Religious System of China* (Taipei: Literature House, 1964), 6: 1110–11; also Heinrich Wallnöfer and Anna von Rottauscher, *Chinese Folk Medicine* (New York: Bell Publishing Co., 1965), pp. 96–99.

7. Ibid., pp. 944–46.

8. E. R. Dodds, *The Greeks and the Irrational* (Berkeley: University of California Press, 1951), pp. 29, 39.

9. Martin P. Nilsson, *Greek Folk Religion* (Philadelphia: University of Pennsylvania Press, 1972), p. 18.

10. Quoted in Paul F. Russell, *Man's Mastery of Malaria* (London: Oxford University Press, 1955), p. 88.

11. Dodds, *The Greeks and the Irrational,* pp. 41–42.

12. L. W. Sambon, "A Medico-literary Causerie: The History of Malaria," *The Practitioner* 66 (1901): 348–59.

13. Norman Longmate, *King Cholera: The Biography of a Disease* (London: Hamish Hamilton, 1966), pp. 86, 179.

14. Charles E. Rosenberg, *The Cholera Years: The United States in 1832, 1849, and 1866* (Chicago: University of Chicago Press, 1962), p. 42.

15. Ibid., pp. 49, 121.

16. Hippocrates, *Of the Epidemics,* bk. 1, sec. 2:11.

17. Russell, *Man's Mastery of Malaria,* p. 84.

18. J. F. C. Hecker, *The Epidemics of the Middle Ages,* 3rd ed. (London: Trübner & Co., 1859), p. 15.

19. Walter George Bell, *The Great Plague in London, 1665* (London: John Lane, 1924), p. 1.

20. J. H. Powell, *Bring Out Your Dead: The Great Plague of Yellow Fever in Philadelphia in 1793* (Philadelphia: University of Pennsylvania Press, 1949), p. 2.

21. Rosenberg, *Cholera Years,* p. 15.

22. Quoted in James Leasor, *The Plague and the Fire* (New York: McGraw-Hill Book Co., 1961), p. 125.

23. Sir Fred Hoyle and Chandra Wickramasinghe, "Does Epidemic Disease Come from Space?" *New Scientist* 76 (November 17, 1977): 402–4.

24. Anna Montgomery Campbell, *The Black Death and Its Meaning* (New York: Columbia University Press, 1931), p. 41.

25. Hecker, *Epidemics of the Middle Ages,* pp. 14–15.

26. Longmate, *King Cholera,* pp. 73–74.

27. Classical writers were sometimes more precise. Varro, for example, warned against swampy grounds because "certain minute animals, invisible to the eye, breed there, and, borne by the air, reach the inside of the body by way of the mouth and nose, and cause diseases which are difficult to get rid of." Quoted in Russell, *Man's Mastery of Malaria,* p. 12.

28. Longmate, *King Cholera,* p. 166.

29. Charles Creighton, *A History of Epidemics in Britain* (Cambridge: University Press, 1891), 1: 175.

30. Saul Nathaniel Brody, *The Disease of the Soul: Leprosy in Medieval Literature* (Ithaca, N.Y.: Cornell University Press, 1974), p. 67.
31. Anthony D. King, *Colonial Urban Development: Culture, Social Power and Environment* (London: Routledge & Kegan Paul, 1976), pp. 108–11.
32. Campbell, *The Black Death,* pp. 3, 61.
33. Hecker, *Epidemics of the Middle Ages,* pp. 58–59.
34. Campbell, *The Black Death,* p. 114.
35. Bell, *The Great Plague,* p. 94.
36. Roderick E. McGrew, *Russia and the Cholera 1823–1832* (Madison: University of Wisconsin Press, 1965), p. 78.
37. Rosenberg, *Cholera Years,* p. 37.
38. McGrew, *Russia and the Cholera,* pp. 75–77.
39. Philip Ziegler, *The Black Death* (New York: John Day Co., 1969), pp. 74–75.
40. Quoted in Leasor, *The Plague and the Fire,* p. 125.
41. Ibid., p. 126.
42. Longmate, *King Cholera,* p. 5.
43. Ibid., p. 85.
44. Thucydides, *The History of the Peloponnesian War,* bk. 2, chap. 7:52. Thucydides is often credited with presenting the first description of plague. It is more likely that he described typhus and possibly typhoid. See Wesley W. Spink, *Infectious Diseases: A History of Their Control* (Minneapolis: University of Minnesota Press, 1978), p. 144.
45. From the *Chronicum Henrici Knighton,* quoted by R. B. Dobson, ed., *The Peasants' Revolts of 1381* (London: Macmillan & Co., 1970), pp. 59–63.
46. Bell, *The Great Plague,* pp. 158–59, 192–94, 281.
47. Quoted in Longmate, *King Cholera,* p. 63

9. Fear of Human Nature: Witches

1. E. H. Winter, "The Enemy Within: Amba Witchcraft and Sociological Theory," in John Middleton and E. H. Winter, eds., *Witchcraft and Sorcery in East Africa* (New York: Frederick A. Praeger, 1963), pp. 278–94.
2. Clyde Kluckhohn, *Navaho Witchcraft* (Boston: Beacon Press, 1967), pp. 74–75.
3. Lucy Mair, *Witchcraft* (New York: World University Library, 1969), pp. 36–37.
4. H. Boguet, *An Examen of Witches,* first published in 1590, trans. E. A. Ashwin (London, 1929), p. 51; quoted by Geoffrey Parrinder, *Witchcraft: European and African* (London: Faber & Faber, 1963), p. 38.
5. Robert A. LeVine and Barbara B. LeVine, *Nyansongo: A Gusii Community in Kenya,* in Beatrice B. Whiting, ed., *Six Cultures:*

Studies of Child Rearing (New York: John Wiley & Sons, 1963), pp. 57–58.

6. T. O. Beidelman, "Witchcraft in Ukaguru," in Middleton and Winter, eds., *Witchcraft and Sorcery,* p. 61.

7. John Middleton, "Witchcraft and Sorcery in Lugbara," in Middleton and Winter, eds., *Witchcraft and Sorcery,* p. 262.

8. R. G. Lienhardt, "Some Notions of Witchcraft Among the Dinka," *Africa* 21 (1951): 303–18.

9. Ernest Jones, *On the Nightmare* (New York: Liveright Publishing Corp., 1971), pp. 233–34.

10. Kluckhohn, *Navaho Witchcraft,* p. 137.

11. H. R. Trevor-Roper, *The European Witch-Craze of the Sixteenth and Seventeenth Centuries and Other Essays* (New York: Harper Torchbooks, 1969), p. 94.

12. Julio Caro Baroja, *The World of Witches* (Chicago: University of Chicago Press, 1965), p. 238. For witchcraft in the mountainous regions of the Savoy and the Jura, see E. William Monter, *Witchcraft in France and Switzerland: The Borderlands During the Reformation* (Ithaca, N.Y.: Cornell University Press, 1976).

13. Nicholas Remy, *Demonology* (1595), trans. E. A. Ashwin (London: J. Rodker, 1930), p. 84.

14. J. R. Crawford, *Witchcraft and Sorcery in Rhodesia* (London: Oxford University Press, 1967), pp. 265–66.

15. *Malleus maleficarum* (1489), trans. with an introduction, bibliography, and notes by Montague Summers (1928; reprint ed., New York: Benjamin Blom, 1970), pp. 91–92.

16. Baroja, *World of Witches,* p. 176.

17. Kluckhohn, *Navaho Witchcraft,* pp. 25, 47.

18. Mair, *Witchcraft,* pp. 54–56.

19. Monica Wilson, "Witch Beliefs and Social Structure," *American Journal of Sociology* 56, no. 4 (1951): 307–13.

20. Robert F. Gray, "Some Structural Aspects of Mbugwe Witchcraft," in Middleton and Winter, *Witchcraft and Sorcery,* p. 163.

10. Fear of Human Nature: Ghosts

1. R. H. Nassau, *Fetishism in West Africa* (New York: Charles Scribner's Sons, 1904), pp. 223–24.

2. Clyde Kluckhohn, *Navaho Witchcraft* (Boston: Beacon Press, 1967), pp. 104–5.

3. T. O. Beidelman, "Witchcraft in Ukaguru," in John Middleton and E. H. Winter, eds., *Witchcraft and Sorcery in East Africa* (New York: Frederick A. Praeger, 1963), p. 66.

4. J. R. Crawford, *Witchcraft and Sorcery in Rhodesia* (London: Oxford University Press, 1967), p. 88.

5. A. Grimble, "From Birth to Death in the Gilbert Islands," *Journal of the Royal Anthropological Institute of Great Britain and Ireland* 51 (1920): 46–48.

6. Clyde Kluckhohn and Dorothea Leighton, *The Navaho,* rev. ed. (Garden City, N.Y.: Doubleday Anchor Books, 1962), p. 184.

7. Gladys A. Reichard, *Navaho Religion: A Study of Symbols* (New York: Pantheon Books, 1963), p. 81.

8. Kluckhohn and Leighton, *The Navaho,* pp. 184–85.

9. W. T. Harris and Harry Sawyer, *The Springs of Mende Belief and Conduct* (Freetown: Sierra Leone University Press, 1968), p. 14.

10. Crawford, *Witchcraft in Rhodesia,* p. 78.

11. R. N. H. Bulmer, "The Kyaka of the Western Highlands," in P. Lawrence and M. J. Meggitt, eds., *Gods, Ghosts, and Men in Melanesia* (Melbourne: Oxford University Press, 1965), p. 139.

12. M. J. Meggitt, "The Mae Enga of the Western Highlands," in Lawrence and Meggitt, eds., *Gods, Ghosts, and Men,* p. 111.

13. Pausanias, *Description of Greece,* bk. 9:31, trans. W. H. S. Jones, Loeb Classical Library (London, 1935), 4: 353, 355.

14. Martin P. Nilsson, *Greek Piety* (Oxford: Clarendon Press, 1948), p. 9.

15. Martin P. Nilsson, *Greek Folk Religion* (Philadelphia: University of Pennsylvania Press, 1972), pp. 91, 113.

16. Arthur P. Wolf, "Gods, Ghosts, and Ancestors," in Arthur P. Wolf, ed., *Religion and Ritual in Chinese Society* (Stanford, Calif.: Stanford University Press, 1974), p. 141.

17. Emily M. Ahern, *The Cult of the Dead in a Chinese Village* (Stanford, Calif.: Stanford University Press, 1973), pp. 199–200.

18. Ibid., p. 171.

19. Ibid., pp. 172–74.

20. Wolf, "Gods, Ghosts, and Ancestors," pp. 146–47.

21. Shen Chien-shih, "An Essay on the Primitive Meaning of the Character *kuei,*" *Monumenta Serica* 2 (1936–1937): 1–20.

22. Wolfram Eberhard, *Studies in Chinese Folklore and Related Essays,* Indiana University Folklore Institute Monograph Series, vol. 23, (Bloomington, 1970), pp. 69–71.

23. Margery Wolf, *The House of Lim: A Study of a Chinese Farm Family* (New York: Appleton-Century-Crofts, 1968), pp. 15–16.

24. James George Frazer, *The Fear of the Dead in Primitive Religion* (London: Macmillan & Co., 1934), vol. 2.

25. Baldwin Spencer and F. J. Gillen, *The Native Tribes of Central Australia* (London: Macmillan & Co., 1899), pp. 498–508.

26. G. M. Sproat, *Scenes and Studies of Savage Life* (London: Smith, Elder & Co., 1868), pp. 159, 160; Frazer, *Fear of the Dead,* p. 128.

27. Alexander von Humboldt, *Personal Narrative of Travels in the Equinoctial Regions of America* (London: George Bell & Sons, 1852), 2: 487.

28. Frazer, *Fear of the Dead,* p. 132.

29. Ibid., pp. 32–36, 47–48.

30. Ibid., pp. 17–18, 36.

31. Cyril Bailey, *Phases in the Religion of Ancient Rome* (1932; reprint ed., Westport, Conn.: Greenwood Press, 1972), p. 39.
32. Arthur F. Wright, *The Sui Dynasty: The Unification of China, A.D. 581–617* (New York: Alfred A. Knopf, 1978), p. 67.
33. Carolly Erickson, *The Medieval Vision: Essays in History and Perception* (New York: Oxford University Press, 1976), pp. 14–16; A. J. Grant, "Twelve Medieval Ghost Stories," *Yorkshire Archaeological Journal* 27 (1923–1924): 365–66.
34. Julia Briggs, *Night Visitors: The Rise and Fall of the English Ghost Story* (London: Faber & Faber, 1977).
35. Katherine Wiltshire, *Ghosts and Legends of the Wiltshire Countryside* (Salisbury, Wiltshire: Compton Russell, 1973).
36. Ralph Whitlock, *The Folklore of Wiltshire* (London and Sydney: B. T. Batsford, 1976), pp. 116–17, 126.
37. Lacy Collison-Morley, *Greek and Roman Ghost Stories* (Chicago: Argonaut, 1968), p. 20.
38. Whitlock, *Folklore of Wiltshire,* p. 125.
39. Christina Hole, *Haunted England: A Survey of English Ghost-Lore,* 2nd ed. (London: B. T. Batsford, 1950), p. 139.
40. Ibid., p. 4.
41. William L. Montell, *Ghosts Along the Cumberland: Deathlore in the Kentucky Foothills* (Knoxville: University of Tennessee Press, 1975), pp. 14, 22, 29.
42. Vance Randolph, *Ozark Superstitions* (New York: Columbia University Press, 1947), p. 238.
43. Montell, *Ghosts Along the Cumberland,* p. 6.
44. Randolph, *Ozark Superstitions,* p. 71.
45. Ibid., p. 217.
46. Elmore Messer Matthews, *Neighbor and Kin: Life in a Tennessee Ridge Community* (Nashville, Tenn.: Vanderbilt University Press, 1965), pp. 68–69; Jack E. Weller, *Yesterday's People: Life in Contemporary Appalachia* (Lexington: University of Kentucky Press, 1966), p. 44.

11. Violence and Fear in the Countryside

1. Put in the mouth of Pacatianus by Luke Owen Pike, *A History of Crime in England* (London: Smith, Elder & Co., 1873), 1: 30. He gives his reason for doing so on p. 431. Of the numerous villas in Roman Britain, only a few had palisades. See R. G. Collingwood and S. N. L. Myers, *Roman Britain and the English Settlements* (Oxford: Clarendon Press, 1937), p. 302.
2. Edwin O. Reischauer, *Ennin's Travels in T'ang China* (New York: Ronald Press Co., 1955), pp. 138–39.
3. Eileen E. Power, "Peasant Life and Rural Conditions (c. 1100 to c. 1500)," *The Cambridge Medieval History* (Cambridge: University Press, 1958), 7: 730.

4. I. A. A. Thompson, "A Map of Crime in Sixteenth-Century Spain," *Economic History Review* 21, ser. 2 (1968): 244–67.

5. Gwyn A. Williams, *A Medieval London: From Commune to Capital* (London: Athlone Press, 1970), pp. 21–22; R. H. Hilton, *A Medieval Society: The West Midlands at the End of the Thirteenth Century* (London: Weidenfeld & Nicolson, 1966), pp. 55, 218.

6. James B. Given, *Society and Homicide in Thirteenth-Century England* (Stanford, Calif.: Stanford University Press, 1977), pp. 35–39, 175.

7. John Bellamy, *Crime and Public Order in England in the Later Middle Ages* (Toronto: University of Toronto Press, 1973), p. 43.

8. G. T. Salusbury, *Street Life in Medieval England* (Oxford: Pen-in-Hand Publishing Co., 1948), p. 151.

9. W. G. Hoskins, *The Making of the English Landscape* (London: Hodder & Stoughton, 1955), p. 91; Alfred Harvey, *The Castles and Walled Towns of England* (London: Methuen & Co., 1911), pp. 1–2. "Medieval Europe abounded in castles. Germany alone had ten thousand and more, most of them now vanished." Friedrich Heer, *The Medieval World* (New York: Mentor Books, 1962), p. 32.

10. Andrea Trevisano, *A Relation of the Island of England,* trans. C. A. Sneyd (London: Camden Society, 1847), 37: 34.

11. J. S. Cockburn, "The Nature and Incidence of Crime in England, 1559–1625: A Preliminary Survey," in J. B. Coburn, ed., *Crime in England, 1550–1800* (Princeton, N.J.: Princeton University Press, 1977), pp. 55–56.

12. Thompson, "Map of Crime in Sixteenth-Century Spain," p. 244.

13. Fernand Braudel, *The Mediterranean and the Mediterranean World in the Age of Philip II* (New York: Harper & Row, 1973), 2: 734–56.

14. Y. M. Bercé, "De la criminalité aux troubles sociaux: la noblesse rurale du Sud-Ouest de la France sous Louis XIII," *Annales du Midi* 76 (1964): 43.

15. M. Dorothy George, *London Life in the XVIIIth Century* (London: Kegan Paul, 1925), p. 97.

16. William C. Sydney, *England and the English in the Eighteenth Century,* 2nd ed. (Edinburgh: John Grant, 1891), 2: 29.

17. Christopher Hibbert, *Highwaymen* (London: Weidenfeld & Nicolson, 1967), p. 13.

18. Richard C. Cobb, *Paris and Its Provinces, 1792–1802* (London: Oxford University Press, 1975), pp. 40–41.

19. E. J. Hobsbawm, *Bandits* (London: Weidenfeld & Nicolson, 1969), pp. 24–33.

20. Cobb, *Paris and Its Provinces,* p. 35.

21. Henri Hours, "Émeutes et émotions populaires dans les campagnes du Lyonnais au XVIIe siècle," *Cahiers d'Histoire* 9 (1964): 137–154; François Billacois, "Pour une enquête sur la criminalité dans la France d'Ancien Régime," *Annales—Économies, Sociétés, Civilisations* 22, no. 2 (1967): 345.

22. Olwen H. Hufton, *The Poor of Eighteenth-Century France, 1750–1789* (Oxford: Clarendon Press, 1974), pp. 360–63; quotation on p. 363.

23. Richard Jefferies, *The Toilers of the Field* (London: Longmans, Green & Co., 1892), p. 109. First published in *Fraser's Magazine* in 1874.

24. Ronald Blythe, *Akenfield: Portrait of an English Village* (New York: Pantheon Books, 1969), p. 170.

25. Roger Lane, "Crime and Criminal Statistics in Nineteenth-century Massachusetts," *Journal of Social History* 2, no. 2 (1968): 156–63; quotation on p. 163.

26. Jefferies, *Toilers of the Field,* pp. 90–91.

27. Robert Coles, *Children of Crisis,* vol. 2, *Migrants, Mountaineers, and Sharecroppers* (Boston: Little, Brown & Co., 1972), p. 337.

28. James Dickey, *Deliverance* (New York: Dell Publishers, 1971), pp. 51–52.

29. Lowry Nelson, *American Farm Life* (Cambridge, Mass.: Harvard University Press, 1954), p. 56.

30. The most famous and influential of these laments appears in Thomas More's *Utopia,* which was first published in 1516.

31. W. E. Tate, *The English Village Community and the Enclosure Movements* (London: Victor Gollancz, 1967), pp. 67, 174.

32. Blythe, *Akenfield,* pp. 47–48.

33. Truman Moore, *The Slaves We Rent* (New York: Random House, 1965), pp. xi, 15–17, 36–37.

34. Coles, *Migrants, Mountaineers, and Sharecroppers,* pp. 457, 459.

35. Dale Wright, *They Harvest Despair: The Migrant Farm Worker* (Boston: Beacon Press, 1965).

36. Coles, *Migrants, Mountaineers, and Sharecroppers,* p. 96.

37. Ibid., p. 95.

38. Raymond Williams, *The Country and the City* (New York: Oxford University Press, 1973), p. 46.

12. Fear in the City

1. Paul Wheatley, *The Pivot of the Four Quarters: A Preliminary Inquiry into the Origins and Character of the Ancient Chinese City* (Chicago: Aldine Publishing Co., 1971).

2. Wolfram Eberhard, "The Political Function of Astronomy and Astronomers in Han China," in John K. Fairbank, ed., *Chinese Thought and Institutions* (Chicago: University of Chicago Press, 1967), pp. 33–70.

3. G. M. Wyburn, R. W. Pickford, and R. J. Hirst, *Human Senses and Perceptions* (Edinburgh: Oliver & Boyd, 1964), p. 66; P. H. Knapp, "Emotional Aspects of Hearing Loss," *Psychomatic Medicine* 10 (July–August 1948): 203–22.

4. Jérôme Carcopino, *Daily Life in Ancient Rome: The People and*

the City at the Height of the Empire (New Haven, Conn.: Yale University Press, 1940), pp. 50, 180; Juvenal, *Satires* III, lines 236–59.

5. D. C. Munro and R. J. Sontag, *The Middle Ages* (New York: Century Co., 1928), p. 345.

6. Quoted in Hugh and Pauline Massingham, eds., *The London Anthology* (London: Phoenix House, 1950), pp. 447–48.

7. Marjorie Rawling, *Everyday Life in Medieval Times* (London: B. T. Batsford, 1968), pp. 68–69.

8. Carl Bridenbaugh, *Cities in Revolt: Urban Life in America, 1743–1776* (New York: Alfred A. Knopf, 1955), p. 243.

9. Rosamond Bayne-Powell, *Eighteenth-Century London Life* (London: John Murray, 1937), p. 33.

10. John Betjeman, *Victorian and Edwardian London* (London: B. T. Batsford, 1969), pp. ix–xi.

11. Carcopino, *Daily Life in Ancient Rome,* p. 31.

12. Juvenal, "Against the City of Rome," *Satires,* trans. Rolfe Humphries (Bloomington: Indiana University Press, 1958), p. 40.

13. M. Dorothy George, *London Life in the XVIIIth Century* (London: Kegan Paul, 1925), pp. 73–74.

14. Charles Dickens, *Bleak House,* chap. 16, quoted in Aldon D. Bell, *London in the Age of Dickens* (Norman: University of Oklahoma Press, 1967), pp. 157–58.

15. Petronius, *The Satyricon,* trans. William Arrowsmith (New York: Mentor Books, 1960), p. 84.

16. G. Woledge, "The Medieval Borough of Leeds," *The Thoresby Miscellany,* 2 (Leeds: The Thoresby Society, 1945), p. 294; quoted in Walter L. Creese, *The Search for Environment: The Garden City, Before and After* (New Haven, Conn.: Yale University Press, 1966), p. 72; Gene A. Brucker, *Renaissance Florence* (New York: John Wiley & Sons, 1969), p. 11.

17. Colin Platt, *The English Medieval Town* (New York: David McKay Co., 1976), p. 48.

18. Sir Walter Besant, *London in the Eighteenth Century* (London: Adam & Charles Black, 1903), p. 90.

19. David H. Pinkney, *Napoleon III and the Rebuilding of Paris* (Princeton, N.J.: Princeton University Press, 1958), pp. 16–17.

20. Lewis Mumford, *The City in History: Its Origins, Its Transformations, and Its Prospects* (New York: Harcourt, Brace & World, 1961), p. 370; Jeffry Kaplow, *The Names of Kings: The Parisian Laboring Poor in the Eighteenth Century* (New York: Basic Books, 1972), p. 16.

21. Bridenbaugh, *Cities in Revolt,* p. 34.

22. Ibid., p. 243.

23. Alex Karmel, *My Revolution: Promenades in Paris 1789–1794, Being the Diary of Restif de la Bretonne* (New York: McGraw-Hill Book Co., 1970), pp. 3–4.

24. E. H. Schafer, "The Last Years of Ch'ang-an," *Oriens Extremus* 10 (October 1963): 137.

25. Jacques Gernet, *Daily Life in China on the Eve of the Mongol Invasion, 1250–1276* (London: George Allen & Unwin, 1962), pp. 34–38.

26. H. F. Jolowicz, *Historical Introduction to the Study of Roman Law* (Cambridge: University Press, 1965), p. 347.

27. Carcopino, *Daily Life in Ancient Rome,* p. 33; Juvenal, *Satires* III, lines 197–98.

28. William Fitz Stephen, *A Description of London (Descriptio Londonie),* trans. H. E. Butler, in F. M. Stenton, ed., *Norman London,* Historical Association Leaflets, nos. 93, 94 (London, 1934), p. 30.

29. D. M. Stenton, *English Society in the Early Middle Ages* (Harmondsworth, Middlesex: Pelican History of England, 1965), p. 193.

30. Charles Pendrill, *London Life in the 14th Century* (London: George Allen & Unwin, 1925), p. 12.

31. Fernand Braudel, *Capitalism and Material Life, 1400–1800* (New York: Harper Colophon Books, 1975), pp. 194–95.

32. Carl Bridenbaugh, *Cities in the Wilderness: The First Century of Urban Life in America, 1625–1742* (New York: Capricorn Books, 1955), pp. 58–59.

33. Howard Emmons, "Fire and Fire Protection," *Scientific American* 231 (July 1974): 21–27; Michael J. Munson, *Urban Neighborhoods and the Fear of Fire,* School of Architecture and Urban Planning, Princeton University, Working Paper no. 13, 1975.

34. Elias Canetti, *Crowds and Power* (New York: Viking Press, 1963), pp. 20, 76.

35. William Smith, "A Breeff Description of the Famous and Bewtifull Cittie of Norenberg," Lambeth Palace Library, ms. no. 508; quoted by Malcolm Letts in his introduction to Theodor Hampe, *Crime and Punishment in Germany* (New York: E. P. Dutton & Co., 1929), p. 17. Smith lived in Nuremberg between 1568 and 1588.

36. Henry Fielding, "An Enquiry into the Causes of the Late Increase of Robbers . . ." (1751), *The Works of Henry Fielding* (London: Frank Cass, 1967), 13: 83.

37. John Larner, "Order and Disorder in Romagna, 1450–1500," in Lauro Martines, ed., *Violence and Civil Disorder in Italian Cities, 1200–1500* (Berkeley and Los Angeles: University of California Press, 1972), p. 39.

38. Stanley Chojnacki, "Crime, Punishment, and the Trecento Venetian State," in Martines, ed., *Violence and Civil Disorder,* p. 214.

39. Diane Owen Hughes, "Urban Growth and Family Structure in Medieval Genoa," in Philip Abrams and E. A. Wrigley, eds., *Towns in Societies: Essays in Economic History and Historical Sociology* (Cambridge: University Press, 1978), p. 111; Brucker, *Renaissance Florence,* pp. 11–13.

40. Ferdinand Gregorovius, *History of the City of Rome in the Middle Ages* (London: George Bell, 1897), 5, pt. 2: 659–60.

41. G. T. Salusbury, *Street Life in Medieval England* (Oxford: Pen-in-Hand Publishing Co., 1948), pp. 139–40.

42. Carl Ludwig von Bar, *A History of Continental Criminal Law* (Boston: Little, Brown & Co., 1916), p. 108.
43. Bridenbaugh, *Cities in the Wilderness,* pp. 66, 79–80.
44. Carcopino, *Daily Life in Ancient Rome,* pp. 47–48.
45. Quoted in George, *London Life,* pp. 10–11.
46. Fielding, "An Enquiry . . ." p. 113.
47. Bayne-Powell, *Eighteenth-Century London Life,* pp. 198–99.
48. Quoted in J. J. Tobias, *Crime and Industrial Society in the 19th Century* (New York: Schocken Books, 1967), p. 24; see also Patrick Pringle, *Hue and Cry* (New York: William Morrow & Co., 1955).
49. Luke Owen Pike, *A History of Crime in England* (London: Smith, Elder & Co., 1876), 2: 252–55.
50. Tobias, *Crime and Industrial Society,* p. 25.
51. Dickens, *Bleak House,* chap. 16.
52. Ichisada Miyazaki, "Les villes en Chine à l'époque des Han," *T'oung Pao* 48 (1960): 376–92.
53. Étienne Balazs, *Chinese Civilization and Bureaucracy: Variations on a Theme* (New Haven, Conn.: Yale University Press, 1964), pp. 68–69.
54. Schafer, "Last Years of Ch'ang-an," pp. 138, 156.
55. Balazs, *Chinese Civilization,* pp. 70–71.
56. Ping-ti Ho, "Lo-yang, A.D. 495–534: A Study of the Physical and Socio-economic Planning of a Metropolitan Area," *Harvard Journal of Asiatic Studies* 26 (1966): 90.
57. Gene A. Brucker, "The Ciompi Revolution," in Nicolai Rubinstein, ed., *Florentine Studies* (London: Faber & Faber, 1968), p. 314.
58. Leon Bernard, *The Emerging City: Paris in the Age of Louis XIV* (Durham, N.C.: Duke University Press, 1970), pp. 156–66.
59. Kaplow, *The Names of Kings,* p. 13.
60. Pinkney, *Napoleon III,* pp. 35–37.
61. Bridenbaugh, *Cities in the Wilderness,* p. 380.
62. John E. Alexander, "The City of Brotherly Fear: The Poor in Late-Eighteenth-Century Philadelphia," in Kenneth Jackson and Stanley Schultz, eds., *Cities in American History* (New York: Alfred A. Knopf, 1972), pp. 79–97.
63. W. Cooke Taylor, "Notes of a Tour in the Manufacturing Districts of Lancashire," as quoted by R. Glass, "Urban Sociology in Great Britain," in R. E. Pahl, ed., *Readings in Urban Sociology* (New York: Pergamon Press, 1968), pp. 67–68.
64. Raymond Williams, *The Country and the City* (New York: Oxford University Press, 1973), p. 221.
65. Louis Chevalier, *Laboring Classes and Dangerous Classes in Paris During the First Half of the Nineteenth Century* (New York: Howard Fertig, 1973), pp. 413–16.
66. Charles Loring Brace, *The Dangerous Classes of New York,* 3rd ed. (New York: Wynkoop & Hallenbeck, 1880), p. 27.
67. Dickens, *Bleak House,* chap. 46.
68. Robert Ernst, *Immigrant Life in New York City, 1825–1863* (New

York: Kings' Crown Press, 1949); Ann Novotny, *Strangers at the Door* (New York: Bantam Books, 1974).

69. Novotny, *Strangers at the Door,* pp. 138, 141.

70. Ernst, *Immigrant Life in New York,* p. 51.

71. Novotny, *Strangers at the Door,* pp. 144, 149.

72. John Higham, *Strangers in the Land: Patterns of American Nativism, 1860–1925* (New York: Atheneum Publishers, 1969), p. 25.

73. Roger Daniels, *The Politics of Prejudice: The Anti-Japanese Movement in California and the Struggle for Japanese Exclusion* (New York: Atheneum Publishers, 1969), p. 17.

74. Stanford M. Lyman, "Strangers in the City: The Chinese in the Urban Frontier," in Amy Tachiki, Eddie Wong, and Franklin Odo, eds., *Roots: An Asian American Reader* (Los Angeles: UCLA Asian American Studies Center, 1971), pp. 159–87; and "Red Guard on Grant Avenue," in Howard S. Becker, ed., *Culture and Civility in San Francisco* (New Brunswick, N.J.: Transaction Books, 1971), pp. 20–52.

75. Victor G. and Brett de Bary Nee, *Longtime Californ': A Documentary Study of an American Chinatown* (New York: Pantheon Books, 1973), pp. 299–300.

76. Ibid., pp. 165–66.

77. David Ley, *The Black Inner City as Frontier Outpost* (Washington, D.C.: Association of American Geographers, 1974), pp. 212–14.

78. Paul Bullock, *Watts: The Aftermath* (New York: Grove Press, 1969), p. 37; Robert Conot, *Rivers of Blood, Years of Darkness* (New York: Bantam Books, 1967), p. 454.

13. Public Humiliation and Execution

1. John A. Wilson, *The Culture of Egypt* (Chicago: University of Chicago Press, 1951), pp. 241–43; see also D. Lorton, "The Treatment of Criminals in Ancient Egypt (Through the New Kingdom)," *Journal of the Economic and Social History of the Orient* 22, pt. 1 (1977): 50–51.

2. H. F. Jolowicz, *Historical Introduction to the Study of Roman Law* (Cambridge: University Press, 1965), pp. 326, 412–13; Grant Showerman, *Rome and the Romans* (New York: Macmillan Co., 1931), p. 410.

3. Adhemar Esmein, *A History of Continental Criminal Procedure* (Boston: Little, Brown & Co., 1913), pp. 26–27.

4. Martin Hengel, *Crucifixion* (London: Student Christian Movement Press, 1977), p. 54.

5. Quintilian, *Declamationes* 274; quoted by Hengel, *Crucifixion,* p. 50.

6. Tacitus, "Germany and Its Tribes," secs. 12, 21, trans. A. J.

Church and W. J. Brodribb, *The Complete Works of Tacitus* (New York: Modern Library, 1942), pp. 714, 719.

7. F. L. Attenborough, ed., *The Laws of the Earliest English Kings* (New York: Russell & Russell, Publishers, 1963), p. 131; Christopher Hibbert, *The Roots of Evil: A Social History of Crime and Punishment* (Boston: Little, Brown & Co., 1963), p. 5; F. M. Stenton, *Anglo-Saxon England* (Oxford: Clarendon Press, 1947), pp. 349–50.

8. John Deane Potter, *The Fatal Gallows Tree* (London: Elek Books, 1965), p. 10.

9. Luke Owen Pike, *A History of Crime in England* (London: Smith, Elder & Co., 1876), 2: 82–84.

10. John Bellamy, *Crime and Public Order in England in the Later Middle Ages* (Toronto: University of Toronto Press, 1973), p. 182.

11. William Andrews, *Old-Time Punishments* (Hull: William Andrews, 1890), pp. 132–33.

12. Durant W. Robertson, Jr., *Chaucer's London* (New York: John Wiley & Sons, 1968), p. 47.

13. Carl Ludwig von Bar, *A History of Continental Criminal Law* (Boston: Little, Brown & Co., 1916), p. 190.

14. Theodor Hampe, *Crime and Punishment in Germany* (New York: E. P. Dutton & Co., 1929), p. 46; Von Bar, *Continental Criminal Law,* pp. 106–10; F. R. H. DuBoulay, "Law Enforcement in Medieval Germany," *History,* 63, no. 209 (1978): 345–55.

15. Bellamy, *Crime and Public Order in England,* pp. 185–86.

16. Thomas Wright, *The Home of Other Days* (New York: D. Appleton & Co., 1871), pp. 356–57.

17. Marc Bensimon, "Modes of Perception of Reality in the Renaissance," in Robert S. Kinsman, ed., *The Darker Vision of the Renaissance: Beyond the Fields of Reason* (Berkeley and Los Angeles: University of California Press, 1974), pp. 223, 225.

18. John L. Pritchard, *A History of Capital Punishment* (New York: Citadel Press, 1960), pp. 61–62.

19. Paul Lacroix, *Manners, Customs, and Dress during the Middle Ages and during the Renaissance Period* (London: Bickers & Son, n.d.), p. 424.

20. John Ogilby, *Itinerarium Angliae, or A Book of Roads . . .* (1675); quoted in Leon Radzinowicz, *A History of English Criminal Law and Its Administration from 1750* (London: Stevens & Sons, 1948), 1: 214.

21. Radzinowicz, *English Criminal Law,* p. 216.

22. Potter, *Fatal Gallows Tree,* pp. 22–23.

23. W. C. Sydney, *England and the English in the Eighteenth Century,* 2nd ed. (Edinburgh: John Grant, 1891), 2: 277.

24. Quoted in ibid., p. 294.

25. Alfred Marks, *Tyburn Tree* (London: Brown, Langham, 1908).

26. David D. Cooper, *The Lesson of the Scaffold: The Public Execution Controversy in Victorian England* (Athens: Ohio University Press, 1974), pp. 7, 20.

27. Jack Kenny Williams, *Vogues in Villainy: Crime and Retribution in Ante-Bellum South Carolina* (Columbia: University of South Carolina Press, 1959), p. 101.

28. Gerald D. Robin, "The Executioner: His Place in English Society," *British Journal of Sociology* 15 (1964): 234–53.

29. Henry Fielding, "An Enquiry into the Causes of the Late Increase of Robbers . . ." (1751), in *The Works of Henry Fielding* (London: Frank Cass, 1967), 13: 123–24.

30. Jeremy Bentham, *The Works of Jeremy Bentham,* ed. John Bowring (New York: Russell & Russell, Publishers, 1962), 1: 549.

31. Philip Collins, *Dickens and Crime* (London: Macmillan & Co., 1962), p. 240.

14. Exile and Confinement

1. Derk Bodde and Clarence Morris, *Law in Imperial China* (Cambridge, Mass.: Harvard University Press, 1967), pp. 81–82, 84–85; Étienne Balazs, *Le Traité juridique du "Souei-Chou"* (Leiden: E. J. Brill, 1954), pp. 23, 59, 66; Grant Showerman, *Rome and the Romans* (New York: Macmillan Co., 1931), p. 411.

2. Michel Foucault, *Madness and Civilization: A History of Insanity in the Age of Reason* (New York: Vintage Books, 1973), p. 47.

3. George Rosen, *Madness in Society* (Chicago: University of Chicago Press, 1968), p. 140.

4. Robert S. Kinsman, "Folly, Melancholy and Madness: A Study in Shifting Styles of Medical Analysis and Treatment, 1450–1675," in Robert S. Kinsman, ed., *The Darker Vision of the Renaissance: Beyond the Fields of Reason* (Berkeley and Los Angeles: University of California Press, 1974), p. 282.

5. Kaspar K. Riemschneider, "Prison and Punishment in Early Anatolia," *Journal of the Economic and Social History of the Orient* 22, pt. 1 (1977): 114–15.

6. Wesley W. Spink, *Infectious Diseases: A History of Their Control* (Minneapolis: University of Minnesota Press, 1978), p. 159.

7. E. Jeanselme, "Comment l'Europe, au Moyen Age se protégea contre la lèpre," *Bulletin, Société Française d'Histoire de la Médecine* 25 (1931): 75–81; Saul Nathaniel Brody, *The Disease of the Soul: Leprosy in Medieval Literature* (Ithaca, N.Y.: Cornell University Press, 1974), pp. 73–75.

8. Kinsman, "Folly, Melancholy, and Madness," p. 293.

9. Peter Richards, *The Medieval Leper and His Northern Heirs* (Cambridge, Eng.: D. S. Brewer, 1977), pp. 33, 51.

10. Rotha Mary Clay, *The Medieval Hospitals of England* (1909; reprint ed., London: Frank Cass, 1966), pp. 50–51.

11. W. K. Jordan, *Philanthropy in England, 1480–1660* (London: George Allen & Unwin, 1959); J. S. Coburn, "The Nature and Inci-

dence of Crime in England, 1559–1625: A Preliminary Survey," in J. S. Coburn, ed., *Crime in England, 1550–1800* (Princeton, N.J.: Princeton University Press, 1977), pp. 60–61; Bronislaw Geremek, "Men Without Masters: Marginal Society During the Pre-industrial Era," *Diogenes,* no. 98 (Summer 1977), pp. 28–54.

12. Frank Ayedelotte, *Elizabethan Rogues and Vagabonds* (1913; reprint ed., New York: Barnes & Noble, 1967): 52–53.

13. C. J. Ribton-Turner, *A History of Vagrants and Vagrancy* (London: Chapman & Hall, 1887), pp. 67–78.

14. D. L. Howard, *The English Prisons: Their Past and Their Future* (London: Methuen & Co., 1960), p. 11.

15. J. Thorsten Sellin, *Slavery and the Penal System* (New York: Elsevier Scientific Publishing Co., 1976), pp. 70–82.

16. Foucault, *Madness and Civilization,* p. 41.

17. Georges Guillain and P. Mathieu, *La Salpétrière* (Paris: Masson, 1925), pp. 20, 35.

18. John Howard, *Prisons and Lazarettos* (4th ed., 1792; reprint ed., Montclair, N.J.: Patterson Smith, 1973), 1: 8.

19. Edward G. O'Donoghue, *The Story of Bethlehem Hospital* (London: Fisher Unwin, 1914), pp. 202, 210.

20. Robert R. Reed, Jr., *Bedlam on the Jacobean Stage* (Cambridge, Mass.: Harvard University Press, 1952), p. 25.

21. R. S. Hinde, *The British Penal System, 1773–1950* (London: Gerald Duckworth & Co., 1951), p. 13.

22. Michael Ignatieff, *A Just Measure of Pain: The Penitentiary in the Industrial Revolution, 1750–1850* (New York: Pantheon Books, 1978), p. 44.

23. Foucault, *Madness and Civilization,* pp. 202–4.

24. David J. Rothman, *The Discovery of the Asylum: Social Order and Disorder in the New Republic* (Boston: Little, Brown & Co., 1971).

25. Albert Deutsch, *The Mentally Ill in America,* 2nd ed. (New York: Columbia University Press, 1949), pp. 64–65.

26. Rothman, *Discovery of the Asylum,* pp. 69–71.

27. Blake McKelvey, *American Prisons: A Study in American Social History Prior to 1915* (Chicago: University of Chicago Press, 1936), pp. 16–21.

28. Rothman, *Discovery of the Asylum,* pp. 79–84; for European cases, see Michel Foucault, *Discipline and Punish: The Birth of the Prison* (New York: Pantheon Books, 1977), and Ignatieff, *A Just Measure of Pain.*

29. Deutsch, *The Mentally Ill in America,* pp. 92–95.

30. Rothman, *Discovery of the Asylum,* pp. 129–130.

31. Gerald N. Grob, *Mental Institutions in America: Social Policy to 1875* (New York: Free Press, 1973), p. 89.

32. Rothman, *Discovery of the Asylum,* pp. 184–85.

33. Deutsch, *The Mentally Ill in America,* pp. 116, 129.

34. Rothman, *Discovery of the Asylum,* p. 237.

35. "The Plight of the 'Deinstitutionalized' Mental Patient," *Science* 200 (June 23, 1978): 1366.

36. A new high-security state prison is planned for Minnesota. It is "a low-slung building nestled against the sloping earth overlooking the St. Croix River, almost invisible from the highway and surrounded simply by chain-link fence. . . . The trend these days is to build prisons that don't look like prisons." *Minneapolis Tribune,* June 17, 1978, p. 11.

15. The Open Circle

1. Jean Cazeneuve, "Jeux de vertige et de peur," in Roger Caillois, ed., *Jeux et Sports* (Paris: Encyclopédie de la Pléiade, 1967), pp. 683–731.

2. Charles Houston, "The Last Blue Mountain," in Samuel Z. Klausner, ed., *Why Man Takes Chances: Studies in Stress-Seeking* (Garden City, N.Y.: Doubleday Anchor Books, 1968), p. 57.

3. William Goldfarb and Irving Mintz, "Schizophrenic Child's Reactions to Time and Space," *Archives of General Psychiatry* 5 (1961): 535–53.

4. Harold F. Searles, *The Nonhuman Environment* (New York: International Universities Press, 1960), pp. 15, 146, 309.

5. Edoardo Weiss, *Agoraphobia in the Light of Ego Psychology* (New York: Grune & Stratton, 1964), pp. 51–52.

6. Isaac M. Marks, *Fears and Phobias* (New York: Academic Press, 1969), p. 134.

7. *Pascal's Pensées,* introd. T.S. Eliot (New York: Dutton Paperbacks, 1958), no. 72; but see also nos. 205, 206, 212, 229.

8. Gregory Bateson and Margaret Mead, *Balinese Character,* Special Publication of the New York Academy of Sciences, vol. 2 (New York, 1942), pp. 6, 11; Margaret Mead, "Children and Ritual in Bali," in Margaret Mead and Martha Wolfenstein, eds., *Childhood in Contemporary Cultures* (Chicago: University of Chicago Press, 1955), pp. 42, 80.

9. Gladys A. Reichard, *Navaho Religion: A Study of Symbols* (New York: Pantheon Books, 1963), pp. 5, 89, 158.

10. E. O. James, *Seasonal Feasts and Festivals* (London: Thames & Hudson, 1961), p. 178.

11. J. Littlejohn, "Temne Space," *Anthropological Quarterly* 36 (1963): 8–9.

12. Vance Randolph, *Ozark Superstitions* (New York: Columbia University Press, 1947), pp. 283–84.

13. Bateson and Mead, *Balinese Character,* p. 20.

14. Earl Cook, review of Gilbert F. White and J. Eugene Haas, *Assessment of Research on Natural Hazards,* in Association of American Geographers, *Annals* 68, no. 2 (1978): 289.

16. Fears: Past and Present

1. John Wain, *Samuel Johnson: A Biography* (New York: Viking Press, 1975), p. 43.

2. Pierre Goubert, *Louis XIV and Twenty Million Frenchmen* (New York: Pantheon Books, 1970), p. 21.

3. Lynn White, Jr., "Death and the Devil," in Robert S. Kinsman, ed., *The Darker Vision of the Renaissance: Beyond the Fields of Reason* (Berkeley and Los Angeles: University of California Press, 1974), p. 31.

4. Georges Duby, *La Société aux XIe et XIIe siècles dans la région mâconnaise* (1953), quoted in Philippe Ariès, *Centuries of Childhood: A Social History of Family Life* (New York: Vintage Books, 1965), pp. 353–55.

5. T. K. Chêng, *Archaeology in China: Shang China* (Toronto: University of Toronto Press, 1960), 2: 53–55.

6. Matthew Luckiesh, *Artificial Light: Its Influence on Civilization* (New York: Century Co., 1920), p. 158.

7. René Grousset, *The Rise and Splendour of the Chinese Empire* (Berkeley and Los Angeles: University of California Press, 1959), p. 171.

8. Alan Macfarlane, *The Family Life of Ralph Josselin: A Seventeenth-Century Clergyman* (Cambridge: University Press, 1970), p. 171.

9. Edward Shorter, *The Making of the Modern Family* (New York: Basic Books, 1977), p. 26.

10. Daniel Bell, quoting Merwyn Jones, in "Technology, Nature and Society," *American Scholar* 42 (Summer 1973): 396.

11. Wolfram Eberhard, *Conquerors and Rulers: Social Forces in Medieval China* (Leiden: E. J. Brill, 1965), pp. 15–16.

12. David W. Orr, "Catastrophe and Social Order," *Human Ecology* 7, no. 1 (1979): 41–52.

Index

About the Author

Yi-fu Tuan was born in Tientsin, China, in 1930. He is a professor of geography at the University of Minnesota, and has been a visiting professor at Oxford University, the University of Hawaii, and the University of California at Davis. He has written for numerous magazines and received many awards in his field. His two most recent books are *Topophilia* and *Space and Place.*